THE MACRO ECONOMIC POLICIES
AND
THE MILLENNIUM DEVELOPMENT GOALS

THE MACRO ECONOMIC POLICIES AND THE MILLENNIUM DEVELOPMENT GOALS

Edited by

Dr. Vibhuti Patel

Dr. Manisha Karne

GYAN PUBLISHING HOUSE

NEW DELHI-110002

The Macro Economic Policies and The Millennium Development Goals

Rs. 690

ISBN: 81-212-0925-0

Published in 2007 in India by
Gyan Publishing House
5, Ansari Road, Darya Ganj,
New Delhi-110002
Phones : 23282060, 23261060
Fax : 011-23285914
E-mail : books@ gyanbooks.com
Website: www.gyanbooks.com

Lassertype Setting by: Rudra Computer Graphics, Delhi
Printed at : Salasar Imaging System, Delhi

Contents

Preface 9
Acknowledgements 11
List of Contributors 13

1 Introduction 17

Section I: Eradication of Poverty and Hunger

2. Battle against Poverty: Some Reflections on Agrarian Economy 29
Vinayak S. Deshpande

3. Urban Poverty Management in India with Special Reference to Micro-finance to Urban Poor in Mumbai 41
G. Y. Shitole

4. Eliminating Poverty: Making Globalization work for the Poor 55
Anjali Masarguppi

5. Poverty Alleviation: A Case Study of Tamil Nadu 71
Harshada Rathod

Section II: Achievement of Universal Primary Education

6. MDG 2: Achieving Universal Primary Education 83
Sangita Kamdar

7. Universal Primary Education: Goal and Reality 99
K. S. Ingole

8. Primary Education in India 113
S.S. Captan and Lata S. Moorthy

Section III: Promotion of Gender Equality and Empowerment

9. Promotion of Gender Equality and Empowerment of Women 127
Vibhuti Patel

10. Empowering Rural Women with Technology 145
Chetna V. Sinha and Amy E. Bean

11. Women's Empowerment: Budget as a Tool to Deal with the Gender Gap 155
Prashant Raymus

12. Gender Equality and Millennium Development Goals (MDGs) 175
Kamayani Bali Mahabal

13. Women's Empowerment through Micro-Credit (With special reference to Nanded District) 201
G.S. Yelne

Section IV: Reduction of Child Mortality, Improvement of Maternal Health, Combat HIV/AIDS, Malaria, T.B.

14. Macroeconomics, Public Health and MDGs 217
Ravi Duggal

15. A Need to Re-emphasize the Role of Public Healthcare in India 247
Manisha Karne

16. Children Infected and Affected With HIV/AIDS 261
Rita Sonawat

17. Combat HIV/AIDS, Malaria, T.B. 277
Mr. Elvis Thomas

18. Combat HIV/AIDS, The Millennium Development Goal 283
Ms. Vaijayanta Anand

Section V: Ensure Environmental Sustainability and Develop a Global Partnership for Development.

19. Ensuring Environmental Sustainability 289
Veena Devasthali

20. Environmental Entrepreneurship Programme for Urban Poor Women 301
Jyoti Mhapsekar

21. Develop A Global Partnership for Development 313
Vibhuti Patel

22. The Emerging Issues from the Seminar 325
Leni Chaudhuri

Index 331

Preface

Examination of macroeconomic policies in the past three decades has shown that the benefits of development have not trickled down to the Third World countries. Moreover the neo-liberal macroeconomic policies emphasising Liberalisation, Privatisation and Globalization (LPG) have widened the economic inequalities and the gap in the standard of living between the haves and have not. The reliance on free forces of market have exacerbated deprivation and structural violence for large majority of the masses and resulted into concentration and centralization of economic power in the hands of microscopic minority. The stabilisation policies imposed on the nation states by the international financial institutions forced withdrawal of state from the social sector.

In this backdrop, scholarly researches of the nineties by renowned economists and the social scientists brought to light that state, civil society and industry needed to work in unison to ensure basic needs— food security, shelter, education, health and peace to the poor. The stark reality of hunger and starvation deaths in African, Asian and Latin American countries; poverty-driven increase in trafficking of women and children for servitude, cheap labour and sexploitation; resurgence of epidemic of tuberculosis, water-born diseases, malaria and dengue due to poor sanitation and lack of safe drinking water as a result of commercialisation of social infrastructure forced sensitive decision makers to persuade the United Nations to take initiative to address these burning problems.

As a result, the millennium summit of September, 2000 organized by the United Nations in which world leaders gathered to deliberate and arrive at common understanding, universally applicable vision statement and give commitment to confront these problems. The Member States of the UN issued the Millennium Declaration, committing themselves to a series of time-bound and quantified targets for addressing extreme poverty in its many dimensions—income, poverty, hunger, disease, lack of adequate shelter, and exclusion—while promoting gender equality, education, and environmental sustainability. Most of the targets are to be achieved by 2015. Known as the Millennium Development Goals (MDGs), they represent a framework for achieving human development and broadening its benefits.

MDGs are adopted by 189 Member Nations of the UN, including India, on 18th September 2000, the Millennium Declaration outlines the signatory countries' commitment to achieving the MDGs.

With a view to create better understanding of interface between macro economic forces and attainment of the MDGs, we decided to organise a national symposium on this theme. We received tremendous response to our concept note. Overwhelming response from researchers, scholars, academicians, NGOs and GOs made our effort worthwhile in spite of several hurdles faced by us due to dislocation of normal life created due to heavy floods in Mumbai.

This book is an outcome of the papers presented and animated discussions during the two-day symposium on "Macro Economic Policies and the MDGs". This book encapsulates major issues handled by the nation states, voluntary organisations and international policy makers and financial institutions vis-a-vis the agenda of human development and rights based approach.

Dr. Vibhuti Patel
Dr. Manisha Karne

Acknowledgements

The papers included in this book were presented at National Symposium on "Macro Economic Policies and Millennium Development Goals" in Mumbai in the on 30th -31st August 2005.

To begin with, we are grateful to the UGC for sponsoring this symposium and also to SNDT University for allocating the required funds and support system.

We are extremely grateful to Honourable Vice Chancellor Prof. Rupa Shah, Registrar Shree. K. G. Bhide, BCUD Director, Dr. A G. Bhalavankar and Dr.Madhuri Chheda, Ex Director PGSR for extending all possible support in organising the symposium. We are extremely thankful to Sayeeda Hameed, Member of the Planning Commission for presenting Keynote address for the symposium and Mr.M.N.Chaini, chairman of MEDC for concluding the symposium and also to Justice Jahagirdar for delivering valedictory address.

We are grateful to the Paper contributors who have worked very hard to contribute their papers for the symposium.

Last but not the least, we express our deep sense of gratitude to our family members (especially to Lara and Maitreyee) for providing us congenial atmosphere to pursue this tedious and laborious work.

DR. VIBHUTI PATEL AND DR. MANISHA KARNE

List of Contributors

Amy E. Bean is a researcher at John F Kennedy School of Government, Harvard.

Anjali Masarguppi is teaching economics in Wilson College, Mumbai.

Chetna V. Sinha is a Founder and Director of Mandeshi Mahila Bank in Mhaswad, Satara.

Elvis Thomas is a Senior Lecturer in Nirmala Niketan, College of Social Work, Mumbai.

Ghanshyam S. Yelne is Reader at School of Social Sciences, Swami Ramanand Teerth Marathwada University, Nanded. He is Ph. D. in sociology.

G. Y. Shitole is Reader, P.G. Department of commerce, SNDT Women's University, Mumbai. He holds doctoral degree in Commerce.

Harshada Rathod is Principal, Maniben Nanavati College, Mumbai. She holds Ph.D. in Economics.

Jyoti Mhapsekar is Director Parisar Viks and Stree Mukti Sangathana, Mumbai.

Kamayani Bali Mahabal is a lawyer and associated with Centre for Enquiry into Health and Allied Themes (CEHAT).

Kisan. S. Ingole is Reader, P.G. Department of Economics, SNDT women's University, Mumbai. He has doctorate in Economics.

Lata S. Moorthy is a Research Scholar.

Leni Chowdhary is research officer at CEHAT. Earlier she was working at Documentation, Research and Training Centre, St. Pius College, Mumbai and also worked for the world Social Forum in 2004.

Manisha Karne is Reader, P.G. Department of Economics, SNDT women's University, Mumbai. Her Ph. D. work is on Transport Economics.

Prashant Raymus is Research Officer at Centre for Enquiry into Health and Allied Themes (CEHAT).

Ravi Duggal is an independent consultant on health issues. He was research officer at Foundation for Research in Community Health (1983-1993) and Coordinator of CEHAT (2000-2005).

Rita Sonawat is Reader at P.G. Department of Home Science, SNDT Women's University, Mumbai. She holds Ph. D. in Home Science.

Sanjay.S. Captan is Professor and Head of Post Graduate Department of Commerce, SNDT Women's University, Mumbai. He is Ph. D. in Commerce.

Sangita Kamdar is Assistant Professor at Economics Department, University of Mumbai, Mumbai. She was awarded Doctor of Philosophy in Economics.

Ms. Vaijayanta Anand is Senior lecturer in Nirmala Niketan, college of Social Work, Mumbai.

Veena Devasthali is Reader, P.G. Department of Economics, SNDT women's University, Mumbai. Her doctoral thesis was in Labour Economics.

Vibhuti Patel is Director, PGSR and Professor and Head of Post Graduate Department of Economics, SNDT Women's University, Mumbai.

Vinayak Deshpande is Reader at Department of economics, Nagpur University, Nagpur. He holds Ph. D. in Economics.

1
Introduction

The central objective of this book is to critically evaluate the Millennium Development goals in the context of the macro economic policies pursued by the Indian States. The MDGs constitute eight major goals that need to be achieved by 2015. They are as follows:

Goal 1: Eradication of Poverty and Hunger

Goal 2: Achievement of Universal Primary Education

Goal 3: Promotion of Gender Equality and Empowerment

Goal 4: Reduction of Child Mortality

Goal 5: Improvement of Maternal Health

Goal 6: Combat HIV/AIDS, Malaria, T.B.

Goal 7: Ensure Environmental Sustainability

Goal 8: Develop a Global Partnership for Development.

As articulated in the Millennium Declaration, the MDGs are benchmarks of development progress based on such fundamental values as freedom, equity and human rights and peace and security. Within this matrix, all papers in this book have examined different MDGs.

The paper by Vinayak Deshpande on poverty titled 'Battle against Poverty: Some Reflections on Agrarian Economy' deals mainly with poverty in the rural areas.As suggested by Dreze and

Sen public action helps to promote extensive social opportunities and the wide spread equitable provision of schooling, health and other basic services. But in country like India as discussed in his paper there are failure of state intervention in provision of essential social services like health and education. In the rural areas there is agrarian distress as more than half the rural households in Maharashtra are farmers and more than half of the farmer households are indebted. Understanding the unfortunate process that led to suicides at micro level is one stage and the second stage involves following this both at micro as well as macro level through policy initiatives. Apart from indebtedness market inadequacy and crash in prices were reported as the major reasons for farmers' distress. The ups and downs in the prices are inevitable in the marketing process. However, sudden crash of prices and consistently lower prices disproportionate to the price level in the inputs causes severe agony and economic stress in the farm family. The prevailing market intervention schemes and MSP do not adequately support the farmers without a time lag and therefore completely ineffective. Therefore, the paper argues for a better support system for the farmers by revamping of the market discipline, providing infrastructure, price monitoring and providing quick information could go a long way in removing the market imperfections. Thus the paper concludes by saying the backward areas need to be focussed more by having suitable schemes and while designing and initiating such schemes, it is essential to understand the resource endowments and economic advantages of these regions to participate in the mainstream growth pattern.

Urban Poverty Management in India with special Reference to Micro-finance to Urban Poor in Mumbai by Dr. G.Y. Shitole focuses on urban poverty which is a multidimensional phenomenon. The urban poor live with many deprivations. Their daily challenges include limited access to employment opportunities and income, inadequate and insecure housing and services, violent and unhealthy environments, little or no social protection mechanisms, and limited access to adequate health and education opportunities. Though there are several poverty alleviation programmes, a proper blending of financial and social intervention is imperative. In this context, the importance of micro finance intervention cannot be over emphasized. Micro finance is an innovative tool. It is concerned with the provision of thrift credit, other financial services and products of very small amounts with an element of social intervention enabling mainly the poor to improve their living standards. Micro finance is generally routed through small groups commonly known as Self-Help Groups (SHGs), which not only serve as a platform to supervise the activities of each other but also provide social collaterals. Loan amount to the member of the SHG is based on the amount of the savings of the SHG and is recovered generally in 12 monthly instalments. Loans are repeated and gradually increased; thus establishing relationship banking.

Eliminating poverty: Making Globalization work for the poor Anjali Masaguppi's paper examines poverty in wider framework. The neo- classical or neo- liberal paradigm no longer considers poverty as an isolated problem of Low- Income Countries and with globalization, 'absolute poverty' is considered as a major global problem. Millennium Development Goals aim at tackling this problem globally and collectively and reducing global poverty at least by half by year 2015. This brings several interrelated issues to the forefront: such as: economic growth, pattern and trends in income distribution, human development index and their impact on poverty reduction. Against this background the paper in order to study the effectiveness and role of foreign aid, this paper tries to establish certain relationships between different macro economic indicators like Economic Growth & Aid and Aid & Poverty Reduction etc.

The paper titled Poverty Alleviation: A Case Study of Tamil Nadu by Harshada Rathod is based on Tamil Nadu. Tamil Nadu is a model of a middle income state that has tried to enhance the level of human development through the formation and implementation of programmes that address the needs of the poor, vulnerable and marginal population of the state. It has made significant strides in terms of poverty reduction and it has also achieved a lot in terms of the social sector. Besides the budgetary reasons for this, the achievements are also due to the implementation of poverty alleviation schemes aimed at income generation and employment creation, the noon meal scheme covering school children and old age pensioners and the implementation of other nutrition programmes such as the ICDS aimed specifically at improving women and children's nutritional status. The main findings reveal that Poverty reduction strategies in Tamil Nadu should lay emphasis on urban areas. As the incidence of poverty is more in urban areas in Tamil Nadu. More emphasis should be also being placed on employment generating schemes. Another important observation made in the paper is regarding the need to evolve Tamil Nadu Afforestation Programme (TAP) into a sustainable poverty alleviation programme from a mere greening project.

Sangita Kamdar's paper on Universalization of Elementary Education discusses in detail the present scenario of elementary education in India. There is a theoretical backdrop to the need to invest in education where the paper discusses the Human Resource Development (HRD) and the Human Development (HD) approaches to investing in education. There is discussion on the factors which contribute to universal enrolment in primary education. The Government policy and factors hindering universalisation of primary education are discussed very well in the paper.There are several problems and constraints in fulfilling this dream of Universalization of Elemetary Education and unless these problems are tackled, the dream of making education as 'joyful learning' will remain a distant dream.

Universal Primary Education: Goal and Reality by Dr. K. S. Ingole deals with some of the vital issues relating to Constitutional provision to achieve the goals of universal education. It discusses in detail the impact of various policies implemented towards achieving this goal by reviewing the present educational status of depressed and oppressed classes in India. The paper also assesses the government's expenditure for achieving the goals of universal primary education in India.

The paper on Primary Education in India by Dr. S.S. Captan and Dr. Lata S. Moorthy focuses on inevitability of education for consciousness and reconstitution of the society. He has examined the planning process from 1950 to 2005 with special focus on resource allocations for education. He has taken a review of District Primary Education Programme (DPEP), Operation Black Borad, Shiksha Karmi Project, Lok Jumbish, Sarva Shiksha Abhiyan with respect to MDG II in this paper

Promotion of Gender Equality and Empowerment of Women is a paper by Vibhuti Patel which has given a very comprehensive treatment to the economic globalization and its impact on different issues related women. The paper argues that free-play of market forces have made majority of Indian women more vulnerable in the factor, labour and product markets. NGOs have provided islands of security in some pockets. In this situation, affirmative action by the democratic institutions and the nation state, in secular areas of human governance is the only answer.

Through World Social Forum, 2004 women for just, sustainable and caring trade are trying to reach out to thousands of women who are voicing the concerns of toiling poor. Women decision makers are striving for agenda setting power to achieve MDGs.. Moreover, stronger efforts are required for evolving strategies to address the vicious circle linking gender inequality, neo liberal macro economic policies and poverty.

Empowering Rural Women with Technology by Chetna V. Sinha and Amy E. Bean is based on the first hand experience of the authors in Mandeshi Mahila Bank. As the women of Mann Deshi Mahila gain exposure to technological advances, it was found that the cycle of empowerment is perpetuated. Each new technology the women use, their confidence grows and their importance in the community is heightened and realized. This increases their desire to accept newer technologies and acquire the skills necessary to operate these advances. Even in rural settings, technology can be used in surprisingly innovative ways to improve lives. The benefits of technology use are two-fold - lives are improved and women gain the confidence and skills to take a more active role in society. The paper finally concludes that women are increasingly becoming technologically and financially savvy. It was found that when women are given both the tools and the opportunity, they seldom fail to capitalize Women have proved their innovation, desire, and dependability. Now, it is vital that policy makers widen their visions to create space for the empowerment of all women.

The paper titled Women's Empowerment: Budget as a tool by Prashant Raymus deals with the Gender Gap. Globalization has dramatically changed the conditions under which the struggle for gender equality must be carried out, especially in developing countries. One of the important tools of gender mainstreaming, aimed principally at poverty reduction, has been the concept of "gender budgeting," i.e. focusing attention in the process of budget formulation in order to assess whether a particular fiscal measure will increase or decrease gender equality, or leave it unchanged. Gendered budget analysis can help to focus on these neglected aspects; it provides women with the vital information regarding the contents and focus of existing government policies. Armed with that, women can confront policy-makers and demand changes in policies as per their needs and choices. The process is for greater transparency and for deepening of democracy. The paper strongly argues that Capacity building workshops on 'Gendering budgets" must be organized for elected representatives, different ministries at state and central government level.

'Gender Equality and Millennium Development Goals' (MDGs) by Kamayani Bali Mahabal elaborates in detail about the concept of gender equality. It identifies three primary domains of equality between men and women which are crucial: capabilities, access to resources and opportunities, and agency or the ability to influence and contribute to outcomes similarly, we also understand from the paper that laws and policies play a significant role in determining the extent of gender inequality that exists in a society. They can serve to protect women's rights or to reduce them. For example, in many countries, women still lack the legal right to inherit or own property and, in many others, violence against women is not considered a criminal offense. Without transformations in economic relations or the implementation and enforcement of legal rights and protection, gender equality and the empowerment of women can certainly remain a distant goal.

'Women's Empowerment through Micro-Credit' (With special reference to Nanded District) by G. S. Yelne in his paper focuses on economic empowerment of the women. Government of India has taken various steps to empower the women out of which various developmental programmes is the out come of it Viz. Indira Awas Yojana, Mahila Samrudhi Yojana, Development of Women and Children in Rural Areas (DWACRA), Maharastra Rural Credit Project (M.R.C.P.), NABARD sponsored SHG programme. Through these various programmes Self-help groups have emerged as a popular method of working with Women for their empowerment in the recent years.

Collectives of individuals, usually small groups of persons, are formed into "self-help groups" that provide mutual aid to each other around common problems and operate under such concepts as self-determination and joint responsibility. They work together to achieve specific behaviour attitudinal or cognitive goals. The group is the central component and everyone. Works with others for the group's further development, and individual needs are met in the process. This process of SHG has brought change among the women to some extent, as they have started to organise themselves in a social group, which is known as SHGs, which was, absent prior to the initiation of SHGs. It shows the increased participation of women at community level in the direction to socio-economic and political empowerment of women.

Ravi Duggal's paper on Macroeconomics, Public Health and MDGs has been one the most comprehensive papers as it takes in to consideration all most all the aspects related to health infrastructure and health care services in India. In the post-economic reforms period India is more exposed to the global market with increasing vulnerability. Against this background, it is important for understanding the impact and changes in the health sector. There is historical dominance of the private health care sector in India in provision of ambulatory care and rising costs could spell disaster for the poor given the fact that the State is gradually reducing its responsibilities in provision of health care. Since the poor too have been active users of private health care their dependence on it makes the case for "right to health care" and health for all is becoming a distant dream.

Manisha Karne's paper on 'A Need to Re-emphasize the Role of Public Healthcare in India' discusses some issues of Healthcare services in India. Due to prevalence of extreme poverty and market failure in providing health facilities at affordable rates the paper rightly emphasizes on the need for increasing the role of state in this sector. State intervention has occurred within a centralized framework especially in regard to infrastructure provision in sectors such as transport, power, health etc. This paper argues that the Government should continue to focus on public health with greater decentralization to increase effectiveness of the public healthcare programmes.

The paper on 'Children Infected and Affected with HIV/AIDS by Rita Sonavat by highlights the issues and problems faced by children affected by HIV. As many as 14 million children have lost one or both parents to HIV/AIDS. Children have dilemmas related to parents, relatives, siblings and friends. Problem becomes serious because it's just not an individual's problem but the entire family, school and community.

Children experience a long period of losing their parents, increasing economic hardship and growing uncertainty about their own future. All this aspect has been well covered in the paper. She also discusses the role that NGOs are playing in addressing some problems in this area. NGO's play a very important role – provide remedial education, celebrity involvement during celebration of festivals, organize physical community events. Education, vocational training, use of therapies, yoga and spirituality are few recommendations or suggestions for working with children with HIV/AIDS.

Similar concerns have been raised about HIV/ AIDS, Malaria, T.B in the paper by Mr.Elvis Thomas in his paper 'Combating HIV/ AIDS, Tuberculosis and Malaria'. The unchecked spread of HIV/ Aids, Malaria, T.B could bring about social disintegration and political instability. Though Govt. of India began programmes to control and eradicate these diseases. There is a need to intensify the efforts as the spread of these diseases is very rapid. The State must not move away from its responsibility of providing health care to the people. The urgent requirement is capacity building to develop and organize people to decide for themselves. According to the author the emphasis should be on 'improving the quality of existing and future programmes and to increase the scope and quantity of future programmes that are implemented for combating these diseases. A strong emphasis should also be placed on enabling more mutual learning from experience'. The tide of HIV/ AIDS, Tuberculosis and Malaria my take some time to ebb, but, through collective action, that time span can be shortened.

The paper on 'Combat HIV/ AIDS, The Millennium Development Goal' by Ms. VaijayantaAnand discusses the serious issue of prevelance of HIV/AIDS among certain marginalized sections.The epidemic of AIDs has become the most serious problem in the country since independence. India's socio-economic status, traditional social ills, cultural myths on sex and sexuality and a huge population of marginalised people make it extremely vulnerable to HIV/AIDS epidemic. Economic growth and urbanization has led to increase in the categories of unorganized labourers. The women among these categories are more vulnerable to this disease as compared to men. Measures are urgently required to effectively protect and control of AIDS in category Otherwise it be major developmental challenge .It will not only affect economy of the country but all aspects of human life. Therefore an urgent and unprecedented response from all the sections of the society is the need of the hour.

'Ensuring Environmental Sustainability' by Dr.Veena Devasthali takes note of the concerns expressed about the environmental sustainability in the Millenium Development Goals (MDGs) integrating the principles of sustainable development into country policies and programmes and reverse the loss of environmental resources. The important issues which are discussed in the paper are reducing by half the proportion of people without sustainable access to safe drinking water and achieving significant improvement in lives of at least 100 million slum dwellers by 2020.

As policy guidelines and action programmes to achieve the

paper emphasises on the need to focus on the grass root level conditions. In the Indian context watershed development programme has the potential to take into consideration and accordingly incorporate the diversities that exist in the natural base of different regions. According to the author this essentially micro level programme can play a leading role in ensuring environmental sustainability.

Dr. Jyoti Mhapsekar's paper on 'Environmental Entrepreneurship Program for Urban Poor Women' focuses on sustainable human development for the workers in the informal economy who mainly belong to the marginal sections of the population. These are an invisible part of the urban landscape providing a variety of the services to ever increasing urban population. "Sustainable human development is development that not only generates economic growth but distributes its benefits equitably; that regenerates the environment rather than destroying it; that empowers people rather than marginalising them. It gives priority to the poor, enlarging their choices and opportunities and providing for their participation in decisions affecting them. This paper discusses the actual action oriented programmes implemented by Stree Mukti Sanghatana through 'Parisar Vikas' empowering such marginalised groups.

'Develop a Global Partnership for Development' by Vibhuti Patel discusses the issues related to the need for global partnership to achieve the MDGs. The MDGs make clear that it is the primary responsibility of poor countries to work towards achieving the first seven Goals. Though they are expected to do their part to ensure greater accountability to citizens and efficient use of resources but for poor countries to achieve the first seven Goals, it is absolutely essential that rich countries deliver on their end of the bargain with more and more effective aid, more sustainable debt relief and fairer trade rules, well in advance of 2015. The greater responsible role can be played by the rich countries which are in a position to deliver outcomes with their resource richness.

We believe that the MDGs are an agreed set of goals that can be achieved if all actors work together- heads of the nation states, civil society organizations, international financial institutions, global trade bodies and the UN system- and do their part. Poor countries have pledged to govern better, and invest in their people through health care and education. Rich countries must stick to their pledged to support the poor countries through aid, debt relief, and fairer and just trade. Only if there is commitment on the part of the rich as well as poor countries to fulfil these promises all the MDGs could be achieved.

DR. VIBHUTI PATEL

DR. MANISHA KARNE

SECTION I

Eradication of Poverty and Hunger

2

Battle Against Poverty: Some Reflections on Agrarian Economy

Vinayak S. Deshpande

For the first time in human history, eradicating global poverty became the part of Millennium Goals. One hundred and eighty heads of State signed the Millennium Declaration in October 2000. For each goal one or more targets have been set, most for 2015, using 1990 as a benchmark. It is now well accepted fact that to accelerate progress in human development, economic growth is, of course, necessary, but is not enough. Poverty has many dimensions. In addition to low income (living less than $ 1 a day) illiteracy, ill health, gender inequality, and environmental degradation are all aspects of being poor. This is reflected in the Millennium Development Goals. The central challenge today is to ensure that globalization becomes a positive force for the entire world's people. It is realized that the benefits of globalization if at all any are unevenly distributed. The countries with economies in transition face special difficulties in responding to this central challenge. In order to ensure equitable distribution of benefits, the efforts must include policies and measures at the global level which correspond to the needs of developing countries and economies in transition. With this objective Millennium Declaration was drafted.

The country like India is on track to achieve the goal of reducing by half the proportion of people living on less than $ 1 a day. But the country is off track in reaching the goals of primary education, gender equality and child mortality. Ensuring basic health and education outcomes is the responsibility of the State. Public spending makes improvement possible, but the improvements will fall short if spending fails to reach poor people-either because it goes for things the poor do not use or because it is diverted along the way-or if services are not made productive.

Public responsibility is one of the important aspects of Millennium Development Goals. The Indian public sector runs almost 2, 00, 000 primary health facilities, but wide public provision does not always translate into substantial use. The use of public hospitals for in patient care has declined from 45 per cent of the cases in 1987 to 31 per cent in 1996 in the state of Maharashtra. The declining use of public health facilities in the context of high levels of poverty is a symptom of the deterioration of the public health system. The urban areas have marginally higher utilization rates in the public sector as compared to rural areas. Classic welfare economics argues for government intervention in key social sectors. Governments demonstrate their responsibility by financing, providing or regulating the services that contribute to health and education improvement. But public spending has trouble creating quality services and reaching poor people. So there appears to be a weak relationship between spending and outcomes. Dreze and Sen suggest that public action helps to promote extensive social opportunities and the wide spread equitable provision of schooling health and other basic services. While citing the example of Kerala they pointed out that, "building partly on mass literacy and the emphasis placed on universal services by early communist and subsequent coalition governments seem to have been crucial in organizing poor people". In Uttar Pradesh on the other hand traditional caste and power divisions, particularly in rural areas, have persisted through more than 50 years of electoral politics and such divisions have come to form the core of political discourse and clientelist politics.

Individuals' abilities to press their demands depend on their information, perceived rights, and literacy.

Table 1
The Great Divide: Human Development and Basic Services in Kerala and Uttar Pradesh

Sr. No.	Variables	Kerala	Uttar Pradesh	India
1.	Infant mortality rate(per 1000 live births)	16.3	86.7	67.5
2.	Total fertility rate (per woman)	1.96	3.99	2.85
3.	Sex Ratio (women per 1000 men)	1058	902	933
4.	Female school enrollment rate (age 6-17 years)	90.8	61.4	66.2
5.	Male school enrollment rate(age 6-17 years)	91.0	77.3	77.6
6.	Rural girls never in school(age 10-12 years)	0.0	31.7	26.6
7.	Rural women never in school (age15-19 years)	1.6	49.3	38.7
8.	Immunization coverage rate(age12-23 months)	79.7	21.2	42.0
9.	Skilled delivery care (% of births)	94.0	22.4	42.3
10.	Rural population in villages with :			
	A Primary school	90.1	75.1	79.7
	A Middle school	87.1	31.9	44.6
	A primary health center	74.2	4.4	12.9
	An all weather road	79.1	46.0	49.2
11.	Medical Exp. per hospitalization in public facility (Rs.)	1,417	4,261	1,902
12.	Poorest 20% of households that prefer a public health facility	55.7	9.5	32.8

Women born in Kerala can expect to live 20 years longer on an average than women born in Uttar Pradesh. Uttar Pradesh's infant mortality rate is five times higher than Kerala. One in three girls in U.P. had never been to school. Kerala has universal enrolment. Education and health services in the two states indicate these differences. Kerala spent more on education and health while Uttar Pradesh spent more on state administration.

Need to Involve Poor in Decision Making:

When publicly provided and funded housing left vacant, when food supplies are not eaten, when free but empty public health clinics are bypassed in favor of expensive private care, this money is wasted. Improving services means protecting the interest of poor and involving them in decision making process. Engaging poor clients in active role-as purchasers, as monitors and as co producers can improve performance significantly. The wide range of services and differences in the situation and circumstances of the countries make it impossible to implement specific measures for all the developing countries of the world. However, millennium development goals would definitely be useful to monitor the various steps and policies undertaken by the country to tackle the socio-economic issues which are listed in the form of 8 millennium development goals.

Agrarian Distress

Agricultural development must be viewed as a core element of the poverty elevation policies, since growth in this sector is likely to lead to the widest spread of benefits especially to the rural poor. The first generation of reforms concentrated on reforms in the industrial economy and the reforms in agricultural sector were neglected. This must change now.

Indebtedness is one of the important aspects which need to be considered while analyzing the poverty issue especially rural poverty. More than half the rural households in Maharashtra are farmers and more than half of the farmer households are indebted. Compared with the all India average, in Maharashtra the proportion

Table 2
Indebtedness of Farmer Households

Sr.No.	*Indebtedness of Farmer Households*	*Maha rashtra*	*Andhra Pradesh*	*Kerala*	*Punjab*	*All India*
1.	2.	3.	4.	5.	6.	7.
1.	Farm HHs among rural HHs	55.7	42.3	43.9	61.8	60.4
2.	Farm HHs indebted	54.8	82.0	64.4	65.4	48.6
3.	ST Farmer HHs	14.1	11.3	2.1	0.4	13.3
4.	SC farmer HHs	10.1	17.4	4.5	31.5	17.5
5.	OBC farmer HHs	32.5	47.0	49.9	16.2	41.5
6.	OC farmer HHs	43.2	24.2	43.6	51.8	27.6
7.	Indebted ST farmer HH	9.3	10.8	1.6	0.2	10.0
8.	Indebted SC farmer HH	8.6	16.8	4.5	26.1	18.0
9.	Indebted OBC farmer HH	34.5	47.7	49.6	15.8	43.9
10.	Indebted OC farmer HH	47.7	24.7	36.4	57.9	28.1
11.	Farmer HHs with cultivation as main income	57.9	53.7	16.8	45.6	57.2
12	Indebted farmer HHs with cultivation as main income	62.6	54.4	14.4	52.7	56.9

(Contd.)

(Contd. Table 2)

1.	2.	3.	4.	5.	6.	7.
13.	Indebted farmer HHs land < 1 Hectare	36.0	55.7	87.7	53.3	61.0
14.	Indebted farmer HHs land 1-2 hectares	26.2	21.8	9.1	15.8	18.9
15.	Indebted farmer HHs, land > 2 hectares	37.9	22.4	3.2	31.0	20.1
16.	Farmer HHS taken loan for farming activities	75.4	61.5	21.4	62.4	58.4
17.	Farmer HHS taken loan from Moneylenders	6.8	53.4	7.4	36.3	25.7
18.	Farmer HHs taken loan from Cooperative Soc.	48.5	10.4	28.3	17.6	19.6

Source: Mishra Srijit (2005) 'Suicide of Farmers in Maharashtra' Paper presented at the Seminar on farmers suicide. ASCI Hyderabad 10th & 11th July 2005.

of farmers is less but the proportion of indebted farmers is more. Within Maharashtra as well as at the all India level a relatively greater proportion of the other backward caste and the other caste farmers households seem to have loans. Nearly three fifths of the farmer households in Maharashtra depend on cultivation as their source of income and this proportion is slightly more among the indebted farmers.

There are three features of Maharashtra which are different from India and other three states:

1. It has one of the lowest proportions of indebted farmer households with less than 1 hectare of land.

2. Nearly three-fourths of the outstanding loan is for farm business. This comes to almost 15% greater than all India average and that of Andhra Pradesh and Punjab and 45% points greater than Kerala.

3. Nearly half of the loans are from cooperative societies compared to about one-fifth for the all India average. Further, the loan from professional moneylenders is about 7% of the outstanding loan compared to more than half in the case of Andhra Pradesh.

Poverty-Alleviation Programmes

Over the years poverty alleviation programmes of various types have expanded in size and today there is a wide variety of such programmes which absorb a large volume of resources. The employment guarantee scheme was one of the programmes of poverty alleviation through the provision of employment and asset creation. The programme is implemented in 33 districts and in 350 Tahsils of Maharashtra. The scheme avoids competing with agriculture; a low EGS wage will keep the non-poor away. But low rates of wages may not help to improve the income levels of poor. This in many cases leads to underutilization of the fund provided for this scheme. In the District Wardha of Maharashtra there is hardly any person who comes forward to accept the work under EGS. The EGS has so far failed to come up with the ways in which skills of the participants can be built up. The failure of the scheme on this count is one reason why the poor especially women even today continue to depend heavily on the EGS for employment and income. EGS can be considered as a relief programme and not as anti poverty programme.

The Employment Guarantee Bill that has been introduced in Parliament in December 2004 has a basic frame of reference which was provided by Maharashtra Employment Guarantee Act 1977. The specific time limit of 100 days per household is imposed in the bill. The presumption is that an open ended guarantee will cost much more than is estimated for a 100 day per household guarantee. This looks absurd and may not be helpful in solving the problem of chronic poverty.

Suicide of Farmers and Agrarian Distress

Agrarian distress caused in some of the districts of Maharashtra and the situation that led to such distress need to be analyzed. Understanding the unfortunate process that led to suicides at micro level is one stage and the second stage involves following this both at micro as well as macro level through policy initiatives. In a pragmatic sense one needs to give more importance to the second stage. The government so far has offered little, apart from attempting to find out "if wrong policies or decisions were responsible for the suicides". Whatever might be the outcome of such probes, no government can be discharged from its responsibility of drawing out the farmers from this vicious cycle of loans and debts.

Commercialization and Existing Support System

There are clear indications that the crop pattern is leaning in favor of commercialization and hence risk of crop loss increased due to both higher proportions of purchased inputs and technology. Second there is also a tendency of adopting monoculture and consequent overexploitation of land in pursuit of higher gross returns. An inevitable externality of this is the added risk and soil degradation. Third, marginal lands are entering under cultivation and this puts pressure on the inputs as well as farming practices. Lastly the cash component in the package of inputs has increased substantially. This has necessitated higher cash needs. The village as an institution has crumbled down under the pressure of commercialization whereby the weak in the villages are exposed to fend themselves and the village institutions which hitherto took care of those under distress have slowly receded and vanished. When the new systems and fresh initiatives were created enough care was not taken to provide built-in check and balance mechanism so as to correct any failures in the process.

The central issue of farmers' suicide is the debt trap. Small and marginal farmers, especially those, who lease in land from others, are not eligible for availing institutional credit and crop insurance. Thus they land at the doorsteps of the usurious moneylenders. This situation has helped in strengthening the merchant capital and the traders cum moneylenders have their fortunes in the absence of supportive institutional mechanisms. For many farmers, a shift from food crops like jawar to cash crops was suicidal. In comparison with jawar, cotton crops require much more fertilizers and chemical inputs, necessitating higher cash requirements.

Market inadequacy and crash in prices were reported as the major reasons for farmers' distress. In an open market economy, prices and arrival will theoretically follow the cobweb principle. Therefore the ups and downs in the prices are inevitable in the marketing process. However, sudden crash of prices and consistently lower prices disproportionate to the price level in the inputs causes severe agony and economic stress in the farm family. The prevailing market intervention schemes and MSP do not adequately support the farmers without a time lag and therefore completely ineffective. The time lag between price crash and market intervention is long enough to cause severe distress among the farming community. Revamping of the market discipline, providing infrastructure, price monitoring and providing quick information could go a long way in removing the market imperfections.

The absence of safety nets should not crush the entrepreneurial spirit of the farmers. This phenomenon will have more difficult outcome for the sector in future if not dealt with systematically. Therefore, the State must come out with a strong safety net programme.

Conclusion

It is difficult to make prediction that globalization will help to achieve labour intensive growth and would help to reduce the poverty in developing countries. However it is difficult to envisage the frontiers of globalization being rolled back in the near future and still more difficult to imagine this being done in a way as to benefit the poor in developing countries. The question is therefore not whether globalization is good or bad, but rather how its benefits can be maximized and its cost minimized.

There are some shortcomings in promoting institutional framework and the developmental strategies:

1. International markets for goods, services and factors of production function in such a way as to widen the gap between developed and developing countries rather than to close it.

2. The development strategies being promoted by the International financial institutions are more of competitive in nature than cooperative.

3. Poverty reduction though is an important priority of policies still considered to be the byproduct of the development process than they promote.

Backwardness of some of the areas as a challenge cannot be ignored and overlooked. This gives rise to an important requirement for these areas that is to facilitate private and public investment in the backward areas of the state. While designing and initiating such schemes, it is essential to understand the resource endowments and economic advantages of these regions to participate in the mainstream growth pattern.

Since trade liberalization policies in agriculture and removal of quantitative restrictions have become a threat to the survival of Indian farmers, import and export must be regulated and when the WTO agreement on agriculture comes up for review, the Government of India should change the WTO rules related to exports, imports and subsidies on the fundamental criterion of the right to life of Indian farmers being a fundamental right which needs to be protected under all conditions.

References

1. Deshpande R.S. (2002) Farmers Distress in Karnataka, Research Report, Institute for Social and Economic Change, Bangalore.

2. Human Development Report Maharashtra (2002)

3. Krishnaraj M, Pandey D, Kanchi (2004) 'Does EGS require restructuring for poverty alleviation and gender equality?' Economic and Political Weekly April 17, 2004.

4. Mishra Srijit (2005) 'Suicide of Farmers in Maharashtra' Paper presented at the Seminar on farmers suicide. ASCI Hyderabad 10th & 11th July 2005.

5. World Development Report (2004) 'Making Services Work for Poor People'

investment in the backward areas of the state. While designing any integrated schemes, it is essential to understand the resource endowments and economic advantages of these regions to participate in the mainstream growth pattern.

Since trade liberalization policies ... agriculture and ... [illegible]

3

Urban Poverty Management in India with special Reference to Micro-finance to Urban Poor in Mumbai

Dr. G. Y. Shitole

Introduction

Poverty has been considered as a social phenomenon in which a section of the society is unable to fulfil even its basic necessities of life. It is absolute poverty, which is prevailing in all the countries of the world and it is a serious problem in developing and underdeveloped countries. The relative poverty is an income distribution of the population of the population in different fractal groups which is in comparison of the levels of living of the top 5 to 10 percent with the bottom 5 to 10 per cent population. Geographically this poverty is again segregated as rural and urban poverty considering the type of area in which poor people are found. India being the developing country, there is existence of absolute as well as relative poverty that to in rural as well as urban areas. An attempt is made in this paper to study the magnitude of poverty in India with causes and remedial measures in general and special focus on micro financing as one of the measures of urban poverty alleviation with special reference to Mumbai City.

What is Urban Poverty

Urban poverty is a multidimensional phenomenon. The urban poor live with many deprivations. Their daily challenges may include:

- limited access to employment opportunities and income,
- inadequate and insecure housing and services,
- violent and unhealthy environments,
- little or no social protection mechanisms, and
- limited access to adequate health and education opportunities.

But urban poverty is not just a collection of above characteristics, it is also a dynamic condition of vulnerability or susceptibility to risks. In order to provide a richer understanding of urban poverty, this study presents these two analytical frameworks (i) a dynamic framework of poverty (vulnerability and asset ownership) and (ii) the multiple characteristics of poverty and its cumulative impacts.

Multidimensional Character of Urban Poverty

Urban poverty is a multidimensional phenomenon. This paper sets out four dimensions of poverty:

- income poverty
- health and education poverty
- personal and tenure insecurity
- Dis-empowerment.

The term income poverty is concerned with dependence on cash for purchases of essential goods and services. There may be employment insecurity or casual working class with lack of qualifications and less payment to urban poor. The concept of health poverty is related with overcrowding and unhygienic living conditions. The residential environments are prone to industrial and traffic pollution due to juxtaposition of residential and industrial functions in cities. The poor in cities settle on marginal lands which are prone to environmental hazards, such as landslides and floods. They have exposure to diseases due to poor quality air, water and lack of sanitation. The concept of **education poverty** refers to constrained access to education due to insufficient school sizes in rapidly growing cities, inability to afford school expenses and personal safety or security risks deterring school attendance. The **personal insecurity** refers to drug or alcohol abuse and domestic violence; family breakdown and reduced support from children; social diversity and visible inequality in cities, which increase tension and can provide a temptation for crime. The **tenure insecurity** results due to land and housing in authorized areas are not affordable; therefore the poor occupy land illegally and construct their houses without construction and occupancy permits. The concept of **dis-empowerment** is related to illegitimacy of residence and work as well as insufficient channels of information for obtaining jobs, knowing one's legal rights to service, etc. as a result the urban poor do not have importance for the rights and responsibilities of citizens.

Poverty Syndrome

According to the census of 2001, of the total population of 15.1 mn in Mumbai as many as 5.82 mn forming about 38.5% of the total live in slums. It is not unrealistic to assume that a great majority of slum/pavement dwellers are poor and are mostly engaged in activities that do not generate adequate income. As scope for generation of wage employment is somewhat limited, reliance is placed generally on self-employment activities like vending, pickle and jam making; papad making; cooking and supplying of meals; carpentry, tailing, driving and plumbing; mechanical and electrical fittings; and provision of other services such as laundry, saloon, courier, etc

Table 1. Estimates of Poverty in India (Percent)

Year	*All India*	*Rural*	*Urban*
1973-74	54.9	54.4	49.0
1977-78	51.3	53.1	45.2
1983-84	44.5	45.7	40.8
1987-88	38.9	39.1	38.2
1993-94	36.0	37.3	32.4
1999-00	26.1	27.1	23.6

Source: Economic Survey of India, (2000-01) Ministry of Finance, Government of India, New Delhi.

The above statistics show that the urban poverty has been alleviated to fifty percent within the period of thirty years. The reduction of urban poverty is faster than the rural poverty in India. Though the government measures are more in number for rural poverty alleviation with big publicity and propaganda as a political stunt, such as Garibi Hatao, Javahar Rozagar Yojana, etc. In actual sense the urban poverty is extension of rural poverty because the rural poor migrate to urban areas in search of jobs and better life which results in urban slums and poor localities. Even Government focus is on rural poverty alleviation as a matter of fact rather than urban poverty. However, the urban poor get some job opportunities and slowly more number of urban poor do not remain poor without much efforts from Government or N. G. Os. Also it is important to note that more reduction in urban poverty is seen during the post reforms period.

Key Factors Affecting Urban Poverty in India:

1. The impact of labor markets on urban poverty.
2. Vulnerability of the Urban Poor.
3. Social Infrastructure.
4. Location of the urban poor.
5. Poverty and basic urban services.
6. The impact of migration on India's urban poverty.

Sponsored Poverty Alleviation Programmes

So far, a number of programmes have been launched to ameliorate urban poverty, which includes the Scheme of Urban Micro Enterprises, Nehru Rozgar Yojana and Prime Minister's Integrated Urban Poverty Alleviation Programme and Urban Basic Services for Poor (UBSP), etc. Within the framework of such multiplicity of schemes, more emphasis was given to individual programme targets and as a result, income generation on sustainable basis was relegated to the place of secondary importance. With a view to rectifying this situation, Government of India has most of these schemes restructured into a Swarna Jayanti Shahari Rozgar Yojna (SJSRY) from December 1997.

This programme provides employment to unemployed or underemployed urban poor by encouraging them to set up self-employed venture. The scheme also gives a special impetus to empowerment and upliftment of the poor women. For this purpose, a special programme for development of Women and Children in Urban Areas, has been launched under which group of urban poor women setting up self-employment are eligible for subsidy up to 50% of the project cost. It must, however, be stressed that all such sponsored poverty alleviation programmes do not generally lead to establishment of relationship banking. Indeed, most of these often remain a one-time activity, wherein loan is given usually at one stroke. In this situation, the borrower tries to get maximum limit of the loan amount permissible under a particular scheme to fetch the maximum amount of loan and subsidy.

Further, it is observed that financing of a large number of small sized loans under poverty alleviation programmes often exacerbates transaction costs. For the banks, the subsidized interest rates make lending under sponsored programmes least attractive. The provision of capital subsidy at times vitiates the effectiveness of poverty alleviation programmes to a significant extent. Further, in the absence of social intervention, benefits of financial intervention often get marginalized. For example, if there is an uncontrolled increase in family size, despite the accrual of projected incremental income, there would be an erosion in the per capita income. Likewise, various social evils like addiction to drinking, smoking, gambling, use of drugs as also other tobacco products may push the poor family towards an enduring poverty. Thanks to these limitations, the sponsored poverty alleviation programmes have not made significant positive impact.

Micro-finance - An Innovation for Poverty Alleviation

As a policy intervention, micro-finance seeks to:

- reduce poverty by increasing the access of poor people to savings and credit so they can invest in physical capital to increase the productivity of existing assets;
- provide working capital for the purchase of inputs;
- allow for consumption smoothing, enabling major expenses such as health treatment or funeral costs to be met.

Micro finance therefore forms part of an asset-based community development strategy with the following features:

- *Savings:* With savings facilities available to them, the poor are able to accumulate cash surpluses, which could be turned into productive assets and make a significant contribution to household livelihood strategies. Cash surpluses can also create a barrier for the foreseen and unforeseen expenses of the future, thus reducing vulnerability to debt traps.

- *Transaction services*: Given the legacy of the migrant labour system, transaction services are an especially important issue in South Africa. The programme outlined in the financial services charter and the recently launched Mzansi account take us some way forward in addressing access to transaction banking.

- *Credit*: In the right circumstances credit can assist the poor in building assets and 'smoothing' the up-and-down nature of their income. Like savings, credit can assist in converting very small, irregular incomes into a large lump sum, which can augment livelihood strategies and reduce vulnerability.

Insurance: Like savings and credit, properly managed insurance services can 'smooth' income. Our people have organised themselves into popular insurance enterprises in the form of burial societies, which indicates the importance of insurance services to the poor.

Lack of access to credit increases the vulnerability of the urban poor by constraining their ability to improve their homes, their work, and to start new businesses. Credit underwriting is a major problem since the poor do not have property to use as collateral and often lack regular incomes. Supporting micro-finance programs and provision of tenure security to support underwriting are possible policy actions at local levels. The poor typically have little access to formal savings programs. Mechanisms to mobilize small savings of the poor are often limited to credit associations and informal solutions such as rotating savings and credit associations. NGOs or other micro-crediting organizations' ability to collect savings and to mobilize other private and public funds is also limited. In many developing and industrial countries, banks do not perceive the poor as worthwhile clients. Outright discrimination in some countries can be seen. Banks are often located so that they are out of reach of the poor. Discrimination can also be seen in how the poor are treated when they try to open savings or checking accounts. Therefore, the poor may tend to accumulate savings in inefficient ways, such as informal credit unions, rotating saving and credit systems, which yield very low or no interest, or by buying tradable goods. However, experience shows that once banks begin servicing savings accounts among the low-income communities, they become more willing to make credit available to the poor. Local authorities can initiate small savings and credit programs for the urban poor. In the Philippines, for example, local governments have small savings and credit schemes for poor women in Barangays (neighborhoods).

Surely, the poor (whether in rural or urban areas) cannot and should not wait for long to get the required assistance. To address all these complex issues, a proper blending of financial and social intervention is imperative. In this context, the importance of micro finance intervention cannot be over emphasized. Micro finance is an innovative tool. It is concerned with the provision of thrift credit, other financial services and products of very small amounts with an element of social intervention enabling mainly the poor to improve their living standards. The concepts 'micro finance' and 'micro credit' are usually used interchangeably; in fact, micro lending per se is at times considered as micro credit in some quarters. However, micro credit is always dovetailed with thrift, and hence, micro finance is a more appropriate expression rather than micro credit.

Micro finance includes a whole gamut of financial services like thrift, credit, insurance, leasing of equipment, remittance etc. required by the poor. Micro finance is generally routed through small groups commonly known as Self-Help Groups (SHGs), which not only serve as a platform to supervise the activities of each other but also provide social collaterals. Loan amount to the member of the SHG is based on the amount of the savings of the SHG and is recovered generally in 12 monthly installments. Loans are repeated and gradually increased; thus establishing relationship banking.

The implicit objective of SHGs is to combat unjust social relationship by increasing people's participation through their empowerment. The emphasis is also on human resource development. The SHGs are generally of small size. Such small sized SHGs not only ensure active participation, but also promote group dynamics in decision-making and greater transparency. Moreover, separate SHGs for men and women are more conducive for addressing the issues of gender imbalance. Also SHGs frame their own rules and regulations to suit the local conditions. Though the primary objective of micro-finance interventions is to help the poor to surmount poverty, they also assist them to undertake financially viable enterprises, which could be taken up by the banks for commercial lending.

Relevance of Micro-finance in Mumbai

Although, micro finance interventions are more popular in rural areas (illustratively, Grameen Bank in Bangladesh; Aman, Ikhatiyar in Malaysia; and MYRADA in India), their relevance in urban and metropolitan areas is more pronounced as these areas actually bear the brunt of the consistently increasing migration of the poor from rural areas. In India, Mumbai has the largest number of slum dwellers (5.82 mn) distantly followed by Delhi (1.82 mn), Kolkata (1.49 mn) and Chennai (1.08 mn). In terms of proportion of slum dwellers to total population, Mumbai again ranked first with 38.5% slum dwellers distantly followed by Delhi (18.8%), Chennai (18.3%) and Kolkata (12.7%).

The concentration of a large number of the poor is not only an incipient threat to the peace and harmony of the city, but also hazardous for the financial health of the city. Against this backdrop, there is an urgent need for a mechanism under which those who migrate to cities have necessary organizational network to fall back upon in times of difficulties. Nonetheless, efforts are in place to help the poor in a number of cities such as "SEWA" in Gujarat (SEWA also operates in several other areas in Gujarat) and Society for Promotion of Area Resources Centers (SPARC) operating in major cities of India, including Mumbai. Besides SPARC, National Slum Dwellers Federation (NSDF) and Mahila Milan Bank together form an alliance to help the poor in Mumbai as also in other cities to organize poor in SHGs and work on the principles of micro finance. There are also quite a few other non governmental organizations (NGOs) operating in Mumbai for the betterment of the poor, but all these initiatives need to be augmented further, given a staggering number of Mumbai's poor. Undoubtedly, various concerned agencies will have to make concerted efforts to cover and assist all the poor within a timeframe. In this context, all those who are interested in equity and social justice, as well as in the betterment of Mumbai, should join together either as co-operative society, trust, company, non-banking finance company (NBFC), mutually aided co-operative society (MACS) or any other type of institutions that offer micro finance services to the poor. Thus, it would be possible to organize at least pavement dwellers (if not slum dwellers) in Mumbai to form of SHGs of homogenous people in different localities. Undoubtedly, proper shelter is the top most priority for all urban poor. Indeed, a better living place is the very foundation for a socio-economic transformation.

Similarly, a proper work place is a pre-requisite for taking up any gainful economic/business activity. It is important to note that the poor generally do not possess proper ownership rights of housing or business site. They are mostly squatters, living and operating businesses without any legal titles. Therefore, the first priority towards reduction of poverty in a place like Mumbai should be of to clearing of pavements or slums by concerned authorities and provision of alternative sites with legal rights. Organizing slum dwellers in SHGs would enable them to sort out problems like purchase of land, construction of dwellings etc., with concerned agencies. The members of the SHGs should be encouraged to save at least a rupee or two rupees per day, and that may be ultimately used for construction of shelter as also to tide over emergencies. This will also relieve them from the clutches of money lending sharks.

It is interesting to note that according to a case study of Mahila Milan Bank, the poor used to borrow in times of desperate need from pathans/money lenders, pawnbrokers at an interest rate of 10% per month. But on joining saving groups of Mahila Milan Bank, they have been completely relieved from the clutches of such sharks. The peer pressure under SHG System will also curb the tendency of selling of newly acquired house/work site and may discourage reverting back to foot-paths, which is not uncommon among pavement dwellers. SHGs will also help them in procurement of raw materials and skill development for processing of raw material and marketing of finished goods processed by the poor.

Support from SIDBI

SIDBI has galvanized its efforts for accelerating orderly growth of micro sector in urban and metropolitan areas. It has established Foundation for Micro Credit in November 1998 to provide a complete range of financial and non-financial services to institutions engaged in delivery of micro finance products and services. SIDBI's Foundation also provides support to Micro finance Institutions (MFIs) for capacity building.

Under its scheme, micro finance institutions having good credibility, track record and professional expertise are eligible for assistance. The loan assistance for micro finance institutions for onlending is need-based, and is subject to a minimum limit of Rs.12 lakh. However, maximum amount of assistance by micro finance institutions to a single borrower/ member of a SHG should not exceed Rs. 25,000.

Policy Initiatives of Reserve Bank of India

While announcing the monetary and credit policy for the year 1999-2000 the RBI Governor, Dr. Bimal Jalan, evinced a great deal of interest in bridging gaps between micro realities and macro policies. Accordingly, the Micro Credit Special Cell was set up in the RBI to suggest policy measures for mainstreaming and upscaling of the micro finance sector. Indeed, it is the first central bank in Asia, which took several policy measures concerning micro finance, the key features of which are:

(i) RBI has allowed banks to formulate their own models or choose any conduit/intermediary for extending micro credit. Banks are allowed to choose suitable branch/pocket/ area where micro credit programmes can be implemented; (ii) Banks are permitted to prescribe their own lending norms keeping in view the ground realities; (iii) Banks are also allowed to devise appropriate loan and saving products and related terms and conditions including the size of loan, unit cost, unit size, maturity period, grace period, margins and purpose of borrowing including for housing and shelter needs; (iv) Interest rates on bank's loans given to micro-finance institutions are completely deregulated; (v) Bank lending under micro finance will be treated as part of priority sector targets as well as under sub-target of lending to the weaker sections; (vi) The micro-finance institutions registered as not for profit NBFCs have been exempted from registration and prudential requirements. RBI has permitted such NBFCs to provide credit not exceeding Rs. 50,000 for business activity and Rs. 1,25,000 for meeting the cost of a dwelling unit to the poor.

This apart, the Government of India has also allowed foreign direct investment in micro credit to encourage foreign participation in various micro finance projects.

A joint project was undertaken by the Department of Commerce, Mumbai University and Department of Economics, S.N.D.T. Women's University involving twenty teachers and two hundred students during early nineties conducting survey of 562 informal sector enterprises in Mumbai to understand their financial problems. All these small informal sector enterprises had micro credit from different sources and their sincere efforts and hard working attitude have obtained some skills either through formal or informal training. Their capacity to do business contributes to the great help in the overall development of the economy as well as that particular urban area. In turn it helps to reduce the urban poverty.

Conclusions

In summing up, micro finance is an innovative mechanism for ameliorating urban poverty. Indeed, it offers an inspiring tool for concerned people be it businessmen, industrialists, professionals, administrators, researchers or students, for making Mumbai a better place to live, work and invest in. All these stakeholders can deploy micro finance institutions to solve the problems of the pavement dwellers first through the conduit of SHGs by availing of assistance of SIDBI and other facilities and freedom given by RBI towards mainstreaming and upscaling of micro finance sector.

The urban poverty alleviation is much easier than the rural poverty alleviation in the country, because the rural poor people remain poor for generations together which is not in case of urban poor. The SEVA experience in Ahmedabad shows that the micro-credit can go long way in alleviating the urban poverty. Similarly the Gramin Bank in Bnagla Desh started as a rural scheme but it is working well in semi urban areas.

References

1. Anagol Malati and Sundaram S.K.G., Problems of Financing Informal Sector Enterprises, Himalaya Publisihing House, Mumbai. (1995)

2. Radhakrishna and Ray Shovan, Poverty in India : Dimensions and Character, India Development Report, Edited by Kirit Prakash and Radhakrishna, Indira Gandhi Institute of Development Research, Oxford University Press, (2004-05).

3. Vyas V. S. and Bhargava Pradeep, Public Intervention for Poverty Alleviation in India : Poverty Reduction in Developing Countries, Edited by Vyas and Bhargava, Institute of Development Studies, Rawat Publications, Jaipur. (1999)

4

Eliminating Poverty: Making Globalisation Work for the Poor

Ms. Anjali Masarguppi

Recent studies emphasize that poverty is no longer an isolated problem of Low-Income Countries and globalization has made poverty as an International Economic Problem that needs to be tackled at a global level with utmost urgency. The World Bank and other International Economic Agencies collectively aim at reducing poverty at least by half by year 2015.

This brings various inter-related issues to the forefront: such as Economic Growth, Pattern & trends of Income Distribution and their impact on Poverty Reduction. The current research work of World Bank is emphasizing on poverty efficient allocation of multilateral aid to various countries. A cross-country study has showed the significant role Foreign Aid has and can play in reducing poverty in various countries, depending on the effectiveness of their internal Macro-economic Policies.

WB research indicates, "If aid allocation is not politically constrained, despite diminishing returns to aid, aid budget would be allocated overwhelmingly to India. Because India has reasonable policies, a very high poverty and a very high population, hence, its capacity to absorb aid is enormous." (WDR 2002).

A TWO – GAP MODEL AND RATIONALE OF AID:

Going back to history, sovereign lending and problems associated with it, has been a feature of International Economic life – international lending & borrowing process has played an integral role in development of most major industrialized countries and continues to play a significant role in the economic transformation of today's developing countries. Infact, many Oil Producing & Exporting Countries face serious balance of payments problems in current account, while their domestic resources lie idle. Since economies are interdependent, to provide growth momentum to the world economy, these deficits require financing.

The need for resource is as acute as ever, because of dominant foreign exchange gap to meet development requirements, to pay interest and amortization on the past borrowings. Countries find it difficult to convert domestic resources into foreign exchange in adequate quantities (through trade), not only cyclically when the world economy is depressed, but also secularly owing to their structure i.e. they produce goods whose demand tends to be both price& income inelastic in the world trade. **An important point to be noted here, is – if growth is constrained by lack of foreign exchange, free trade can not guarantee simultaneous internal & external equilibrium and gain from trade may be offset by the underutilization of domestic resources.**

A TWO – GAP MODEL:

Income = Consumption + Investment + Exports - Imports

Therefore,

Saving = Investment + Exports – Imports

Investment – Saving = Imports – Exports.

Identity between the gaps – the investment – saving (I-S) gap and import – export (M-X) gap is more of an accounting nature, because there is no reason, in principle, why two gaps should be equal.

The basic underlying assumption of dual- gap model analysis is lack of substitutability between foreign and domestic resources. Therefore, dual gap, then emphasizes the role of imports and foreign exchange in the development process, which synthesizes traditional and more modern view concerning aid and development – i.e. on the one hand, it emphasizes the traditional view of foreign assistance as merely a boost to domestic savings and on the other hand, it makes more modern view that many goods necessary for growth cannot be produced by developing countries themselves, must therefore, be imported with the help of foreign assistance.

Rationale of Aid has undergone change over a period of time:

1. The first justification of aid was put forth in 40s & 50s, linking to the view that increase in the rate of GNP was essential for economic development, which depends upon investment rate. Since domestic savings in LDCs were low, inflow of private investment and aid will be needed to support domestic savings.

2. Emphasis shifted in 60s from physical capital to technical assistance to move from dependency to self- sufficiency. This was a transfer model of aid- it still underlies much thinking in aid and aid- policy.

3. Some criticized this as a leverage to keep neo- colonial links or neo- imperialist dependency intact on metropolitan countries. '80s was marked by conditionality, adjustment policy and aid consortia that was seen as continuation of control.

4. **The new paradigm views international aid as a catalyst and a source of countervailing power in favor of global**

commitments, development cooperation, rather than aid merely as a supplement to savings to enable higher investment, more rapid growth and take-off to self-sufficiency. Aid as a catalyst and countervailing power has been larger and more influential in certain areas of human development.

Recent evidence on the effectiveness of aid based on detailed study of seven countries (Bangladesh, Columbia, India, Kenya, Malawi, Mali) shows that most aid achieves its development objectives, although in several instances performance could be improved. Although, aid allocation has multiple objectives, poverty reduction is the most applicable objective of aid.

In order to study the effectiveness and role of aid in poverty reduction, we try to establish certain relationships between:

1. Economic Growth and Aid.
2. Aid and Poverty Reduction.
3. Poverty Reduction and Income Inequalities.
4. Income Inequalities and Economic Growth.

I. ECONOMIC GROWTH AND AID

The first step to estimate impact of aid on poverty reduction is to estimate the impact of aid on growth.

AID – GROWTH RELATIONSHIP

An early study by Papanek (1973) suggested that aid and growth are positively correlated across countries, despite the paltry level of assistance received per head. Papanek relates domestic growth to three types of foreign capital inflow: aid (a), foreign direct investment (f), and other foreign inflows (o). Taking 85 countries and including the domestic saving ratio (Sd) as an additional explanatory variable, a following equation is estimated:

$$Y = 1.5 + \underset{(6.0)}{0.20\,(Sd)} + \underset{(5.8)}{0.39\,(a)} + \underset{(2.5)}{0.17\,(f)} + \underset{(2.1)}{0.19\,(o)}.$$

r2 = 0.37

Aid coefficient is highly significant and is also higher in absolute value than any other coefficient, suggesting that aid is more productive than domestic resources and other capital inflows. Sub – samples of countries also yield similar results.

For a large number of countries, Burnside and Dollar (1997) have developed a growth function:

$$G = c + b_1 X + b_2 P + b_3 A + b_4 AP$$

G – Growth
X – Exogenous conditions
P – Level of Policy
A – Level of net receipt of aid relative to GDP
AP – Interaction of aid and policy

The OLS results estimated for this equation by Burnside and Dollar is:

- Policy is directly significant in the growth process.
- Policy is also significant via its interaction with aid.
- At the mean of policy (= 0); marginal impact of aid is zero.
- At the mean of policy (= 1); marginal impact of 1% real PPP GDP increase in assistance is 0.3% point.
- For a country with very good policy i.e. mean of policy (= 2); return to aid reaches zero, which is about 5% of real PPP GDP (since PPP measure of GDP are typically 3-4 times higher than GDP at nominal exchange rate, this corresponds to 15 – 20% of GDP evaluated at nominal exchange rate – which is very high).

The equation indicates that aid is more effective in raising growth, the better the policy environment. A single most important component in the aid- growth relationship is that efficiency of aid depends upon policy but beyond a certain point, marginal efficiency of aid diminishes i.e. diminishing returns to aid begin.

Although the overall absorptive capacity might well be higher in the 1990s. than before mainly due to improvement in policy environment, yet the presence of diminishing returns to aid is not controversial.

Dia. WDR. 2005.

Figure 1.14 Poverty reduction is closely associated with growth

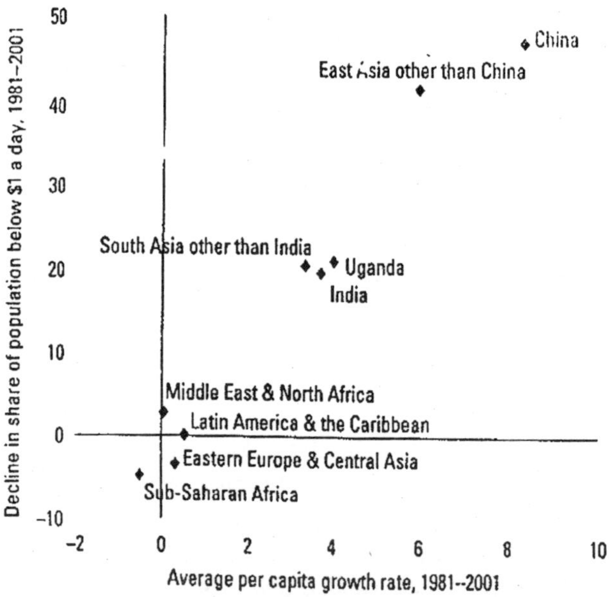

Note: Data for Uganda are from 1992–2000 and uses its national poverty level due to data availability.
Source: Chen and Ravallion (2004); World Bank (2004k)

A major reason of concern here, is whether in reality there are countries with good policies and mass poverty – because it is possible that two variables are negatively correlated. But the empirical measure and head count poverty rate of 113 developing countries show that, there are 32 countries in good policy - high poverty quadrant and a large majority of the world's poor live in these 32 countries (i.e. 2 billion people out of 2.7 billion poor in these 113 countries) and most of the countries in this quadrant are the ones that have reformed in 10 years and aid will have more impact on poverty reduction in this quadrant where there are 2 billion people and policy makes aid effective.

II. AID AND POVERTY REDUCTION

WB research paper (Collier and Dollar) estimate that, if the present allocation of aid is made more poverty efficient it will succeed in sustainably lifting 80 million people per annum vis-à-vis currently estimated 30 million people per annum of absolute poverty.

In case of the efficient allocation for a given level of poverty, aid is supposed to taper – in with reforms but in actual allocation, aid tapers-out with policy reforms.

Reduction in poverty is said to be the function of: aid, initial evel of income, its distribution and sustained long-term growth rate. This yields a unique function for each country, in which aid reduces poverty but is subject to diminishing returns.

For aid to be effective, the precondition is the existence of mass poverty. The WB working papers observe that, if aid were not politically constrained, despite diminishing returns, aid budget would be allocated overwhelmingly to India. The marginal cost of poverty reduction, given the current allocation of aid, varies enormously. For around twenty countries, additional aid would not reduce poverty where as on the other end of the spectrum the marginal cost of poverty reduction is only $333 per person in Bangladesh, India, and Ethiopia.

There is significant relationship between policy and aid, but it is non-monotonic. For a given level of poverty, in the range between bad policy and mediocre policies, aid is positively related to policy, but in the range between mediocre policies and good policies, aid sharply declines (tapers-in); and in the last stage where policy moves into the realm in which aid becomes ineffective in reducing poverty, aid starts phasing out.

Dia. Thirlwall A.

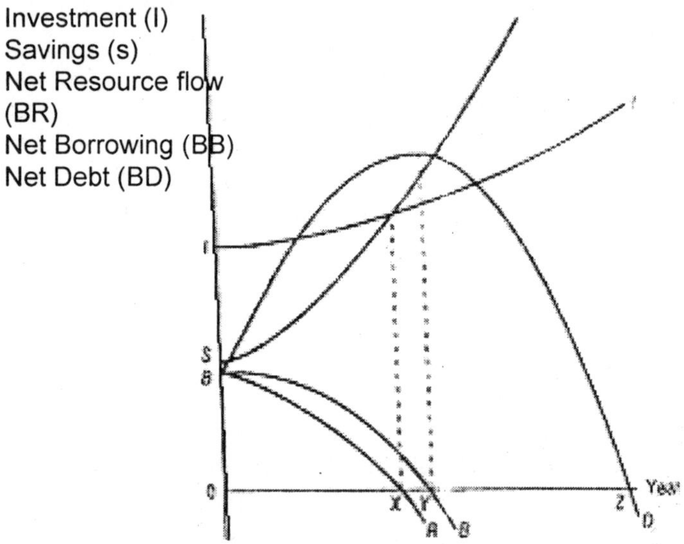

5.1 Debt-servicing interrelationships

The investment- saving gap is given by the difference between the curves II and SS. The net resource flow (BR) required to bridge the investment – saving gap to maintain a target rate of growth declines steadily, becoming a net resource out flow after X years. Net borrowing goes on a little longer in order to cover interest charges on accumulated indebtedness. Net borrowing (BB) is zero after Y years, at this point net indebtedness (BD) starts declining. Debt repayment, in theory, take place by converting the excess saving over investment into balance-of – payments surplus until all debts are repaid by the year Z, after which a country becomes a net creditor.

Policies that matter for aid to be effective in poverty reduction are not purely macroeconomic but include both distributional policies and the provision for social safety net.

III. POVERTY REDUCTION AND INEQUALITY OF INCOME

There exist a close relationship between macro performances indicated by p.c.y (Per Capita Income) economic growth, income distribution and poverty.

For any income distribution, poverty will move broadly in direct relation to changes in p.c.y.; while if growth in p.c.y. stagnates, changes in poverty is a reflection of changes in income distribution. Of course, poverty can increase despite improving income distribution if p.c.y.s are falling rapidly or decrease despite worsening income distribution if p.c.y. is rising rapidly. Although, changing incidence of poverty is more significant than changes in income distribution (A.K.Sen, 1983), but distribution is a major determinant of poverty index.

Cross- country evidence has showed a variety of results e.g. given the relatively high p.c.y. in Latin America, the poverty found here is significantly attributed to extreme inequality which characterizes most Latin American countries.

Contrary to this, in China, during the phase of market reforms or liberalization although inequality increased (indicated by Gini-coefficient), there was a remarkable fall in poverty, the reason was that per capita income rose very fast.

IV. INCOME INEQUALITY AND ECONOMIC GROWTH

" It is not necessary that growth raises incomes of the poor- by about as much as it raises incomes of everybody else."- The Economist.

Finding that the share of income going to the poor does not change on average with growth, does not mean that growth raises the incomes of the poor as much as for the rich. Given the existing inequality, the income gains to the rich from distribution- neutral growth will of course be greater than to the poor. For example, income gain to the richest 10% in India would be four times higher than the gain to the poorest 5%. **This trend that, on an average, the rich will tend to capture a much larger share of the increment to national income from growth, than poor, has been well supported by empirical results (Dollar and Kraay 2000)**

Some other observations show that, the higher the proportion of poor people in the economy, the lower is the growth rate. This is further elaborated under Human development section later.

Inequality also matters to the pace of poverty reduction that is achieved at any given rate of growth. This is also further analyzed later.

Underlying the heterogeneity in the gains to the poor, from a given rate of growth lies in the fact that during spells of growth or contraction one sees changes in inequality overtime. In most developing economies changes are in both directions.

Developing countries with a tendency for rising inequality since late 1980s include Bangladesh, China, Columbia, India, the Philippines and Vietnam, where as declining trends are found in Brazil, Honduras, Jamaica, Thailand (Ravallion 2000b). In India 1999-2000 WB data shows that Gini- coefficient was 32.5 (lowest 20% of the population shared 8.9% of income and the highest 20% shared 41.6% of income).
Dia. WDR. 2005.

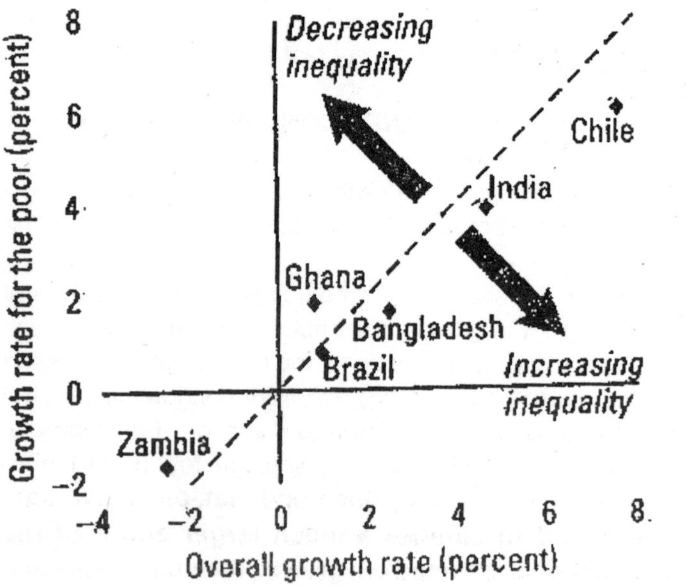

Inequality as an Impediment to Growth

Cross- country comparison of growth rates supports the claim that countries with higher initial inequality in incomes experienced lower rates of growth, controlling the other factors – such as initial p.c.y., rate of inflation and openness to trade. Of course, this does not imply that any reduction in inequality will automatically enhance growth: infact, it can have the opposite effect if it comes at the expense of other factors that are also known to matter to growth. Reducing inequality by adding further distortions to external trade or domestic economy will have ambiguous effects on growth and poverty reduction.

An important determinant of poverty reduction is **the distribution corrected rate of growth in average income,** given the measure of initial inequality i.e. (1 – Gini coefficient x rate of growth). One can represent this in the form of a very simple model, which gives the proportionate rate of change in measured poverty (PR)
over a given interval of time as:

PR = b (1- I) g

where, I is an index of inequality (between 0 and 1) , at the beginning of time period of the time over which average income grows at a rate 'g'. Measuring PR by annual percentage change in the proportion of population living below $1 per day; *I* by the Gini index, and measuring 'g' by the rate of growth in the real per capita income. Therefore,

PR - proportionate rate of change in measured poverty
I - index of inequality (between 0 and 1)
G - rate of growth average income
b - estimated parameter.

Indeed, the distribution corrected growth rate knocks out the simple rate of growth when both are used in a regression for the rate of poverty reduction between surveys across countries and time (Ravallion 1997). Therefore, it is not the rate of growth that matters but the distribution corrected rate of growth. Data indicates that economic growth has tended to reduce poverty in India.

In this context, one may point out that, the world Gini Index increased from 63% in 1988 to 66% in 1993, which has wiped out a large share of the gains to the world's poor from global economic growth – an important reason for this is rising inequality between countries – mainly because growth rates have tended to be lower in poor countries (Prichett, 1997).

Growth and Human Resource Development

HRD is the most closely related issue to poverty reduction, and economic growth. Modern study based on international comparison emphasizes the importance of human capital growth. There is no trade-off between Human Development and sustainable economic development. Although results reported by Prichett (1996) and Caselli et al (1996), indicate that human capital accumulation would exert a negative influence on growth. But these findings are said to suffer from specification bias.

It is true that countries with higher average income tend to have High Human Development Index (HDI), although much depends upon how economic growth is shared.

A comparison is drawn between Chinese and Indian experience since 1960s on the basis of two criteria- strong HD / weak EG and weak HD / strong EG (HD- Human Development, EG- Economic Growth). During 1960-80 China concentrated on education and health and did not pay much attention to economic growth, resulting into healthier and more productive labor force enabling them to adapt better technology and production practices leading to rise in EG.

On the other hand, since 1960s India had low EG and low HD- with reforms we tried to have big push for higher economic growth, but with low HD. ADB database of 1999 shows that adult literacy rates for females and males in India were 44% and 68%. For China the comparable figures were 78% and 91%. Health and other HD indicators across the two countries tell a similar story. **Therefore, a high EG has not led to better HD because linkage between EG and HD are weak in India – due to resource crunch devoted to HD. The need of the hour is to establish a strong EG – HD link to avoid low equilibrium trap. Therefore, a key to sustained higher economic growth in India is investment in HD. But studies are showing that the required 7% p.a. growth rate is hard to sustain in India that can lead to secular rise in unemployment.**

"Investing in people" has become the World Bank slogan in the '90s derived from Neo-Classical paradigm that a strong evidence links productivity to investment in human capital. Lucas (and subsequent contributors), of endogenous growth theory, reinforce the importance of education by postulating that returns to aggregate accumulation of human capital do not diminish, so that sustained per capita income growth can come from endogenous human capital alone. " Market may be impressive economically or technologically. But they are of little value if they do not serve human development. Markets are the means and human development is the end."- (UNDP 1992). **This indicates that free markets should be modified through public policy to redistribute income and assets and safety nets and measures to smoothen the flow of finance to poor countries and reduce their indebtedness. This once again supports poverty reduction and humanitarian relief consistent with the most preferred focus of aid and brings us to the issue of allocation of aid.**

Conclusion

With assistance comes a certain amount of 'leverage' that can be an influence for good as well as for bad. This raises the issue of debt servicing. Therefore, current efforts are on in many of the world's poorest countries to develop **Poverty Reduction Strategy Papers (PRSP) that reflect increased emphasis on mainstreaming poverty reduction process.** As policy instruments and procedure, they immediately ralate to aid, concessional lending and debt relief. But they also embody a set of principles in mainstreaming poverty concerns into national development strategies, which can open an entirely new area for debate.

(This paper is dedicated to late Dr. M.J.Manohar Rao. under whose able guidance I had started my research in this area.)

References

1. Burnside, C and Dollar, D., 1997."Aid, Policies and Growth" Policy Research Working Paper no.1777, World Bank.

2. Chwn Shaohua and Martin Ravallion, 2000,"How did the World's Poorest Fare in the 1990s?" Policy Research Paper 2409, World Bank.

3. Datt, Gaurav, 1999," Has Poverty in India Declined since the Economic Reforms?" Economic and Political Weekly 34(December 11-17

4. Dollar, D. and Autrr Kraay, 2000." Growth is good for the poor". World Bank Washington DC.

5. Ravallion M and Dutt G., 1999, " When is Growth Pro-Poor? Evidence from the Diverse in Experience of India's States". Policy Research Paper 2263, World Bank.

6. Sen,A.K. , 1983 "Choice, Welfare and Measurement," Oxford University Press, New Delhi.

7. Silvera, D.M. 1990, "Human Resource Development - The Indian Experience."

8. Thirlwall A.P., "Growth and Development with special reference to developing economies." Macmillan Publication.

9. United Kingdom Secretary of State for International Development, 1997, "Eliminating World Poverty: A Challenge for the 21st Century. White Paper on International Development."

10.White H., 1992, "The Macroeconomic Analysis of Aid Impact," Journal of Development Studies,28.

11.World Bank, 2000b, World Development Report, Attacking Poverty, New York; Oxford University Press.

12.World Bank, 1990, World Development Report: Poverty, New York : Oxford University Press.

Websites:
www.oecd.org.
www.worldbank.org.

5
Poverty Alleviation: A Case Study of Tamil Nadu

Harshada Rathod

Introduction

In 2000, the UN General Assembly had set eight goals for development, known on Millennium Development Goals, to be achieved by 2015. Most of these goals have quantifiable, monitorable targets to measure progress against standards set by the international community.

Not only the WDR 2000-01 very aptly recommends action on three complementary and synergistic fronts for poverty alleviation- promoting opportunity, facilitating empowerment and enhancing security. This paper mainly focused on sustainable poverty alleviation through Afforestation Project – a case study from Tamil Nadu.

The paper is divided into the following sections:

Section I	: Southern state of India – Tamil Nadu.
Section II	: Basic Macro Economic Frame Work of Tamil Nadu.
Section III	: Poverty Alleviation and reviving the primary sector.
Section IV	: Case study of Afforstration.

Tamilnadu, the southern state of India has a geographic area of 13 million hectares, which constitutes 3.96 % of the land area of the country. The total population of the state is 55.86 million (1991 census) accounting for 6.60 % of the country's population. The recorded forest area is 2.26 million hectares, which makes 17.40 % of the land area of the state. But the actual forest cover as assessed through remote sensing is only 1.71 million hectares- a mere 13.13 % of the land area. More over, half of this actual forest cover has a crown density of less than 40 %.

There are 15822 villages in the state of which 1405 are bordering the forests. The total population of these forest villages is estimated to be 3.11 million.

Section I

Southern State of India

Tamil Nadu is the sixth state in the Indian Union and second South Indian state to prepare an SHDR. The Tamil Nadu SHDR is important as it provides insights into the process of development in a state characterized by heavy industrialization, urbanization, better growth rates and poverty levels which are below national average. In short, Tamil Nadu is a model of a middle income state that has tried to enhance the level of human development through the formation and implementation of programmes that address the needs of the poor, vulnerable and marginal population of the state.

Section II

Basic Macro Economic Framework of Tamil Nadu

Growth: The all round development of the state over the last five decades can be seen from the increased contribution from the industries (secondary) and service (tertiary) sectors to the real income of the state's economy.

Tamil Nadu's performance during the different plan periods compared to the performance of the country as a whole (at constant prices) shows that the rate of growth of the state's economy has been marginally higher than that of the country during the First & Fourth plans, Fifth to Seventh plans and in the first three years of the Ninth plan and marginally lower than that of the country during the Second, Third and Eight plan periods. Tamil Nadu's NSDP growth rate was 6.3% per annum during the 1990's,ahead of the NSDP growth rate of 5.99% of the 15 major state in the country.

Annual Growth Rate 1980-81 Prices , Tamil Nadu and India.

Plan Period	*I*	*II*	*III*	*IV*	*V*	*VI*	*VII*	*VIII*	*IX*
Tamil Nadu	4.45	2.90	1.58	3.40	7.00	6.01	4.94	5.97	5.46
India	3.6	4.0	2.2	3.3	5.2	5.2	5.8	6.8	5.34

Source : Tamil Nadu at fifty – A statistical compendium – Department of Eco. & Stats.

Tamil Nadu's PCI was below the nationai average during the 1980's but crossed the all Indian average marginally in 1991-92. Even since the early 1990's this higher PCI has been maintained. Tamil Nadu ranks fourth among major states in terms of PCI (at current prices Rs. 19,889 in 2000-01)

Sectoral Share : There is a close relationship between employment, income & poverty. Moreover, economic development is invariably associated with structural changes in GDP (income) and employment. A characteristics feature of a developing economy is declining trend in the share of the primary sector in GDP in the process of diversification of the economy. One would expect a shift in the share of workers from the primary sector to the secondary and tertiary sectors.

An analysis of the trends in the sectoral share in income and employment in Tamil Nadu shows that though there has been a decline in the share of the primary sector in income, this has been accompanied by a significant shift in the share of employment. Consequently a very sizeable section of the labour force (nearly 50%) continues to depend on the primary sector. The average income of persons depending in the agricultural sector

Sectoral Share of NSDP, Employment and Per Worker Output, (At 1993-94 prices)

Sector	*GSDP (Rs. Million)*				*Employment in million)*				*Per Worker output (Rs.)*	
	1993-94	% Share	*1999-2000*	% Share	*1993-94*	%	*1999-2000*	%	*1993-94*	*1999-2000*
Primary	142646.6	24.82	155072.6	18.16	15.4	54.1	14.5	50.3	.9263	10695
Secondary	193809.3	33.72	291323.8	34.12	6.2	6.8	6.8	23.6	31260	42842
Tertiary	238364.2	41.46	407515.3	47.72	6.9	7.5	7.5	26.1	345546	543335
Total	574820.1	100.00	853911.7	100.00	28.5	100.00	28.9	100.00	20169	29547

Source : Planning Commission, Govt. of India.

is considerable less than that of those working in the secondary and tertiary sectors. The prevalence of poverty in rural areas is widespread mainly due to the low productivity of workers in the agricultural sector and the seasonal nature of employment.

Even though agriculture continues to account for the bulk of employment, this is not reflected in the income originating from the sectors. The agriculture income declined from 24.82% in 1993-94 to 18.16% in 1999-2000, whereas the share of income from secondary and tertiary sectors improved from 33.72% to 34.12% and 41.46% to 47.72%, respectively. In Per Capita terms this means that the average output per worker in the primary sector increased only marginally compared to other sector where significant increase were noticed.

The low Per capita output in the primary sector has wider implication in terms of distribution of income and consumption. As employment in the secondary and tertiary sectors is concentrated in the urban areas, high differentials in per worker output would create an acute rural / urban dichotomy in the state.

PCI / Health and Education : The PCI of the Tamil Nadu was Rs. 15,929 at current prices in 1996-97 as compared to an all India PCI of Rs. 11,554. Tamil Nadu's recent better performance in terms of PCI was been due to an annual growth rate of 6.3 % between 1990-91 and 1996-97, higher than the growth rate of the other 14 major states. An analysis of district wise estimates of PCI reveal wide divergence. Kancheepuram has the highest PCI (Rs. 23,075 in 1996-97) and Villupuram the lowest (Rs. 10,000). In terms of contribution to overall NSDP, Chennai district contributes the maximum (1996-97) namely 11.38% and Coimbatore contributes the next largest share of 9.07 %. These two districts together account for approximately 1/5 th NSDP in Tamil Nadu.

District with high PCI would generally be expected to have better education and health standards. A close examination of data, however, reveals that this relationship does not necessarily hold true in Tamil Nadu. While Chennai with a high PCI does have a high level of literacy (above 80%) district such as Salem and Erode which have relatively high income levels have quite low literacy levels (below 70%)

On the health side, in a district like Chennai, a positive relationship between income and health holds as also in districts like Dharmapuri, where low income levels translate into low longevity.

Trends in Poverty : According to the 55th round of NSS, 26.10% (or 260 million) of India's population still lives below the poverty line. There are wide divergences in the head count ratios in the country. In 1999-2000, Orissa had the dubious distinction of having the highest percentage of people below the poverty line, 47.15 %. Whereas Haryana and Punjab have less than 10% of the population below the poverty line.

Trends in Poverty levels in Tamil Nadu

Year	*Population BPL (%)*			*No. Persons BPL (million)*		
	Rural	*Urban*	*Combined*	*Rural*	*Urban*	*Combined*
1973-74	57.43	49.40	56.94	17.26	6.69	23.95
1977-78	57.68	48.69	54.79	18.25	7.30	28.95
1983-84	53.99	46.96	51.16	18.25	7.85	26.10
1987-88	45.80	38.64	43.39	16.18	6.93	23.11
1993-94	32.48	39.77	35.03	12.17	8.04	20.21
1999-2000	20.55	22.11	21.12	8.05	5.00	13.05'

Source : Planning Commission, Govt. of India.

While poverty levels remained relatively static in the 1970's and 1980's and well above the 50% level, as mentioned above, there has been a dramatic decrease in poverty levels since that time. Where as in 1987-88, the poverty levels was 45.80%. it declined to 32.48% in 1993-94 and further to 21.12% in 1999-2000. The estimated number of people living below the poverty line in Tamil Nadu in 1999-2000 was 13.5 million (8.05 million in rural areas and 5 million in urban areas). Where as poverty rates declined from 32.38% to 20.55% in rural areas, the decline in urban areas was from 39.77% to 22.11 %. Thus the levels of poverty are almost equal in rural & urban areas.

Inequality in consumption : There is considerable inequality in terms of consumption as well. Whereas the poorest 10% of the population account for a mere 3.5 and 4.0% respectively to total urban and rural consumption expenditure (1993-94), the top 10% account for 26 and 24 percent of consumption expenditure respectively. It is also noticeable that consumption inequalities are greater in urban areas.

The relationship between income, poverty and inequality therefore, seems quite complicated. While Chennai fare well in terms of income, it has quite high level of poverty as well inequality. On the other hand, Dharmapuri which forms poorly not only in income terms but also interms of education and health indicatory, fares better in terms of poverty and inequality.

Section III

Poverty Alleviation and Reviving the Primary Sector

Tamil Nadu has made significant strides in terms of poverty reduction and it has also achieved a lot in terms of the social sector. Besides the budgetary reasons for this, the achievements are also due to the following factors. The implementation of poverty alleviation schemes aimed at income generation and employment creation, the noon meal scheme covering school children and old age pensioners and the implementation of other nutrition programmes such as the ICDS aimed specifically at improving women and children's nutritional status.

A number of points specifically in terms of employment and income are highlighted below.

1. Poverty reduction strategies in Tamil Nadu should lay emphasis on urban areas. While at the national level the incidence of poverty is more in rural areas, in Tamil Nadu the reverse is true.
2. More emphasis should be placed on employment generating schemes. Unemployment rates are quite high in Tamil Nadu especially in terms of daily unemployment.

3. Specific attention is required for inter district variation, the problems that districts face in terms of income, poverty and inequality are significantly different and with specific interventions.
4. Given the structural changes taking place in the economy, employment creation will have to focus increasingly on non-farm employment in the manufacturing and service sectors.
5. An agri-clinical approach should be adopted to evaluate each farmer and his land. See how knowledge inputs can be provided to live cultivation of wastelands.
6. Encouragement should be given to rainwater harvesting to replenish ground water and surface water sources.
7. Remodel and upgrade Remodelling and upgrading should be done to surface water sources such as irrigation tanks village ponds with a basin wide approach.
8. Promotion should be given for rural self employment.
9. Better market intelligence and communications to farmers, should be developed.
10. Fishery mission activities alongwith animal husbandry to be promoted.
11. Women should be involved in farming.
12. Better farm intelligence and communications to farmers should be developed.
13. Promotion should be given to capital investment in agriculture & revamp the cooperative credit system for better outcomes.

Section IV

Case Study of Afforstation

Project Outline :

Tamilnadu Afforestation Project (TAP) is a Japan Bank for International Cooperation funded100 million $ Joint Forest Management (community forestry) Project being implemented in Tamilnadu state since 1997-98. In the project, degraded forest micro watersheds along with adjoining hamlets or habitation or revenue villages are selected. The forest area is divided into three zones – Lower zone or Utility zone, Middle zone or Asset creation zone and Upper zone or Eco-restoration zone. Normally, the area for all three zones is 250 ha. in which the zone-wise gap planting is taken up. The uniqueness of the project is that it has a provision of 12000$ for village development alone under buffer zone activities over a period of three years. The aim is to reduce the dependence of villagers on forests by alternate income generation activities.

The Government order sanctioning the funds from JBIC soft loan gave the objective of the programme to increase the tree cover through involvement of people. But once the programme was launched it was continuously reviewed, modified, and broadened in consonance with the feedback from people and field officers. The amount for buffer zone (development of forest dependents) was increased to 12000$ from 6000$. The individual grants were converted into interest free loans so that VFC can build up its corpse fund and extend loans to the remaining forest dependents for acquiring productive assets.

TAP and poverty alleviation

Though it was never explicitly intended even at later stages, but broadening of the TAP in response to field needs evolved it into a sustainable poverty alleviation programme from a mere greening project. As elucidated below, at the local level it abundantly provides all the three elements of comprehensive poverty alleviation strategy devised by World Bank study group recently.

Benefits generated by the project

1. Opportunity

Tree Assets: Tree assets, promotion of alternate income generation activities and the water harvesting structures have provided security by reducing the vulnerability to natural vagaries, particularly the drought. In this project the people development and forest regeneration go hand in hand in a synergistic way which makes it a scintillating example of "win-win" logic and worth replicating elsewhere in the world with suitable modifications.

2. Wage work:

Out of 60000 $ spent in each programme micro watershed, around 36000 $ go for wage work of planting or civil structures (remaining for materials) . The local people do this wage work. In initial 3 years this substantial wage employments available at their doorstep gives a big boost and enables them make full use of the infrastructure and productive assets.

3. Empowerment:

The entire planning, execution and monitoring of the programme is done by the village Forest Councils, whose day-to-day affairs are looked after by its Executive committee headed by an elected President. The annual NTFPs revenue of some of the VFCs has already crossed 4000 $ and from the initial money of 12000 $ for buffer zone some VFCs have developed a corpus fund of 24000 $.

4. Security:

Improvement of village infrastructure and diversification of income generation activities have enhanced the security. The reclothing of the forests and water harvesting structures have reduced the vulnerability to drought, which is the most common risk. The training in alternate livelihoods has also made significant contribution in reducing the vulnerability to the natural vagaries.

Thus TAP amply provides the three elements -opportunity, empowerment and security at the local level for effective poverty alleviation. No other government programme in India has such a comprehensive approach for poverty alleviation.

Conclusions.

This project very vividly demonstrates the role of forest development in sustainable poverty alleviation, which is hitherto not adequately appreciated in the developing countries. Further it emphasizes that the ultimate solution for forest conservation in India and other developing countries lies in not mere community forestry but keeping a broad approach to alleviate poverty in the most comprehensive and sustainable way through promotion of opportunity, facilitating empowerment and enhancing security. It also underscores the need for present day foresters to comprehend social and economic issues in addition to the technical ones for taking up forestry projects successfully. However, growing of trees and poverty alleviation are long drawn processes hence the duration of forest development projects should not be less than 10 years.

References

1. Bhalla Surjit (2002), Imagine There's No Country – Poverty, Inequality and Growth in the Era of Washington Institute for International Economics, Washignton.

2. Battacharya Rakhee (2002), Rural Poverty in India, A Review – India Journal of Regional Sciences, Vol.34 , No. 27.

3. Govt. of Tamil Nadu (2003), Tamil Nadu Human Development Report, Social Science Press, Delhi.

4. Govt. of Tamil Nadu (2003), Tamil Nadu: Development Imperatives and Reforms; Finance Dept., Tamil Nadu.

5. Indira Rajaraman (2003), Poverty and Globalisation, 'The Economics Times', August 14, 2003.

6 K.K. Kaushal & Kala J.C. (2003), Sustainable Poverty Alleviation Through Afforestation Project – A Case from India, South Asia conference on Technologies for Poverty Reduction, New Delhi, 10-11 October, 2003.

7. Rao P.K. (2000), Sustainable Development, Economics and Policy, Blackall , Publication OXFORD.

8. Thakur R. N. (2002), Economy of Tamil Nadu, Marching Ahead, Deep and Deep Publication, New Delhi.

9.UNESCAP (2003), Anti Poverty or Anti Poor? The Millenium Development Goals and the eradication of extreme poverty and hunger,

UN Economics & Social Commission for Asia & Pacific, Bangkok.

10.World Bank Report (2001), Attacking Poverty, WDR.

SECTION II

Achievement of Universal Primary Education

6

MDG 2 : Achieving Universal Primary Education

Sangita Kamdar

I. Introduction

The paper discusses the Millennium Development Goal 2 which outlines the need to universalize primary education. It begins with a theoretical backdrop to the need to invest in education. Here, it discusses the Human Resource Development (HRD) and the Human Development (HD) approaches to investing in education (Section II). This is followed by the factors which contribute to universal enrolment in primary education (Section III). Government policy and factors hindering universalisation of primary education are discussed in Section IV and Section V respectively.

II. Investing in Education: The Human Resource Development (HRD) and the Human Development (HD) Approaches

There are two approaches to the study of education, health and nutrition - the Human Resource Development approach (HRD) and the Human Development approach (HD). The human-resource developers stress the productivity aspect of investments in education, health and nutrition. The acquisition of education, health and nutrition is in the context of enhancing 'human capital' which has been defined as the stock of skills and productive knowledge embodied in people (Rosen, 1987, p. 682). The basic premise of the HRD approach is that human beings invest in themselves by means of education, training or other activities, which raises their future income by increasing their lifetime earnings (Woodhall, 1985). Macro-level analysis as reflected in the neo-classical growth theories, however, ignored the role of human capital till recently. It is only since the late 1980s that human capital variables have been considered important in explaining the differences in growth rates across countries (Romer, 1986; Lucas, 1988).

The other approach is that of Human Development that stresses the quality of life or well-being dimension of such investments. The Human Development approach considers the acquisition of education, health and nutrition as an end in itself and as essential components that ensure better quality of life rather than as a means to ensuring higher productivity and earnings. They are considered as 'humanitarians' as this approach is concerned also with the 'unproductive, the lame ducks, and the unemployables: the old, infirm, disabled, and chronically sick' (Streeten, 1994, p. 233). Human Development calls for projects and programs that look upon nutrition, education and health as ends in themselves rather than as means to higher productivity, even when the conventionally measured rates of return on these investments turn out to be zero.

Sen terms the 'two distinct but related areas of investigation in understanding the processes of economic and social development as the accumulation of "human capital" and the expansion of "human capability"'. Education helps a person to add to the value of production in the economy as also to the income of the person who has been educated. But even with the same level of income, a person may benefit from education, in reading, communicating, arguing, in being able to choose in a more informed way, in being taken more seriously by others, and so on. The two perspectives are, therefore, closely related but distinct (Sen, 1997).

The Human Resource Development approach argues for investment in social sectors like education and health for reasons of increasing productivity of the individual and thereby contributing to increased economic growth. However, what is important is not mere economic growth, but the quality of economic growth. The role of economic growth lies in improving the quality of lives people lead. Hence, economic growth must result in the expansion of opportunities leading to human well-being or 'capabilities'. The Human Resource Approach is narrow and needs supplementation, as human beings are not merely means of production but their well-being is the goal of development.

The Human Development approach is wider in yet another sense. It has incorporated income within the ambit of the concept of human development and its measurement. This approach is different from other attempts which have also quantified well-being using non-income dimensions such as Basic Needs approach (Streeten et al, 1981). By incorporating control over resources as one of the important dimensions of human development, the approach becomes the most comprehensive so far.

It may thus be argued that the need to invest in primary education may be argued from any perspective, be it the HRD or the HD approach.

Millennium Development Goal 2 thus outlines the need to universalize primary education in the following words:

'Lack of education robs an individual of a full life. It also robs society of a foundation for sustainable development because education is critical to improving health, nutrition and productivity. The education goal is thus central to meeting the other goals' (UNDP, 2003, p.6).

III. Factors Contributing to Universal Enrolment in Primary Education

It is possible to examine the factors which determine universal primary education from the demand and the supply side.

On the demand side:

1. Income or the level of economic development at the macro level. There exists a direct relationship between incomes and the demand for education at the individual or family (micro) level. At the macro level, the threshold level of education rises with economic development.

2. Secondly, female literacy directly contributes to universalizing education.

3. Third, a growing economy in which productivity increases result in increase in real wages of the labor feeds into the system by increasing incomes and creating a demand for education. The East Asian economies are an example.

On the supply side,

4. Government policy should encourage the spread of primary education. The government may use direct or indirect measures.

5. Access to schools in terms of availability of schools and the means of transportation.

6. Quality education attracts children to school and this may be construed to mean quality teachers and infrastructure facilities conducive to learning.

IV. Government Policy Towards Universal Primary Education

Given the low attainment levels in education, the government has taken various initiatives to universalize primary education.

The Indian Constitution has enjoined upon the Government to provide free education to all children up to the age of 14 years. Universalizing primary education is therefore a key to the discharge of a fundamental responsibility enshrined in the Constitution. Education to begin with was the subject matter of the State Government till education was made a concurrent subject through the 42nd amendment in the year 1976. Primary education though continues to be the primary responsibility of the State government, has also been receiving significant support from the Union Government.

Universality cannot be made only a matter of right, it has also to be a matter of policy. The attainment of universality requires not only the removal of disabilities but also the creation of abilities. The neglect of elementary education has been the most costly failure of policy since Independence.

-Andre Beteille

- Universal access and enrollment;
- Universal retention of children up to the age of 14 years; and
- Substantial improvement in quality of education to enable all children to achieve essential level of learning.

To achieve these objectives the State government identified some action areas for special attention in the 10th Plan, which are as follows:

(a) Accelerate the tempo of universalisation particularly in tribal, hilly / inaccessible areas and other areas lagging behind.

(b) Reduce the drop out rates by launching special campaigns for motivation of weaker sections.

(c) Involve local bodies in the villages to create congenial atmosphere in rural areas for education.

(d) Seek involvement of teachers organizations, voluntary organizations and various other non-government bodies.

(e) Encourage families of weaker sections to send their children to Primary schools by taking measures for their economic upliftment.

(f) Take special campaigns to target illiterates within the age group 15 to 35.

These identified thrust areas are backed by means of the following schemes and programs :

(1) Opening of Primary Schools in School-less Villages

The Government revised its earlier policy and decided to open new schools wherever necessary to ensure that there is a school for a habitation of at least 200 population within a distance of 1.5 km and for a habitation of 100 population in hilly and inaccessible areas within a distance of 1 km.

(2) Opening of 'Vastishala'

In rural areas it is noticed that some habitations do not have a school within the specified distance of 1.5 km or 1 km as the case may be, but new schools can not be opened as the population is less than the prescribed norms. For such habitations the government has decided to start 'Vastishalas' with a minimum requirement of students strength of 15 in standard I to IV. These schools are run by Gram Panchayats or Gram Shikshan Samitis of the village.

(3) Mahatma Phule Shikshan Hami (MPSH) Yojana

This scheme has been introduced to rope in child labor and shelter-less children deprived of primary education within the fold of education. Under this program school centres are opened through voluntary organizations and are run by voluntary teachers on contract basis at a honorarium of Rs.1000/- per month.

4) Opening of Balwadis

In order to create familiarity with school environment from early age the government has adopted a policy to open Balwadis for age group 3 - 5 years in the campus of Zilla Parishad primary schools. This is also expected to reduce the drop out rate.

(5) Attendance allowance for the Girls from Weaker Sections of the Society

This scheme is being implemented in the State from 1992 for the girls from below poverty line families. The attendance allowance paid is Re.1 per day to the parents of the girls studying in the Standard 1 to 4. Tribal students in standard V to X are paid a stipend if they attend school at least 75 per cent of the working days (Rs. 40 per month to boys and Rs. 50 to girls in standard V to VII and Rs. 50 per month for boys and Rs. 60 per month for girls in standards VIII to X).

(6) Operation Black Board

This Centrally sponsored scheme, originally launched by Government of India is meant to strengthen the school infrastructure of building, number of teachers and teaching material. Currently this scheme primarily aims at construction of 2 room units of primary school buildings. 60 percent of the expenditure is provided by Government of India (GoI) under Prime Minister Rojgar Yojana while the balance 40 percent is provided by the State government.

(7) District Primary Education Project (DPEP)

The Government of India started in 1997, a centrally sponsored scheme with the assistance from the World Bank called DPEP. GoI has provided extra resources for accelerating the development of districts which are identified as educationally backward. The districts having percentage of literacy especially of persons below the national average were identified as educationally backward. Nine districts in Maharashtra (later became 11 due to creation of new districts) were identified as educationally backward. This program has begun in two phases in the State.

The GoI laid down detailed guidelines for micro level planning and preparation of Project reports. DPEP envisaged that 85 percent of the cost of the project would be provided by GoI while the State will bear the balance 15 percent. It is expected that with this assistance the State will improve the operational efficiency of Primary education scheme in the district by way of providing additional physical amenities as well as undertake specially identified programs for universalisation of education. It also desires that a strong effective supervision and control mechanism will be in place in the district. DPEP provides for 70 percent of the expenditure on project programs, 24 percent on construction and 6 percent on establishment. More specifically for improving the quality of education a grant of Rs.500 per annum per teacher is provided to the school for teaching, learning aids and consumables. A further grant of Rs.2000 per annum is provided to be given jointly to the school and Village Education Committee for improving facilities in the school. This project was last extended up to 30th June 2003 and has now been followed by the scheme called "Sarva Shikshan Abhiyan" a specially designed program funded by GoI.

Achievements

During the field visit to the some of the villages in Maharashtra, it was observed that the drop out rate has fallen significantly due to implementation of this program. This has also been corroborated by the follow up Cohort study conducted in 2003. Comparison of the Cohort studies undertaken at the outset of the DPEP program with that after its completion has indicated that retention rates have improved.

The rooms constructedunder the DPEP program were not of very good quality as seen in the height of the room, tin roofs, flooring which had tiles without cement. However, on the positive side schools have been provided with rooms due to this external funding.

(8) Sarva Shikshan Abhiyan

Based on the experience gained from the DPEP program which was implemented with World Bank assistance in selected districts in the country, a National Program has been launched through out the country by name "Sarva Shikshan Abhiyan" . Under this program about 17/18 specific activities have been identified to be taken up. To implement this scheme, a governing body under the Zilla Parishad President and an Executive Committee under the Chief Executive Officer (CEO) has been constituted. The funds come directly from GoI to the District Executive Committee with 25 percent contribution from the State government.

(9) Other activities

The State Government has started a scheme of Book Banks in primary schools to provide a set of books to the needy students. These sets are required to be replaced periodically. Free text books are also to be given to all the students studying in standard I to IV of Zilla Parishad primary schools of the 103 Panchayat Samiti areas where female literacy rate is below the national average.

Free Uniforms are provided to all students belonging to SC/ ST categories for standard I to IV studying in Zilla Parishad schools. Free uniforms are also provided to all the students of Standard I of the primary schools in 103 blocks where female literacy is below the national average. The Zilla Parishad has also started 31 summer "Shetu Shala" to cover the boys and girls who are left out of the educational main stream. They have informed that during last summer 1093 students have taken advantage of this "Shetu Shala" scheme.

(10) District Institute of Education and Training (DIET)

For strengthening teachers training, the District Institute of Education and Training has been set up. The National Policy on

Education, 1986 has described a vital role of DIET in the improvement of the quality of elementary education. In practice, the role of DIETs have been limited to imparting pre-service training programs and in-service training programs.

V. What ails Universalisation of Primary Education?

As outlined above government policy has been trying to universalize primary education by improving access to schools and providing special incentives to attract children to schools. In that case what are the problems that hinder universalisation of primary education in India?

It is possible to examine the problem from two angles. One is the issue of increasing enrolment. The other, is retaining children in schools.

There has been an increase in enrolment at all levels of education since Independence. The gross primary enrollment rate which was only 43 percent in 1950-51 reached 100 percent by 1990-91 (Deolalikar, 2005). Gross enrolment rates obtained from school administrative data tend to overstate the actual enrolment rate. Household survey data show smaller net, gross and age-specific enrolment. The data of the 55th round of the National Sample Survey (NSS) undertaken in 1999-2000 suggests that only 78 percent of children aged 6-11 years were attending school in 1999-2000. At 61 percent, the gross enrollment rate and at 52.5 percent, the net primary enrollment rate was significantly lower in 1999-2000 (ibid). There are reasons for discrepancy between household survey-based and school administrative records-based enrolment rates, including the fact that household surveys obtain information on school attendance during a short reference period while administrative data refer to students actually enrolled in the registers of the school at the beginning of the school year.

Retention of children in schools is a major task facing policy makers. Retention means to ensure that the entire cohort of children who begins grade 1 remains in school until grade 5. School retention is an indicator of the quality of schooling, though imperfectly. In the rush to expand access to schooling, often policy makers compromise on quality of schooling which is likely to show up in lower rates of student retention and primary school completion. Using NSS 55th round data for current and completed schooling level of each child, Deolalikar (2005) estimates that in 1999-2000, at the national level, the primary completion rate for children aged 12 years was 61.4 percent. In Maharashtra, data for school year 1998-99 indicate that by the time children reach Standard IV only 85 percent of the boys and 86 percent of the girls out of a cohort of 100 who started in Standard I four years ago remain in school. These fractions dip further in Standard VII where 69 percent of boys and 66 percent of girls survive and by Standard X only 47 percent of the original group of boys and 40 percent of the same for girls remain (Government of Maharashtra, 2002).

Based on field work in Maharashtra the following factors appear to be some of the leading problem areas which need to be attended to.

Access and Availability

Availability and accessibility of schools is a major determinant of educational attainment. Since 1960, the growth of educational institutions in Maharashtra at all levels has been impressive. Primary schools doubled in their numbers in 40 years even as secondary schools have grown phenomenally by fivefold (Government of Maharashtra, 2002). Despite this increase in the availability of schools which has improved access to schooling, there is a need to have more schools. An example follows.

In accordance with the policy of opening new schools to ensure that there is a school for a habitation of at least 200 population within a distance of 1.5 km and for a habitation of 100 population in hilly and inaccessible areas within a distance of 1 km., the district of Jalna requires about 70-80 new primary schools to be opened in 2003. During the year 2003-04, a target of opening 200 new schools has been kept. During field visit to the district, discussions with district officials indicated that at present there are around 20 schools where student population has gone below

10. These schools having become uneconomical and need to be re-deployed in other villages. Vastishalas need to be opened in these villages which have been vacated of schools.

Teachers

Retention of students in primary schools depends upon the type and caliber of instruction they receive, primary school completion rates are likely to be more sensitive to teacher absenteeism. Several other studies have highlighted the problem of teacher absenteeism and shirking. Dreze and Gazdar (1997) observed that two-thirds of the teachers were absent from their positions during announced visits to 16 schools in Uttar Pradesh. A study by PROBE (1999) based on visit to over 200 primary schools across the country, found that the head teacher (principal) was absent in nearly a third of the schools on the day of the survey team's visit. One reason for the high rates of teacher absenteeism may be extensive involvement of teachers in politics as suggested by Kingdon and Muzammil (2003) based on their study in Uttar Pradesh (cited in Deolalikar, 2005). In Maharashtra, it was given to understand the saddling of teachers with non-teaching duties such as census work and the like. The problem of teacher absenteeism reflects a general lack of accountability of teachers and schools and the entire educational system to students and the society.

Absence of teachers was observed during field visits in Maharashtra. Several schools are one-teacher schools and had only recently been provided with teachers. One-teacher schools adversely affect enrolment and attendance levels of the students. More importantly, it also affects achievement levels of the students. In schools where appointment of teachers had been a problem, it was observed that while students could read in Marathi they could not do complicated jobs like the mathematics expected of that age and level of schooling.

Not only is the availability of teachers important but the motivation level of teachers is also equally important in determining the quality of education. In the village Kolhapur, in Jafferabad taluka, the lack of availability of teachers had affected the studies of the students. The Headmaster was an elderly person with no interest in the future of the school. The Sarpanch indicated that the cleanliness observed was done just prior to the visit. The school was used as a marriage hall and hence there was no compound wall and this meant the misuse of teaching material. The room in which we were seated had huge cracks and the additional room given under DPEP was made use of to show the visitors. Lack of appointment of teachers and the lack of interest of the teachers in the school had affected the performance of the students. Standard V students were not able to write 3-digit numbers. The anganwadi was dirty. The toilet was very small, barely sufficient for children to enter and lacked privacy.

Our field visit highlighted the role of non-income factors in determining educational attainment in a society. In the villages we traveled, it was obvious that the teacher had an important role to play. *A good teacher could change the society.* Educational attainment depended on the zeal and the work of the local school teacher. *Motivation* of the teacher emerged as an important factor which affected the performance of the students and others in the village.

The lack of performance and the motivation of the school teacher is to a great extent influenced by the fact that they live outside the village in which they teach. About 70 percent of the teachers do not live in the locality in which they teach. Many of them are also from outside the district and hence are constantly making efforts to return back to their district. It is for this reason that they have no long term interest in the development of the village.

In the village Sanjol in Jafferabad, which consists mainly of Scheduled Caste and Scheduled Tribe population, the villagers expressed confidence in the Headmaster, D.B. Shelke, who was a young, energetic man. He had instilled a sense of discipline in his team of teachers and students as reflected in the clean environment, cleanliness of students and uniforms for students and teachers. He had encouraged the women of the village to save. There was no self-help group. However, every woman of the village saved their day's saving with the headmaster, be it Re. 1 or 2. When the accumulated amount stood at Rs. 100, the headmaster would then deposit the amount in the post office. Every woman had a post-office saving account and every child had a similar account. Besides this, the achievement levels of the students were high. There is hardly any drop out.

Lack of Infrastructure Facilities

Field visits however revealed a different story. Lack of drinking water facilities and lack of toilets are major problems faced by the schools in Jalna. Although figures in these tables show increased availability of these facilities, ground level realities point out to the reverse. *When there are no toilets for children in schools, where is the question of separate toilets for girls? Even drinking water was not available in most of the schools visited.*

The school had an apathetic environment in the classrooms too. Cramped classrooms, poor lighting such that there was difficulty in reading, no ventilation, dull walls.........We wondered how teachers and students worked under such circumstances. And then, where is 'joyful learning' ? That is a distant dream.

Involvement of Gram Panchayats

Our overall impression was that the Vastishala scheme has performed better than the Mahatma Phule Hami Yojana Scheme (Mahatma Phule Education Guarantee Scheme). The MPHYS is meant for child laborers in the age group 6 to 14 years and is managed by NGOs (Non-government organization) of that village. The funding comes from the state government to the NGO – The teacher's salary at the rate of Rupees 1000 per month for a period of 10 months (Rupees 10,000), Rupees 2,000 and 1,000 annually for teachers training and stationery respectively. The Vastishalas on the other hand are managed by the Gram Panchayats and this local control contributes to proper functioning of schools.

Community Participation

Field work done during a review of an UN program, *Janshala*, revealed the importance of community participation and teaching learning material (TLM). This program was being implemented in the tribal districts of Nashik and Thane. These communities in the face of severe adversities such as lack of water even in the month of October were able to have a school functioning with complete enrolment. It was observed that community participation in education had helped universal enrolment in the villages and helped prevent drop outs. There was 'ownership' of the school and that feeling encourages the spread of schooling and education.

Children in Need of Special Care

There are children in need of special care in almost all the schools we visited. However there are no special educators nor a separate curriculum for them. These special children sit with the rest of the students and are then said to be lagging behind in studies. School facilities for such children may be available at the district level. However, it is difficult to send these children with disabilities over long distances and hence this is a section of children who are neglected and a wasted lot.

References

1. Deolalikar Anil B., 2005, *Attaining the Millennium Development Goals in India*, Oxford University Press and the World Bank, New Delhi

2. Dreze Jean and H. Gazdar, 1997, 'Uttar Pradesh: The Burden of Inertia', Jean Dreze and Amartya Sen (ed.) *Indian Development: Selected Regional Perspectives*, Clarendon Press, Oxford.

3. Government of Maharashtra, 2002, Human Development Report Maharashtra 2002, Mumbai.

4. Lucas, Robert E., Jr., (1988) 'On the Mechanics of Economic Development', *Journal of Monetary Economics*, 22 (1988) 3-42 North-

Holland, as reproduced in Becker, R. and Burmeister, E., *Growth Theory* Volume I, The International Library of Critical Writings in Economics 10.

5. PROBE, 1999, *Public Report on Basic Education in India*, Oxford University Press, New Delhi.

6. Romer, Paul M., (1986) 'Increasing Returns and Long-Run Growth', *Journal of Political Economy*, 94(5) October, 1002-37 as reproduced in Becker, R. and Burmeister, E., *Growth Theory* Volume I, The International Library of Critical Writings in Economics 10.

7. Rosen, S., (1987) 'Human Capital' J. Eatwell, M. Milgate and Peter Newman (Ed.), *The Palgrave Dictionary of Economics* Volume 2, pp. 681- 690, (London, U. K.: Macmillan Press).

8. Sen Amartya (1997) 'Editorial: Human Capital and Human Capability', *World Development*, Volume 25 (12), pp. 1959 – 1961

9. Streeten Paul (1994) 'Human Development: Ends and Means', *Asian Journal of Economics and Social Studies*, Volume 13 (1), pp. 21 – 41.

10. Streeten Paul, Shahid Javed Burki, Mahbub Haq, Norman Hicks and Frances Stewart (1981) *First Things First: Meeting Basic Human Needs in the Developing Countries* World Bank, (Oxford: Oxford University Press).

11. United Nations Development Program (UNDP), *Human Development Report 2003*, Oxford University Press, New York.

12. Woodhall, M., (1985) 'Human Capital', Torsten Husen and T. Neville Postlethwaite (Ed.). *The International Encyclopedia of Education Research and Studies* Volume 4, F-H, (Oxford: Pergamon Press).

7

Universal Primary Education: Goal and Reality

K. S. Ingole

Introduction

The universal primary education is one of the most important goals of Millennium Development. In a segmented and stratified society like India the importance of education to the disadvantaged social groups such as scheduled castes and scheduled tribes can hardly be exaggerated. They suffered for centuries from deprivation and destitution of every kind viz social, economic, political and cultural, due to the ill effects of the caste system. Such a deplorable scenario that all along prevailed in the case of the SC/STs can mainly be attributed to the denial to them of the access to education. It was this lack of the access of education that kept them socially segregated, economically immobile and dependent and politically powerless. This paper deals with some of the vital issues relating to Constitutional provision to achieve the goals of universal education, present educational status of depressed and oppressed classes in India and government's expenditure for achieving the goals of universal primary education in India.

Importance of Education

The importance of education in economic and social development is well known and can hardly be over-emphasized.

Education plays a key role in both economic and social development. It develops basic skills and abilities and thereby boosts productivity. It also fosters a value system conducive to the national development goals and preserves and promotes the cultural ethos of the country. It is such a wonderful key that, transforms the person from unproductive status to highly productive status from low efficiency to high efficiency and from local attitude to a global attitude. Education has always acted as an emancipator of the individual. For it imparts to the individual occupational mobility, creates awareness about the new values and self-respect and also reveals the nature and strength of various socio-economic forces that act against the progress, dignity and prestige of the individual, and also equips him to fight against these forces. Education creates a strong sense of scientific temperament that enables the individual as also the society at large, to fight superstitions that seek to perpetuate the state of ignorance. Literacy also works as a basic tool of self-defense in a society where social interaction often involves the written media. An illiterate person is that much less equipped to defend himself in court, to obtain a bank loan, to enforce her inheritance rights, to take advantage of new technology, to compete for secure employment, to take part in political activity. Thus, education is a strong and potent force that keeps the society permanently on the path of all round development. The relationship between education and social change was also well understood by many social leaders during the independence movement. In India, the development of human resources constitutes a central objective of all development efforts from the very beginning of the planning era. The basic importance of education in promoting economic and social development has explicitly recognized. The significance of education was realized even during the National movement and stress was laid on the need to provide a quality education, which was commensurate with the economic aspirations as well as social and cultural milieu of India.

Gokhale, for instance, was a strong advocate of the promotion of basic education. Dr. Ambedkar, whose own scholarship helped him to overcome the stigma of low caste and saw education as a cornerstone of his strategy for the liberation of, oppressed castes in India, Education was also of paramount concern to Ram Mohan Roy, Maharshi Karve, Jotirao Phule, and Rabindranath Tagore, Mahatma Gandhi and numerous other social reformers and political thinkers of the pre-independence period.

Constitutional Provisions

The fathers of the Constitution of India were in no doubt as to central role of education in promoting equity and justice for all its citizens. On the issue of compulsory education, it was decided that education should be available free of costs and that attendance in school should be compulsory for all children up to the age of 14 years as incorporated in article 45 of the directive principles of state policy. This was a farsighted provision in contrast to the view that education should only be universalized up to the primary level, about 10 years. Keeping in mind the need to combat the educational and economic disadvantage of scheduled castes and scheduled tribes along with other disadvantaged sections of society in the past, special emphasis was given to their needs in article 46. This article makes a commitment to protect these groups from social injustice and all forms of exploitation. All these provisions indicate a clear commitment to giving Indian children in this freedom and dignity and recognizing their essential contribution to building a democratic nation.

It was stipulated that the state should provide free and compulsory education to all children up to age of 14 within 10 years of independence that is by the year 1960. This added a sense of urgency to the measure and is the only provision in the constitution of India that has specified a time limit. However, reality has failed to match the vision of India's first legislators. There has been a gross violation of children's right to education in spite of it being clearly protected in the constitutional frame work of India's polity and being an honorable and cherished goal of the Indian Constitution[1] this was an ambitious goal, and the practical measures that were taken to implement it have fallen for short of what was required. To this day, compulsory education has not been actually implemented any where in India, even though state governments and even local authorities are empowered to make primary education compulsory.

Educational Status of Depressed Classes in India

The empowerment value of basic education is so obvious that there is something puzzling in the fact that the promotion of education has received so little attention from social and political leaders in the post-independence period. Given the tremendous amount of inequality in our country, there is also a great deal of variation across different sections of population with regard to the nature of access they have to education. Basic education continues to remain a privilege enjoyed by some and there is tremendous variation among the social groups. Universal primary schooling is still a distant goal, particularly for females amongst the socially disadvantaged groups, i.e. the SC / STs and Other Backward castes and Muslim in remote rural areas and urban slums. Table No. 1 shows the comparative educational level among the SC /ST and others. As per the Report of Ministry of HRD Government of India 1998-99 that literacy level among the SC females was 23.76 and for ST females it was 18.19 and for others 44.81 per cent and males literacy rate shows 49.91 for SC and 40.65 for ST and 69.53 for others. It shows the literacy disparity and urgency to take steps to spread the education among the SC/ST particularly. Further to if we observe in the rural area literacy then the condition is worst. Literacy rate among the SC female in rural areas shows that 19.46 percent and for ST 16.02 and for other 35.38. With such a vast illiteracy how can we compete with the global economy? Therefore it is imperative that government must take some serious steps to spread the education to general and particularly to the depressed classes.

In India we have an average low literacy rate and there are also large inequalities in educational achievements between males and females, between urban and rural areas, and between different social groups. These diverse inequalities, combined with low average literacy rates, are responsible for the persistence of extremely low level of education for disadvantaged sections of the population. Therefore, it is hard to overstate the need for unequivocal rejection of these and other skeptical views of the value of education.

Table 1
Comparative Literacy Rates of SC / ST and Others

	Scheduled Castes	*Scheduled Tribes*	*Others*
Male	49.91	40.65	69.53
Female	23.76	18.19	44.81
Total	37.41	29.60	57.69
Rural Male	45.95	38.45	63.42
Rural Female	19.46	16.02	35.38
Total	33.25	27.38	49.56
Urban male	66.50	66.56	83.40
Female	42.29	45.66	67.48
Total	55.11	56.60	75.93

Source: Ministry of HRD Government of India Report, Selected Educational Statistics 1998-99.

A firm commitment to the widespread and equitable provision of basic education is the first requirement of rapid progress in eradicating educational deprivation in India[2]. Low levels of education in India reflect both the low duration of schooling for children who are enrolled at some stage and a large proportion of children are never enrolled at all. Several ideological convictions have contributed to this educational neglect in India, including the conservative upper-caste notion that knowledge is not important or appropriate for the lower castes, the belief, held in some radical quarters, that the present educational system is a tool of subjugation of the lower classes or vestige of the colonial period. Due to the inconsistency in educational policy of government and lack of appropriate measures to spread the education the drop

Table 2

Drop out rate among the SC/STs

Classes 1st to 5th	*1960-61*	*1970-71*	*1980-81*	*1990-91*	*1992-93*	*1998-99*
Boys	61.70	64.50	56.20	40.10	43.93	40.63
Girls	70.90	70.90	62.50	46.00	46.67	44.66
Total	64.90	67.00	58.70	42.60	45.01	42.39
Classes 6th to 8th						
Boys	75.00	74.60	68.00	59.10	58.23	54.40
Girls	85.00	83.40	79.40	65.10	65.21	60.09
Total	78.30	77.90	72.70	60.90	61.10	56.82

Source: Government of India HRD Report 1998-99

out rate among the disadvantaged classes is very high this shows the Table 2

Table 2 revealed that the drop out among the SC/ST is very high though it is gradually declining yet it is very high. Girls are leaving school early then boys. The drop out rate among the girls shows 44.66 percent as compare to boys 40.63 per cent in 1998-99. But when they go for upper classes their drop out rates goes up. For instance in 1998-99 the drop out rate shows 60.09 per cent among the girls and 54.40 for boys up to the class 8th. The most common reasons for non-attendance or non-enrolment reported household surveys are

(a) high opportunity cost of children's time and
(b) lack of interest in education due to ignorance

With this reality naturally the question will arise in mind that how can we achieve the goal of universal education unless right vision and commitment to the cause.

The 2005 Global Education Monitoring Report which incorporates the 2001 Census data shows the India's ranking 106th out of the 127 countries surveyed. On this basis, India is home town in every three illiterate persons in the world India with 34 per cent of the illiterate population in the world has the largest number of illiterates. Further report said that, India on enrolment ratio is 82.35 and it's close to the world average ranking 94th, but it does badly on the rest. There has been a jump in India's adult literacy ranking from 121 in 2003 to 105 in 2004 because of the change from 1991 figures to 2001. Yet, the adult literacy rate at 61.3 per cent is still way below the 76 per cent average for developing countries and the 81.7 per cent global average.

The gender specific index is the most worrying. The average years spent in school for boys at 10 years is close to the global norm (10.7 years) and the average for developing countries (10.1 years). But for girls the figure drops to 7.9 years way below the global average of 9.8 years and even the developing country norm of 8.9 years.

At the world education forum in Dakar Senegal in 2000 over 160 countries pledged to achieve universal primary education, gender equality and an improvement in quality of education by

2015. The UNESCO report notes that while 91 countries are making some progress, a group of 35 countries including 22 sub Saharan countries and India are vary far from achieving the goals[3].

Inconsistencies in education policies:

Educational policies are full of inconsistencies of ends and means. It can found in a series of commission reports and policy statements that have appeared since 1947. The elusive goal of providing free and compulsory education until the age of 14 within a few years has been regularly reiterated without any effective steps being taken to reach it. The resolution of national policy of education adopted in 1968 emphasized the need for a radical reconstruction of the educational system in India. The resolution stressed the need:

(a) to transform the educational system so as to relate it more closely to the life of the people,
(b) to make continuous efforts for expanding educational opportunities,
(c) to make sustained efforts for raising the quality of education at all levels,
(d) to give a special emphasize to the development of science and technology and
(e) to promote and cultivate moral and social values.

In the year 1986-87, less than half of all enrolled children managed to complete the initial cycle of 5 years of primary education barely one third completed the 8 years corresponding to the stated goal of compulsory and free education and nearly half of all rural children in the 6-11 age group had never been enrolled in any school.This did not prevent the National policy of education of 1986 from declaring with blind optimism that by 1995 all children will be provided free and compulsory education up to 14 years of age without giving any sense of the revolutionary policy on education, 1992 ,is in line with imperative for the Government to formulate and implement a new education policy for the country, the policy did little more than to repeat the old credo with a different time frame: it shall be ensured that free and compulsory education of satisfactory quality is provided to all children up to 14 years of age before we enter the twenty first century. Once again the policy gave no limit of the practical steps that would make this so-called "resolve" a reality, and did not go much beyond a remarkable collection of platitude such as all teachers should teach and all students should study .One implication of these vague pieties is that they have opened the door of further inconsistencies between stated goals and actual policy. This has made it possible, in particular, to combine the highly egalitarian slogan of free and universal education with extreme inequality in practice[7].

In short, the lamentable history of post-independence education policy has suffered from diverse kinds of in consistencies, and contradiction including

(1) A confusion of objectives,
(2) Inconsistencies between stated goals and actual policy and
(3) Specific contradiction between stated goals resources allocation .The formulation of a more effective policy must begin with the elementary tasks of setting clear that are adequately ambitious yet realizable, devising practical measures to meet them, and providing the resources required to implement these measure.

Government's Expenditure on Education :

Inadequate public expenditure is one important reason for India's poor educational achievements. From 1968 onwards, successive versions of the national policy on education have resolved to raise the proportion of public expenditure on education to 10 percent but this target has not been approached to this day.

As per the constitutional division of powers in India, education mainly comes under the purview of state government. The Central Government has also been increasing its expenditure on education and allied services in various directions, namely co-ordination and determination of standards in institutions for higher education and research and scientific and technical institutions. In India Central and States Governments, Local Bodies fees from students and other sources including endowments, donation and voluntary contribution finance on education.

The proportion of public expenditure that goes to the education sector is indicative of the relative importance assigned to that sector. These figures from table 3 are indicative of the relative lack of public commitment to developing the education system. The public authorities in India have neglected the importance of education in the formation of human capital and economic growth.

Table 3
The percentage of Total Plan Expenditure on Education

Year	*% of Total plan expenditure on education*
1985-86	2.65
1989-90	4.54
1990-91	3.96
1991-92	4.01
1995-96	4.98
1996-97	5.90
1997-98	5.90
1998-99	6.38
1999-2000	6.22
2000-01	7.10
2001-02	6.07
2002-03	4.79

Source: Hand Book of Statistics, RBI 2003-04.

Education is being increasingly looked on as a "market "for major national and multi-national corporations where immense profits are to be made instead of public service vital for the overall development of the country. Notably, the Ambani-Birla Report (2000) had made a case for full cost recovery from students of public higher education institutions and immediate privatizations of entire education except these areas of education involving disciplines that have no market orientation. In this regard, the national level meeting on trade in education services expressed concern that the socio-economic implication of opining the education system globally and making education service for profit needs to be carefully examined[8].

The problem of inadequate aggregate resources is compounded by imbalances in allocation. Table 3 and 4 indicate the government's intention to spend on education. These figures are self explanatory, it was told by the government that after new economic policy introduction since 1991 government will increase the education but, this is not happing.

Table 4

The percentage of GDP expenditure on Education

Year	% of GDP of Education
1985-86	0.35
1990-91	0.45
1995-96	0.50
2000-01	0.61
2001-02	0.62
2002-03	0.30

***Source*: Handbook of Statistics Reserve Bank of India, 2003-04.**

Because education expenditure is born primarily by individual states rather than by the central government, there are large inter state variations in per- captia expenditure on education, and states with lower educational achievements, where the need for public investment is most acute, tend to be those where financial resources are particularly scarce. Another from of imbalances is the relatively low share of elementary education in total expenditure. This share, is not only low in terms of the stated objective of universalizing elementary education, it has also declined significantly[9]. Education expenditure in India needs to be increased, especially at the primary level and in the educationally backward states. In this regard the views of Professor Amartya Sen are very important he vehemently criticized the Indian government for neglect of basic education and infrastructure .He said that" taking the underprivileged into account was particularly important when framing economic policies in the contemporary world. Global economic interaction brings benefits for many, but can also create problems for some because of inadequacies of global arrangements as well as limitations of appropriate domestic policies[10].

These answers, of course, have to be interpreted in the light of the current functioning of the schooling system in different regions of the country. Interest in education for instance, is likely to be a function of the quality of teaching. Bearing in mind the low standards of teaching in large parts of the country, it is no surprise that many children quickly lose interest in going to school. But these responses also tell us that in sufficient valuation .This issue may be particularly relevant in the case of social groups for whom education has traditionally been considered unimportant whatever survives of this notion cannot but effect.

(a) The educational aspirations of children from these depressed castes
(b) The parental and social support which they receive in pursuit of these aspirations and
(c) The strength of public commitment to the promotion of education among these disadvantaged groups.

There is, indeed, some evidence that school attendance levels are particularly low among disadvantaged castes even after controlling for other relevant variables such as household income and educational facilities[11]. Compulsory education is frequently advocated means of intervention. On this issue, the inconsistencies of official policy makers are of the view that compulsory education is a bad idea, or that it will take many years before compulsory education is feasible or desirable[12] .It is time to address these inconveniences, and to initiate a reasoned debate on compulsory education and the forms it might take.

Ultimately, the expansion of basic education in "India depends great deals on the political factors. There is no question that, even in a country as poor as, India means can be found to ensure universal attainment of literacy and other basic educational achievements at least in the younger age groups. There are important strategic questions to consider in implementing that social commitment, but the primary challenge is to make it a more compelling political issue. The governments have to be involved in education by way of continues investment and through regularity measures. The private sector too must develop a better understanding with the government .For India to actualize its true and full potential in a knowledge economy, it's imperative that there be trust among different stakeholders .For our education system to grow, public investment must go up. The narrow pyramid with a small base of quality widened unless and until we enlarge the base with quality education, we won't be able to feed into the knowledge economy. The market won't make the correction: it's up to state[13] .On this issue Pranab Mukerjee said that, we do need spend more, we need about 10 percent of the GDP on primary education to achieve universal literacy[14] .However, in practice we are far away from the goal targeted .The Central Advisory Board of Education (CABE) on the draft free compulsory education till generated more heat than light. That states have been inept at providing education of equitable for the masses was brush under carpet. The draft Bill does not make any explicit provision for the state to ensure that adequate resources are provided for implementing the bill. The draft Bill protects the interest of the powerful private school lobby, just as the imperial assembly tried to protect the powerful lobby of maharajas, landlords and other privileged sections. No wonder that Kothari Commission's recommendation and the 1986 education policy call to establish a common school system stands ignored .For its charity ,the draft bill provides for reimbursement out of public funds to rich societies and trust that own theses schools. An earlier provision had required all state governments to regulate private schools, as they do now.

As an afterthought, this provision, too, was withdrawn. In another unauthorized change, a provision was added to enable the government to provide resources to the private unaided schools for their infrastructural development. Yet, they would continue to be treated as unaided schools[15] .So all these are inconsistency to the goals of Universal primary education .Therefore, I conclude with the hope that government will take this issue seriously and increase the adequate allocation in budget regularly with a proper monitoring the implementing of the schemes. Good governance is essence for any success of the plan.

References

1. Shantha Sinha, Emphasizing universal principles towards deepening of democracy actualizing childern's right to education, Epw Vol XL No 25, June 18, 2005. P.2571.

2. Jean Dre'ze Amartya Sen, India Economic Development and Social opportunity , Oxford University Press, 1995, Delhi P111.

3. Times of India daily News Paper dated 9th November 2004

4. Jean Dre'ze Amartya Sen, India Economic and social Opportunity, Oxford University Press 1995, p-117, Delhi.

7. Ibid p.119.

8. T.RAVIKUMAR , VIJENDER SHARMA ,Downsizing Higher Education An Emerging crisis, EPW, Vol XXX VIII no 7 February 15,2005, p607

9. Ibid p.121

10. Times of India, Wednesday February 21, 2001.

11. Ibid p .130

12. Ibid p.131

13. R Govinda. The Economic Times Mumbai , Tuseday 2 August 2005

14. Times of India, Tuesday 18 July 2000.

15. Anil Sadgopal, Times of India 3rd August 2005.

8

Primary Education in India

S.S. Captan and Lata S. Moorthy

Education is the basic tool for the development of conciousness and reconstituition of the society

Mahatma Gandhi

The Importance of Primary Education

Education is considered as one of the potential instrument for human resources of the country. There is a growing consensus worldwide that all children need to be educated to become productive adults and primary education forms the foundation of the entire super structure of education. Education plays a key role in the economic development of the country and investment in primary education by any government gives a high return in the long run. Since human resources are the most important factor in any economic endeavor, any expenditure to enhance their knowledge and skill will directly increase the value productivity and bring positive returns to the individual as well. Education is considered as the powerful instrument to remove the hurdles on the way to nation al reconstruction. The basic objectives of primary education is to bring about the harmonious development of a child's personality by catering to various needs, to inculcate a sense of belonging to the country, to develop scientific skills and prepare the child for the future.

Scenario after Independence

Till the advent of the British rule, the Indian educational institutions were run by voluntary organizations, which were funded by various princes and public and provided free education. With the advent of British rule in India there was a change in the educational system where importance was given to educating Indians in English for administrative purposes. After independence, the organization of government schools came under the state government.

At the time of independence in 1947, India inherited a quantitatively small education system compounded by regional imbalance and acute gender and regional disparities. Only 14% of the population was literate and one out of every third child was enrolled in primary school. Mahatma Gandhi, viewed education as the basic tool for development of national consciousness stressed on the importance of basic education even while leading a struggle against the colonial power and evolved a community based system of education

Just after the independence the decision to reorient the education system of the country to pave the way for national upliftment was taken. The central and state government directed their attention towards reconstruction of the educational system by appointing various committees and commissions to recommend ways of structuring a national pattern of educational system to bring about national progress.

The progress in the field of education was further hurdled with problems such as influx of refugees and administrative reorganizations during the period 1944 to 1951. But the government of India implemented a few schemes for educational promotion as recommended by the sergeant plan and separate ministry of education was created. Inspite of these problems, the statistics showed an increase in the enrollment of primary education, which was due to the awakening created by the attainment of independence.

Government Measures for Development of Primary Education

Independent India gave a lot of importance to education, as an educated citizenry is an essential condition for democracy. Article 45 of the constitution provided in the year 1950 stated that ' the state shall endeavor to provide universal, free and compulsory education to all children upto the age of 14 by 1960'. Education for all (EFA) in the Indian context aims at expansion of childhood care and development activities, eradication of illiteracy, improving the quality of education and specially universalization of elementary education.

The goals of Universalization of elementary education (UEE) constitute the following components:

Access to elementary education to all children up to 14 years of age;
Universal participation till they complete the elementary stage through formal or non-formal education programmes; and
Universal achievement of at least minimum levels of learning.

Government of India wanted to design an educational system, which would not only pave the way for economic development but would also cater to the directives of the constitution, which gave importance to democracy and secularism. Hence a resolution was passed at the parliament, which led to the setting up of planning commission in March 1950. This led to the era of planned development which was ushered in since 1951-52.The main emphasis of five-year plans was to provide elementary education to all.

Five Year Plans

During the first, second and third fiver plans which covered the period from (1951-55, 1956-60, 1961-65) the number of students enrolled in primary classes increased from 191 lakhs to

511 lakhs, the number of teachers increased by 40% and the number of primary schools rose from 210 lakhs to 400 lakhs. The share of expenses too rose from 36 lakhs to 122 lakhs.

But the progress in primary education was too slow due to allocation of a meager sum to primary education when compared to secondary and technical education and expansion in the population of the country. Further Universalization of primary education did not gain momentum due to the slow progress of social and economic development and the worst affected were the poor and socially disadvantaged classes, as they never viewed education as a gateway towards employment opportunities.

The original fourth five-year plan was converted into three annual plans comprising of years (1966-67, 67-68, and 68-69). Progress in Primary education was not as good as it was expected due to severe shortfall in the outlay due to recession in the economy. The central government undertook various measures for reduction in wastage, stagnation and removal of disparity in the primary education.

The fifth five-year plan gave top priority to provision of universal primary school for all children in the age group of 6-11 at least by 1975-76. The economic situation reduced the original allocation for primary education but government of India sponsored special programmers such as qualitative improvement, educational technology project etc for development of primary education. NCERT gave training to primary teachers in science education but overall the entire primary education sector was hit hard due to inadequate allocation of finances.

The sixth and the seventh five-year plan (1980-90) allocated Rs 110.61 crores towards primary education and implemented the reorganization of teacher education, and development of 400 elementary teacher training institutes in various districts. During the year 1987-88 central government provided 32.47 crores to teacher education programmes to 15 states and one union territory.

The eighth plan and the ninth plan aimed at provision of universalization of primary education as the basic objective by attempting to make primary education compulsory. The plan also envisaged a vision of reduction in wastage, and improving the enrolment of girls especially in tribal areas and backward castes.

District Primary Education Programme

The government of India launched the DPEP in 1994 as major educational initiative where're different districts with poor educational indicators were selected to receive financial assistance towards improvement to school infrastructure, teacher training, textbook improvement etc. The principal objective of DPEP was to provide access for all children to primary schooling, decreasing drop out rates and reduce gaps in enrollment and learning achievement among gender and social groups

DPEP is a centrally sponsored scheme where 85% of the approved cost and the balance are borne by the respective state government. Currently more than 271 districts in over 18 states are covered by DPEP with 51.3 million children, 1.1 million teachers and 375000 schools. More than 40000 new school buildings have been constructed with 66000 contracts have been given for construction of toilets and drinking water etc.

Operation Black Board

Operation blackboard was launched in 1987 in pursuance of NPE_POA. to provide minimum essential facilities to all primary schools in India and revised gain in 1992-93. The main objective of the scheme was to improve on teacher training, providing three teachers and three rooms to all primary schools with enrollment of more than 100 children and improving on infrastructure and instructional aids for children. This scheme sought to bring about quantitative and qualitative improvement in primary education.

Central Government will provide funds for equipment and teachers' salary for the plan period. The State governments will mobilize resources for construction of school buildings, including Headmaster-cum-office room and toilet facilities. The State Governments will also provide contingency and replacement funds for equipment.

At the time of initiation operation black board was to cover all schools by 1993-94. Other two sub-schemes will be started in the second half of the 8th Plan. About 30 per cent of the eligible schools will be provided three rooms and three teachers under the expanded OB by the end of 8th Plan and the remaining schools to be covered by the year A.D. 2000.

Shiksha Karmi Project

SKP was initialized with the aim of universalizing primary education to all children especially girls in Rajastan. As the project identified teacher absenteeism as the main reason behind the high drop out rates efforts were made to appoint locals who were less qualified but specially trained as teachers. The project aimed at bringing the local community and NGO's together for its successful implementation. The two schemes launched under SKP were:

> The Prahar pathasalas which provide educational facilities to out of school children, who were tied down with their occupation at home during the day, at their convenient time. The Angan pathasalas, which gave importance to primary education of girls. The success of this scheme is mainly due to the motivation of mahila sahayogis in the respective districts.

The government of Rajastan shared the equal expenditure with Swedish international agency. After the completion of Phase II on 2003, it has been proposed to cover 4100 villages or day schools and 7335 prahar pathasalas.

Lok Jumbish (LJP)

This project was implemented exclusively for the State of Rajastan during the period 1992-1994, with the assistance from Swedish International development Authority for bringing about the achievement of Education for All through people's participation and mobilization. The LJP has improved management and quality of textbooks. Further it has organized regular in service training programmes for primary teachers and has created cluster groups for academic support.

Sarva Shiksha Abhiyan (SSA)

SSA was launched in 2000 with the primary objective of achieving Universalization of elementary education before 2010 with time bound integrated approach in participation with the states. The project aimed at completion of five years of primary schooling for all children by 2007 and completion of eight years of schooling by 2010 along with reduction of gender and social gaps. The expenditure was to be shared in the basis of 85:15 in the ninth plan and 75:25 from the tenth plan onwards. The SSA wanted to bring about the change in the following areas: Teacher training, improvement in quality of education, provision of teacher training materials, and establishment of cluster groups for support and education guarantee centers.

The Current Situation in India

Though the constitution of the country had made a commitment to providing free and compulsory education to all children up to the age of 14, the task of providing basic education for all received high priority after the National Policy on Education was launched in 1986 and revised in 1992 which has been reflected in the higher allocation of resources as well as in terms of clearly defined strategies to achieve the goals of education for all. The World Declaration on Education For All – 1990 adopted in Jomtien together with several positive developments within the country has given the need for viewing basic education as a fundamental right of every citizen.

Achievements during the last fifty years are not insignificant. An estimated 95% of the rural population living in 826,000 habitations has a primary school within 1 km. and about 85% population have an upper primary school within 3 km. More than 150 million children are currently enrolled covering around 90% of the children in the age group of 6-14 years. From 1950-1998 numbers of schools quadrupled and school enrollment increased six fold. Despite such significant achievements and positive goal orientation in the recent years, it is realized that there are serious problems of gender, regional, sectional and caste disparities in

UEE. A significant proportion of students continue to dropout due to socio-economic and cultural factors as also due to lack of adequate infrastructure, shortage of teachers and unsatisfactory quality of education provided. There are still more than 300 million illiterates in India. Though the progress made is not insignificant, the country realizes that the challenges ahead at the turn of the century are quite daunting, demanding not only continued commitment but also an enhanced attention and resources to meet the challenges in the coming years because of the 200 million children aged 6-14 only 120 million attend primary school and 60% of them are girls. Further more than half of all the students do not complete basic education.

The efforts of Government of India and the results are summarized in Table 1.1 and Table 1.2.

Table 1.1
Number of Primary/Upper Primary Schools (1990-1997)

Year	*Primary*	*Increase*	*Upper Primary*	*Increase*
1990	560935	57172	151456	29079
1991	566744	5809	155926	4470
1992	571248	4504	158498	2572
1996	598354	27106	176772	18272
1997	**610763**	**12409**	**185506**	**8734**

Source: Education in India 1992, & Selected Educational Statistics, 1997-98, Dep't. Of Education.

The problems faced by the primary education in India in terms of expansion today are:

1. The geographical conditions of hilly deserted and forest regions in India have led to isolation of people in one area to another. Hence it is not economically feasible to have primary school for very few children and lack of proper

Table 1.2
Growth in Primary School Enrollment (in millions)

Year	*BOYS*			*GIRLS*			*TOTAL*		
	I-V Primary	*VI-VIII Upper Primary*	*I-VIII Eleme-ntary*	*I-V Primary*	*VI-VIII Upper Primary*	*I-VIII Eleme-ntary*	*I-V Primary*	*VI–VIII Upper Primary*	*I-VIII Eleme-ntary*
1951	13.79	2.98	16.77	5.51	.67	6.18	19.30	3.65	22.95
1961	25.98	5.62	31.6	13.12	1.87	14.99	39.10	7.48	46.58
1971	36.78	9.64	46.42	22.03	4.04	26.07	58.82	13.68	72.50
1981	46.71	14.69	61.40	29.39	7.25	36.64	76.11	21.95	98.07
1991	58.64	22.05	80.69	42.30	13.60	55.90	100.94	35.65	136.59
1992	57.87	21.22	79.09	41.75	12.87	54.62	99.62	34.09	133.71
1996	62.5	24.7	87.20	47.9	16.3	64.20	110.4	41.0	151.50
1997	61.83	23.7	85.53	47.59	15.80	63.39	109.41	39.50	148.91

Source: Growth of School Enrolment 1950-1993 MHRD, Government of India

transport facilities have added to the woes in the rural areas, which constitute 70% of India's population.

2. Local bodies such as municipal boards, and district boards handle primary education in rural areas. The lack of co-operation among government officials and these local bodies for compulsory and free education has created hurdles in expanding primary education.

3. The paucity of funds required for expansion is a main hassle in implementing free education programme.

4. Social problems such as untouchables, caste differences and conservatism have resulted in opening of schools only for children of a particular community or children.of low caste not allowed to join in school with children of upper caste etc. Further conservative parents are reluctant to send girls to co-education schools.

5. People living below the poverty line are never willing to meet the involved expenses of sending children to school, which has resulted in increasing gaps between educated people among rich and poor.

6. Child labor, which is rampant among the masses due to the need of supplementing their income, has led to drop outs from school or non-enrollment.

7. Failure on the part of education system to attract children to school by way of providing appropriate teaching materials and suitable teachers have led the parents regard primary education as valueless.

8. Increased dropout after or before completion primary education is termed as wastage. This is due to lack of methodological approach, faulty administration and lack of suitable curriculum.

9. Stagnation means failure to complete the prescribed course within a prescribed time. This is caused by unattractive courses, defective examination system and malnutrition.

10. The non-availability of suitable teachers in the primary education has led to number of school, which have a single teacher handling all the classes of primary classes. Thus lack of teachers vitiates he atmosphere.

Reforms Required for Expansion of Primary Education

1. New schools need to be opened within the easy approach for all children.
2. Trained teachers for each class need to be appointed.
3. The curriculum needs to be vocational oriented to stimulate the interests of rural areas.
4. Private enterprises, which come forward to open schools, which cater to the needs of each social and cultural tradition, need to be encouraged.
5. Suitable buildings with proper school ground attached need to built for attracting children.
6. Focus must be directed on locals who can be trained to become teachers to avoid absenteeism etc.
7. The number of teachers needs to increase to cater the needs of increasing children and stress to be laid on appointing one teacher for every primary class.
8. The curriculum in rural areas need to be different in urban as they cater to the needs of two different categories of people.
9. Co-operation between public and government is of high importance for expansion of primary education.
10. Research in the areas to locate problems in primary education need to be encouraged.
11. Ban of child labor need to be taken at a serious note as it the main cause of dropouts or wastage in schooling.
12. Child marriages. Though banned under act of 1930 is not able to produce desired results due to lack of co-operation

from the respective communities. The communities must be encouraged to have a more liberal and progressive outlook to patronize girl's education.

13. Education of adults/ guardians/parents is an absolute necessity to make them realize the importance of education.
14. An examination pattern, which decides the progress of a child in the entire session he/she has undergone, should be followed instead of one, which tests the ability in few hours.
15. Finally the physical health, which develops the mental health, should be given importance. Nutritious food needs to be supplemented by the respective state to prevent stagnation.

Conclusion

Building a credible and a concrete educational policy with achieving "education for all" is a mammoth task and must include critical analyzation of performance of teachers in class room to national priorities given to financing the primary education. Government of India must focus on creating an educational policy which links education to economic development and employment in the country. Since the percentage of Indians who have been educated into unemployment is steadily increasing, the faith in the educational system is on the decline. Hence, selection of an appropriate policy and curriculum is the need of the hour to inculcate faith on education in parents.

As India is emerging largely as market economy, the darker side reveals that India's population of illiterates is larger than its population as was in 1947. Though the share of elementary education spending is increasing the share of elementary education spending does not exceed one third of total public education spending. The Ministry of Human resources development in 2002 had put up an proposal for hypothecated tax to be used solely for elementary education and the government levied a 2% in central budget. Since the gap between available and needed resources is on the rise a similar tax need to be levied by states as well.

References

1. New Education in India, B R Purkait. Associated Publishers, Ambala Cantt. 1999.

2. Education in India, Today and Tomorrow S N Mukerji, Acharya Book Depot 1964.

3. Primary and Elementary Education, Jagannath Mohanty, Deep and Deep Publications Pvt. Ltd.
New Delhi 2000.

4. Land marks in the History of Modern Indian Education,
K Aggarwal, Vani Educational Books, New Delhi 1984.

5. Development of Education in India, Socio economic and Political Perspective, SK Saini, COSMO Publications, New Delhi.

6. Education for All – The Indian Scene, Ministry of Human Resources Development, Govt. of India, Dec. 1993.

7. Elementary Education in India, Myth, Reality,Alternative, John Kurrien , Vikas Publishing House, 1993.

8. Primary Education in India, World Bank Publication, Washington DC, March 1997.

SECTION III

Promotion of Gender Equality and Empowerment

9

Macro Economic Policies and MDG III: Promotion of Gender Equality and Empowerment of Women

Vibhuti Patel

"We need a vision of mankind not as patients whose interests have to be looked after, but as agents who can do effective things- both individually and jointly. We also have to go beyond the role of human beings specifically as 'consumers' or as 'people with need', and consider, more broadly, their general role as agents of change who can- given opportunity- think, assess, evaluate, resolve, inspire, agitate, and through these means, reshape the world."

Prof. Amartya Kumar Sen

Introduction

MDG 3 challenges discrimination against women, and seeks to ensure that girls as well as boys have the chance to go to school. Indicators linked to this goal aim to measure progress towards ensuring that more women become literate, have more voice and representation in public policy and decision making, and have improved job prospects. But the issue of gender equality is not limited to a single goal; it applies to all of them. Without progress towards gender equality and the empowerment of women, none of the MDGs will be achieved. Prioritizing women and girls offers a compelling, and in many cases, win-win approach for policy makers and planners towards implementing the MDGs.

Analysing from this perspective, experiences of last one and half decades have shown that the macro economic policies (MEPs) pursued by the nation states are not in consonance with the MDGs.

Bleak Scenario

Neo-liberal MEPs have accentuated inequality and poverty[1] and has had massive influence on the urban, rural and dalit /tribal poor women as paid, underpaid and unpaid workers of the economy.[2] As homemakers the poor women have shouldered disproportionate (triple) burden of G due to commercialisation of day-to-day survival needs such as drinking water, degradation of environment and health services[3] and cash controlled and privatised education by corporate driven G[4]. Expensive transport, erosion of public distribution system that provided grains, fuel, cloth material, soap, etc., have reduced chances of schooling, nutritious diet and healthy growth of poor women's children. *Laissez-faire* in the labour market has threatened the employment opportunities of the adult and married women. During the last one decade, there has been drastic increase in the girl child labour

The Impact of MEPs on Women Workers in India

Women of the third world are seen as the most flexible of the world's labour force. The lower supply price of these women provides a material basis for the induction of poor working-class urban women into export industries such as electronics, garments, sports goods, toys and agro-industries.[5] In the export-oriented industries, the production of leather goods, toys, food-products, garments, diamond and jewellery, piece-rate female labour is employed, working from sweatshops or from home.[6] Outsourcing is name of the game. The relationship between the formal sector and the decentralised sector is a dependent relationship where the formal sector has control over capital and markets and the 'informal' sector works as an ancillary. In India, 96% of the urban and rural poor women work in the decentralised sector, which has a high degree of labour redundancy and obsolescence. These women have less control over their work and no chance for upward mobility because of temporary, routine and monotonous work.[7]

Women constitute only 14% of the total employment in the organized sector. It is concentrated in Maharashtra, Delhi, West Bengal, Uttar Pradesh and Tamilnadu. In the urban areas, Female Economic Activity Rate (FEAR) in tertiary sector has increased, from 37.6 % in 1983 to 52.9 % in 1999. (Economic Survey, 2002, GOI).

Here too, though women workers and employees get relatively better wages, there is gross violation of labour standards. Much applauded recommendations of the IInd Labour Commission grant increased freedom to the employers to hire and fire workers at their whims and fancies.

Perpetuation of Wage Differential (WD) by economic G is such that for identical tasks done by both men and women, women are paid less. And women are also confined to relatively inferior tasks, casual work. The Trans National Corporations (TNCs) and Multi National Corporations (MNCs) are cashing on patriarchal attitude and myths about women's low productivity. Effects of WD have been subordination of women, son preference, man being treated as a "bread winner" and a Head of the Household (HoH). Affirmative Action to remove these prejudices is a need of an hour. Both, the state and the social action groups need to join hands to provide gender justice in the labour market.

Primitive Accumulation of Capital for Expansion of World Capitalism

Marked feature of neo liberal policy is enlightened self-interest activated through market forces in the era of economic Globalisation (G). **G** rides on the back of cheap labour of women and children. Landscape of urban and rural informal sector in dozens of South Asian (India, Pakistan, Bangladesh, Srilanka, Nepal) and South East Asian (Thailand, Indonesia, Philippines, Malaysia) countries, Indochina (Laos, Kampuchea and Vietnam) and China is flooded with sweatshops, ghetto labour markets and stigmatised migrant workers.

ASEAN countries have recently discussed establishment of Special Economic Zones that would ensure flexibalisation of the labour force to attract Foreign Direct Investment (FDI).

During the 1990s employment of adult women decreased and employment of adolescent girls and child labour increased. Women were and are given less skilled and underpaid jobs. Budgetary cuts for balwadis and crèches enhanced the burden of poor working women. FTZs and EPZs thrive on young women's super-exploitation. The employers overlook occupational health hazards.

Displacement in the Name of Development: The most disturbing aspect is the very space to live and work is withdrawn from the urban poor in favour of parking spaces and flyovers. Throughout the 20th century, the urban poor women have been employed in food, beverage, tobacco, textiles, and wood / bamboo / cane and ceramics industries. Here too, they have been targets for retrenchment and forced to join the unorganised sector. Women are squeezed out of the marketing, vending spaces because global traders have made local labour and skill obsolete.

Sizeable section of the informal sector goods and services are produced, frequently by means of contracting and subcontracting, which are paid for on piecework rather than a time-rate basis. Much of the economic activity in the informal sector is founded on capital from the formal sector and given the low cost of labour and taxed minimally or not at all, return to where it came from with tidy profit. Primitive accumulation in its classical form included plunder, slavery and colonialism, while primitive accumulation in the contemporary period includes sweat- shops, labour concentration camps and criminalisation of the working class. In 1998, the world economy had 1.2 billion poor i.e. population with an income of less than 1 dollar per capita per day.

As a result of Structural Adjustment Programme, sacked/ retrenched formal sector workers and employees are forced to work in the informal sector. Victims of Voluntary Retirement Scheme have downward economic mobility. Rationalisation, mechanisation and automation have had labour reducing implications. Massive urban unemployment and rural underemployment and disguised unemployment have resulted into social tensions in terms of ethnic and religious chauvinism in several Asian countries. Women pay the heaviest price due to communal and ethnic conflicts. Incidents of economic crimes have risen drastically.

Labour Standards as set by the ILO under the impact of Economic Globalisation have been violated resulting into erosion of workers' rights and collective bargaining process due to informalisation, casualisation and marginalsation of the working class as a result of economic liberalisation policies adopted by the nation states in the region. Trade union workers from all Asian countries expressed their anxiety about countries competing with each other to cut costs by compromising labour standards. In the name of labour flexibility, exploitation of the workers is enhanced and feminisation of poverty has taken place. The social action groups **must demand of uniform labour standards for all countries that are part of World Trade Organisation so that the nation-states stop competing for cutting the cost by violating workers rights.**

Co-existence of high wage islands in the sea of pauperised working class has enhanced human misery and social conflict in the context of massive reduction in the welfare budgets of the nation states in South Asia and South East Asia. With rising ethnic and communal tension jeopardising economic activities, visible and invisible activities of underground extra-legal economy is displaying a tendency to expand. Introduction of contract system in public sector has institutionalised neo-liberal dual economy model.

Immigrant women face job discrimination in pre-entry phase & wage discrimination in post entry phase. They remain the first to be fired and the last to be hired. They are the major victims of casualisation of the labour force. Dualistic Models in the urban

India promotes differentiation based on language, caste, religion, ethnic background and exclusion from informal network for upward economic mobility. Majority of the toiling poor rot in the external sector in which real wages change at disparate rates. Institutions like extended family, caste and village nexus play an important role in providing safety nets to migrant workers. **Forced Eviction to Accommodate Mega Projects:** Capital driven globalisation has perpetrated tremendous human miseries by resorting to forced eviction of poor people from their dwelling place and work-place. "Women...and other vulnerable individuals and groups suffer disproportionately from the practice of forced eviction. Women in all groups are especially vulnerable given the extent of statutory and other forms of discrimination which often apply in relation to property rights (including home ownership) or rights of access to property or accommodation, and their particular vulnerability to acts of violence and sexual abuse when they are rendered homeless."(UN Committee on Economic, Social, and Cultural Rights, Sixteenth Session, 1997)[8]

Displaced Population due to Natural as well as man-made disasters: Women victims of natural disasters such as floods, earthquakes and social disasters such as caste, communal, ethnic conflicts and war and economic disasters in the name of development (building 350 flyovers in Mumbai, mega plants, shopping plazas displacing people) need rehabilitation in terms of proper housing, civic amenities, safe transport and work.

Girl Child Labour and Globalisation

Nearly 10 % of girls were never enrolled in schools due to paid and unpaid work they had to do in homes, fields, factories, plantations and in the informal sector.[9] Sexual abuse at the work place is a hidden burden that a girl worker endures. The child labour policies, however, do not spell out anything specific to girl child workers. There is no implementation of prohibition of girls working in hazardous occupations as per Child Labour (Prohibition and Regulation) Act, 1986. About 6% of the males and females in rural areas and about 3% males and 2% females in age group 5-14 in urban areas were found to be working during 1993-94.[10]

HIV AIDS and STD among Urban Poor Girls: Tourism driven Globalisation has promoted sex-tourism and child prostitution. Tourists seeking uninfected short-term sex partners increasingly pursue young girls based in the urban centres as well as on the national highways and have paid sex with child prostitutes.[11] Young girls may be forced into sex or otherwise have little power in sexual relationships to negotiate condom use, particularly if their sexual partner is older —a double risk since older men are more likely to be infected. Belief that the sex with virgin girls cures STDs among men has intensified trafficking of girls from rural hinterland to the urban red light areas.

STD pathogens can more easily penetrate the cervical mucus of girl than that of older women. The cervix of a girl is more susceptible to gonorrhoeal and chlamydeous infection as well as to the sexually transmitted human papilloma virus (HPV), which causes cervical cancer. They may be even more reluctant than the adults to seek treatment for STDs because their sexual activity is frowned upon. Also, they may not know that they have a disease. They may be too embarrassed to go to a clinic, have no access to a clinic, or be unable to afford services. They are instead taken to unqualified traditional healers or obtain antibiotics from pharmacies or drug hawkers without proper diagnosis. Improper and especially incomplete treatment of STDs may mask symptoms without completely curing the disease, making it more likely that STDs will be transmitted to others and that complications such as infertility will occur. In our country millions of adolescents live or work on the street, and many are forced to sell sex under extremely barbaric and unhygienic conditions that increase their exposure to STDs.

Criminalisation of day-to-day Survival Needs in the Urban Slums and Predicaments of Poor Women: The urban slums are getting increasingly criminalized due to the working of land-sharks, violent political rivalries and youth unemployment. Violence against women such as rape, kidnap, induction of girls for pornographic filming, child sexual abuse, kidnapping of girls in the urban slums have increased many fold in the recent years. Globalisation has made it extremely easy to import XX and XXX pornographic films and literature that promotes sado-masochistic relationship between men and women and escalates male violence, paedophilia and child sexual abuse.

MEPs and Educational Needs of Women: Liberalisation of educational services under General Agreement on Trade and Services has given a major blow to the state supported educational institutions. Privatisation of education is oriented to profit and commodification of educational services. Women are the main losers as parents channelise financial resources for son's education, daughter's education is considered to be less important. There has been massive retrenchment of women teachers from schools and colleges. Foreign educational institutions operating within purely commercial parameters are expanding their tentacles all over the country. At present, all educational institutions are thriving on super-exploitation of workers, employees and teachers working on a contract basis where totals control over hire and fire policy rests with the management; majority of contract workers happen to be women.

Health Sector Reforms and the Poor Women: In the name of cost- efficiency patients are discharged earlier from the public hospitals. This has increased women's invisible labour, whose stretchablity has limits. Their physical and mental health suffers. Now, medicines are not freely available. Only contraceptives and high potency tranquillisers to check mental illnesses are easily available.

Women's health is determined by the forces working at homes, work places, society and the state. According to Dr. Amartya Kumar Sen, "Burden of hardship falls disproportionately on women" due to seven types of inequality- mortality (due to gender bias in health care and nutrition), natality (sex selective abortion and female infanticide)), basic facility (education and skill development), special opportunity (higher education and professional training), employment (promotion) and ownership (home, land and property).[12] Economic G has accentuated all 7 types of inequalities faced by women from womb to tomb.

As a result of sex-determination and sex-preselection tests, sex ratio of the child population has declined to 927 girls for 1000 boys. Sixty lakh female infants and girls are "missing" due to sex-selective abortion of female foetuses and pre-conception rejection of daughters. Sex-ratio (number of women per 1000 men) of Greater Bombay has reduced from 791 in 1991 to 774 in 2001 in spite of rise in its literacy rate.

Violence and Health Issues of Women over the Life Cycle: As unborn children, they face covert violence in terms of sex-selection and overt violence in terms of female foeticide after the use of amniocentesis, chorion villai biopsy, sonography, ultrasound, imaging techniques.[13] IVF (In Vitro Fertilization) clinics for assisted reproduction are approached by infertile couples to produce sons. Doctors are advertising aggressively, "Invest Rs. 500 now, save Rs.50000 later" i.e. if you get rid of your daughter now, you will not have to spend money on dowry.

As girls under 5 years of age, the urban poor women face neglect of medical care and education, sexual abuse and physical violence. As adolescent and adult women in the reproductive age-group, they face early marriage, early pregnancy, sexual violence, domestic violence, dowry harassment, infertility, if they fail to produce son, then face desertion, witch hunt. The end-result is a high maternal mortality. Causes of maternal deaths in our country are haemorrhage, abortion, infection, obstructed labour, eclampsia (blood pressure during pregnancy), sepsis, and anaemia.

Escalating number of cases of domestic violence, dowry deaths and bride burning has motivated Bombay Municipal Corporation (BMC) run K.B. Bhabha Municipal General Hospital to collaborate with an NGO, CEHAT to launch a project ***Dilaasa*** (means **reassurance)** to provide social and psychological support to women facing domestic violence. On March 8, 2002, the BMC declared its intention to replicate this model in all BMC run hospitals in the Greater Bombay.

Sexual harassment at work place should be treated as an occupational health hazard as it causes damage to both physical and mental health of women.[14] Women workers working in foreign land have often reported sexual harassment and torture by employers and agents.

Home and Work Conditions Affecting Women's Health: Pollution of air and water, noise pollution and chemicalisation of environment affect everybody. Scarcity of fuel, water and food-grains as a result of commercialisation has taken heavy toll of women's health. Urban poor women have to take up 2-3 jobs to supplement their income to meet the basic survival needs of their family members. Floods create deaths, destruction and epidemics. Global warming has resulted in resurgence of older epidemics such as cholera, typhoid, malaria, dengue, and haemorrhagic fever. Burgeoning sex-trade have made 2 million sex-workers potential carriers of HIV, STD, and AIDS. Moreover, women in prostitution may suffer from T.B., other STDs, malnutrition, malaria and skin diseases.[15] At present, there is an evidence of rising HIV rates among young married women who are infected by their husbands. Data from 7 cities in India of ante- natal clinics reveals that HIV-AIDS prevalence rates among pregnant women are 2% to 3.5 % in Mumbai and 1% in Hyderabad, Banglore and Chennai.[16]

Modern lifestyle and environment has increased breast and uterine[17] cancer among Indian women. Techniques meant for detecting cancer (e.g. self-examination of breast and pap- smear) are rarely used by the urban poor women. As a result, detection of cancer and its treatment at earlier stage becomes impossible. All types of fruits are cornered by liquor industry and alcoholism is aggressively promoted among the toiling poor. As a result, men don't contribute for daily necessity of the households. Women have to shoulder major burden of household expenditure. Use of bio-fuels- wood, dung, crop residue resulting into indoor air-pollution takes away the lives of 5 lakh women annually.[18]

Health-care Facilities for Women: Profit motive of five star hospitals and multinational pharmaceutical industries determine the health agenda, not the public health concerns. As a result, in India, only 49.2 % of total pregnant women received ante-natal check-up by health professionals. Health workers visited only 21% of pregnant women. Tetanus toxoid coverage of pregnant women was 53.8% and Anaemia prophylaxis coverage among pregnant women was 50.5%. [19] Majority of Indian women are left with no choice than to deliver at home.[20] Every 5000 population has an auxiliary nurse midwife (ANM) with responsibility to attend childbirth. Only negligible parts of home-births are attended by ANMs. [21]

Institutional deliveries constituted only 22 % of total deliveries at the national level. Urban areas were better covered: 55 percent as against a very megre 18% in rural areas.[22]

New Reproductive Technologies (NRTs) and the Urban Poor Women: Profit obsessed MEPs have given boost to bio-medical research that lacks ethical standards. NRTs perform 4 types of functions. In Vitro Fertilisation (IVF) and subsequent embryo transfer, GIFT (Gamete Intra Fallopian Transfer), ZIFT and cloning assist reproduction.[23] Contraceptive Technologies prevent conception and birth. Amniocentesis, chorion villai Biopsy, niddling, ultrasound are used for prenatal diagnosis.[24] Foetal cells are collected by the technique of amniocentesis and CVB. Gene technologies play crucial role through genetic manipulation of animal and plant kingdoms.[25] Genomics is "the science of improving the human population through controlled breeding, encompasses the elimination of disease, disorder, or undesirable traits, on the one hand, and genetic enhancement on the other. It is pursued by nations through state policies and programmes".[26] The urban poor women are treated as genie pigs for experimentation of the NRTs.

It is important for the social action groups to examine scientific, social, juridical, ethical, economic and health consequences of the NRTs. G has facilitated NRTs that treat women's bodies as site for scientific experimentations. G had also accentuated a process by which the poor women from Africa, Latin America and Asia have been treated as raw material for bio-medical researches.

Contraceptives targeted at women, with serious side effects are Quinacrine, Net-en, Norplant, Depo-Provera, anti fertility vaccine and RU 486. Side effects of long acting hormonal contraceptives are menstrual disturbance, circulatory and cardio-vascular problems, thyroid, chest-pain, giddiness, migraine, increased risk of cancer and infertility[27]. Aggressively promoted HRT (Hormone Replacement Therapy) i.e. oestrogen therapy for menopausal women has generated opposition as several studies have shown that HRT has carcinogenic implications for women.[28] Modus operandi of contraceptive research in the Asian countries treats coloured women as raw material for experimentation for eugenics.

Population Policy The focus of health programme should change from a population control approach of reducing numbers to an approach that is gender sensitive and responsive to the reproductive health needs of women/ men. Women groups have raised hue and cry against sexist, racist and class biases of the population control policy, which perceives uterus of coloured women as a danger zone. They have opposed genetic and reproductive engineering, which reduce women to reproductive organs and allow women being used as experimental subjects by science, industry and the state.[29] They believe that instead of abusing reproductive biology, responsible reproduction is an answer to overpopulation and infertility. Any coercion, be it through force, incentives or disincentives in the name of population stabilisation should be rejected. Instead enabling women to have access to education, resources, employment, income, social security and safe environment at work and at home are precondition to small family norm. Reproductive Rights of Women which guarantee women healthy life, safe motherhood, autonomy in decision-making about when, how many and at what interval to have children are a central axis around which a discourse on population policy should revolve. Several groups have prepared manuals to assist women leaders to reach out to poor illiterate women and teach them about fertility and infertility, giving them knowledge of their anatomy, to teach women to use fertility awareness as a means of family planning and to use natural family planning as an entry point to women's health and development.[30]

Worsening Socio-economic and Political Situation and Mental Health of Women: Experiences from both industrialised and developing countries have revealed that the prevalence of common mental disorders or minor psychiatric morbidity is high among the urban low income and marginalized population. Women among them are even more vulnerable. G, structural Adjustment Programmes, increasing conflict with neighbouring countries and ongoing sectarian violence on caste, ethnicity and communal lines within the country have put the population of our country at high risk of mental illnesses. Alert India is a large NGO with 550 community workers working among the marginalized sections of Mumbai metropolis. Their women health workers found that women who have to deal with financial hardship, experience tremendous stress. Multi-tasking is name of the game. At a time women are doing 3-4 types of economic activities- tailoring, assembling of eletric spare-parts, packaging of medicines, food processing, etc. Moreover, women within community are affected differentially depending on their own place in the Indian socio-economic hierarchy. In this regards, female-headed households are most vulnerable to mental distress. The mental health professionals are only geared for the episodic disasters and not the enduring disasters. Urban poor women have also become the victims of 'mental health' agenda shaped by multinational pharmaceutical giants. With liberalisation of economies drug cures have become established as sure cures for mental illness. World Bank has offered 'template' for a predominantly psychiatry driven mental health services all over the world.

Need for Rural-Urban Linkages: Dismantaling of PDS has heaped enormous misery on the poor women. The reason lies in onslaught on agriculture and food-security. 84% of all economically active women are in agriculture, majority into subsistence farming. Opening up of market since 1-4-2000 for 729 new commodities (240 are agrarian products including rice, meat, milk powder, fruits) that can be imported unrestrictedly have resulted in enormous tragedies resulting into suicides and starvation deaths among farmers and weavers. Prices of rubber, cotton, coconut, coffee, cardamom, pepper, tomatoes, sugarcane and potatoes have crashed. Urban poor women in Kerala and Karnataka are fighting desperate struggles against imports of these items to express their solidarity with their rural and tribal sisters.

Conclusion

MEPs have increased power of economic and financial transnational actors. MEPs have also increased armamentisation and militarisation. As a result insecurity for poor women has increased. They have been the first victims of downsizing and rationalisation. Their subjugation and exploitation have enhanced thro' retrenchment, unemployment, increases in contract/ subcontract work, home working and loss of livelihood. There is an urgent need to address globalisation of poverty, violence, expanding zones and techniques of violence (as experienced in the Gujarat Carnage), consumerism and glocal cultural industry, strengthening partnership of market and global fundamentalism. Globalisation has made civil society more inward looking. Caste, religious and kinship networks are activated to bring reforms within the community. Without ensuring women's rights, globalisation can't have a human face. We should not forget that globalisation has widened income gap between the resource poor and resource rich countries. ICE of G i.e. Information, communication and entertainment in favour of economic globalisation has nothing to offer the common women except deprivation, degradation and dehumanisation. Free-play of market forces have made majority of Indian women more vulnerable in the factor, labour and product markets. NGOs have provided islands of security in some pockets. In this situation, affirmative action by the democratic institutions and the nation state, in secular areas of human governance is the only answer.

Women's rights organisations and social action groups were the most vociferous during the Asia Social Forum, 2003 against Trans National Corporation and Multinational Corporation driven G.

Through World Social Forum, 2004 women for just, sustainable and caring trade are trying to reach out to thousands of women who are voicing the concerns of toiling poor.

Women decision makers are striving for agenda setting power to achieve MDGs. At the same time, they are aware about the failure of MDGs to reaffirm women's human rights, access to secure land tenure and action to stop violence against women and reproductive rights of women. Moreover, they are evolving strategies to address the vicious circle linking gender inequality, neo liberal macro economic policies and poverty.

References

1. Mungekar, B.L. "Globalisation and the Dalits," Global Conference Against Racism and Caste Based Discrimination, New Delhi, March, 2001.

2. Dietrich, Gabriele "Globalisation and Women in India in the Nineties", *Vikalpa,* Vol.1, No. 3, 2001.

3. Ravi Kumar, T. "Downsizing Higher Education- An Emergent Crisis", *Economic and Political Weekly*, Vol. XXXVIII, No.7, Feb.2003.

4. Ambani, Mukesh and Kumarmangalam Birla "A Policy Framework for Reforms in Education", report submitted to the prime minister's Council on Trade and Industry, 2000, Website: http://www.nic.in/pmcouncil/reports/education.

5. Jeong, Joo-Yeon & Choi, Seung-Min "Neo-liberalism Through the Eyes of Women", Policy and Information centre for international Solidarity (PICIS), Korea, Nov, 2001.

6. Committee for Asian Women, Moving Mountains-25 years of Performance, Bangkok, 2003.

7. Patel, Vibhuti ***Women's Challenges of the New Millennium***, Gyan Publications, Delhi, 2002.

8. Websites: www.cohre.org

9. National Sample Survey Organisatoion, Table 21-2, Delhi, 1991; s70-s119.

10. Jawa, R *Girl Child Labour*, N. Delhi: Manak Publications, 2002: 157

11. Fernandes, G and Stewart C *Raids, Rescue, Rehabilitation*, Research Unit, College of Social Work, Mumbai: Nirmala Niketan, 2002.

12. Amartya Sen: "Many Faces of Gender Inequality", an inauguration Lecture for New Radcliff Institute at Harvard University, 24-4-2001.

13. Vibhuti Patel "Girl Child: An Endangered Species?", in Viney Kripal (ed*) The Girl Child in 20th Century* Indian Literature, Sterling Publications Pvt. Ltd., New Delhi, 1992. p.9.

14. Thelma Narayan: "Gender and Power Issues in Medical Education **Consultation on Gender and Medical Education,** Understanding Needs for Gender Sensitisation, Critiquing Content and Method of Medical Education- Developing Long Term Strategies for

Intervention, organised by Achutha Menon Centre for Health Science Studies in collaboration with CEHAT, at SNDT Women's University, Bombay, on 31-1-2002.

15. Gracy Fernandes and Cecily Stewart Ray: *Raids, Rescue, Rehabilitation, The Story of Mumbai Brothel Raids –of 1996-2000*, The College of Social Work, Nirmala Niketan, Mumbai, 1991.p.75.

16. Sameera Khan: "The Indian Women: Confronting HIV/AIDS", SANKALP, The Newsletter of the International AIDS Vaccine Initiative in India, Nov.-Dec. 2001.p.7.

17. S. Wal and Ruchi Mishra; op.cit., pp. 27-30.

18. Sarla Gopalan and Mira Shiva: *National Profile on Women's Health and Development*, Voluntary Health Association of India and World Health Organisation, Delhi, 2000, p. 213.

19. International Institute of Population Sciences, Bombay, 1995.

20. Kalyani Menon Sen and A.K. Shivakumar: *Women in India-How Free? How Equal*? Report Commissioned by the United Nations Resident Coordinator in India, New Delhi, 2001. p. 37.

21. Shyam Ashtekar: *Health and Health Care Systems-Observations From China, Philippines and Thailand and Reflections on India*, Bharat Vaidyak Sanstha, Nasik, p.128.

22. Registrar General of India, 1997.

23. Tarala D. Nandedkar and Medha S. Rajadhyaksha: *Brave New Generation*, Vistas in Biotechnology, CSIR, Department of Biotechnology, Government of India, 1995.

24. Vibhuti Patel: Sex Selection, in *Routledge International Encyclopedia of Women- Global Women's Issues andKnowledge*, Vol. 4, 2000. pp.1818-1819.

25. Jyotsana Agnihotri Gupta: *New Reproductive Technologies-Women's Health and Autonomy, Freedom* or *Dependency*? Indo Dutch Studies in Development Alternatives-25, Sage Publications, New Delhi, 2000.

26. Chee Heng Leng "Genomics and Health: Ethical, Legal and Social Implications for Developing Countries", Issues in Medical Ethics, Bombay, Vol.X, No. 1, Jan.- March, 2002, pp.146-149.

27. Chayanika, Kamakshi, Swatija: We and Our Fertility, Research Centre for Women's Studies, SNDT Women's University, Bombay, 1990.

28. Sherril Sellman: "Osteoporosis- the bone of contention", Drug Disease Doctor, Quarterly Journal on Rational Drug and Therapy, Drug Action Forum, Kolkata, Vol.14, No. 2, April, 2001.

29. Feminist International Network of Resistance to Reproductive and Genetic Engineering (FINRRAGE) - UBINIG-Policy Research for Development Alternative- DECLARATION OF COMILLA, Bangladesh, 1989.

30. Mahila Samooh: Fertility Awareness, published by Jagori, Delhi, 1995.

10

Empowering Rural Women with Technology

Chetna V. Sinha and Amy E. Bean

When founding the Mann Deshi Mahila Sahakari Bank, we strove to provide basic financial services to women in the drought-prone area of western Maharashtra. After seven years of service, we find ourselves facing a radically different kind of 'customer.' In today's environment, our bank must work hard to meet the increasingly sophisticated and progressive demands of our clients. The women of Mann Deshi Mahila handle both household and enterprise-related finances, own and manage assets, found businesses, and increasingly control family savings and expenditures. Success in these financial matters has made the women self-reliant, powerful, and confident. This newfound confidence spills over into both domestic and civic matters and makes them eager to embrace change.

One change that is occurring throughout India, both urban and rural, is the technological revolution. As the women of Mann Deshi Mahila gain exposure to technological advances, we find that the cycle of empowerment is perpetuated. Each new technology the women use, their confidence grows and their importance in the community is heightened and realized. This increases their desire to accept newer technologies and acquire the skills necessary to operate these advances. Despite our rural location, Mann Deshi Mahila has found that the continued utilization of technology provides for the maximum the empowerment of our women.

"Reliable Banking Improved My Life, Not Charity"

Every day, Nakusa is reminded of her painful childhood, as her name in Marathi means unwanted. Nakusa was the fifth daughter born to her mother and father. Soon after her birth, Nakusa's father married another woman. She recalls with sadness how her entire family was thrown out of their home and onto the street.

With no one to turn to, the family travelled to the nearby city of Karad in search of work and shelter. They lived on a footpath in Karad City and found it exceedingly difficult to find work. Nakusa had not eaten in two days and was hungrily watching some men have tea and snacks. "I realized then, that if you watch people while they are eating, they will give you food because they want to get rid of you." This is how she learned to beg.

Nakusa did not allow her dismal upbringing to predestine her future. Several years ago, she approached Mann Deshi Mahila Bank for an Rs. 10000 loan, which she used to free herself from the clutches of a moneylender. After repaying that loan, she took an Rs. 30000 loan to purchase land and an Rs. 60000 loan to develop that land into a farm. Today, she is the proud owner of 3 acres of land, 1 cow, 2 buffalo, and 100 chickens. Nakusa no longer toils painfully as a construction laborer because she owns and manages productive assets. She is now assisting other women like herself by acting as Director of our Self-Help Group Federation and coordinating three self-help groups of her own. She has learned to manage these accounts with the assistance of a calculator and portable computer.

Our bank is proud to help women like Nakusa – women who dare to dream dreams, and act to make those dreams happen. These women are the inspiration for our products and the motivation behind our continued innovations and improvements.

Mann Deshi Mahila envisions a future where financial services are available to all women who aspire to make life better for themselves and future generations.

Mann Deshi Mahila Sahakari Bank

The Mann Deshi Mahila Sahakari Bank is a regulated cooperative bank run by and for women. Founded in 1997, it is India's first rural financial institution to receive a cooperative license from the Reserve Bank of India. Our bank has 3058 members and serves 24,244 clients. Based on women's increasing interest and involvement, we estimate the bank will reach 50,000 clients by 2007. We operate 3 branches, 1 extension counter, and 2 administrative offices - covering an area which includes the districts of Satara, Solapur, and Sangli. We also have a direct linkage to over 300 rural Self-Help Groups. Each stage of the bank's development has presented our members with unique challenges. Without fail, the women have confronted each trial and surpassed all expectations.

Prior to the founding of the bank, we bemoaned the stories of hundreds of women who kept their savings hidden by burying it in the earth. More often than not, that hard-earned money was eaten by ants. We thought, why couldn't women start a bank? Intially, our proposal was rejected by the Reserve Bank of India on the grounds that many of the promoting members were illiterate women. The Reserve Bank of India was understandably concerned - if women cannot read or write, how can they start a Bank? The women reacted to this news by appealing the decision and requesting that an RBI Officer come out to test them on interest calculations and simple accounting. When the women accepted the first banking license of its kind in 1997, it was the harbinger of many future empowering successes.

Wage Laborers and Calculators

The calculator was the first technology to reach the rural women of Mann Deshi Mahila Bank. After proving to the Reserve

Bank of India their ability to calculate interest by hand, it was time to introduce the initial technological advance. Surekha Chourumle remembers learning to use the calculator for her work as a collection agent.

I didn't trust the calculator for several days. At first, I only trusted my head to do the calculations correctly, so I would refigure each calculator calculation by hand - to make sure it was accurate. After time, I realized that it was accurate and it was also extremely fast! Using the calculator has allowed me the speed to increase my clients from ninety, to three hundred. My business is now very successful and I am able to earn much more since I started using the calculator.

A majority of Mann Deshi women quickly adapted the new technology into their routines. They were pleased by the reduction in time spent doing the calculations and with the newfound sense of self-confidence. For a group of previously illiterate and marginalized women, using the calculator was a momentous and unprecedented stride.

Palm Computers for the Field Agents

Self-help group leaders are responsible for moving around the countryside and collecting the savings of their group members. Most of these women completed 7th or 8th standard and have extremely basic writing skills. Even with practice, the act of filling out information in the register is slow and tedious. Since the women are paid on commission, the register dilemma was complicated by their need to increase speed for profitability.

In 1999, Mann Deshi Mahila introduced palm computers to our self-help group leaders. The technology of choice was carefully selected in order to be effective in our taxing rural conditions. We often face electricity shortages of up to eight hours per day, so it is critical that the palm computers are easily chargeable or battery operated. They should also be lightweight and easy to operate. Our experience has shown that in order to be empowering, technologies must be chosen carefully. The act of introducing 'just any' technology is not necessarily beneficial.

Our field agents are now adept at operating the palm computers and their livelihoods have improved as a result. They are now quicker and more mobile, thereby increasing profits and standard of living.

Street Vendors and Cell Phones

Sonale Awade, a street vendor, recently came into our Vaduz Branch Office and asked for a loan in order to buy a cell phone. The Manager was a bit surprised and asked her why she wanted a cell phone – was it for her son? Sonale replied, "No!"

As a street vendor, I vend on the road all day, from morning until night. Having easy access to a phone allows me to place orders for additional fruit without leaving my business. It's also important that I be able to keep in touch with my family throughout the day and that my children can reach me if they need me. I've also heard that women in other villages who are earning extra money by lending their cell phones to other street vendors who need to make personal calls.

The Mann Deshi Mahila Bank has listened closely to these stories and has responded by providing a special loan product for cell phones. The cell phone empowers women by increasing their mobility and freedom, while simultaneously allowing them to remain in contact with children and household responsibilities. To date, we have given cell phone loans to numerous women. Street vendors use the cell phones to order additional product, goat herders keep in touch with children while they are on the road, and a rural greenhouse owner now takes flower orders directly from her clients.

Mann Deshi Mahila Bank could not have possibly predicted these innovative uses for rural cell phones. Empowered women had the confidence to embrace technology, and the insight to make this technology work for them. This example is perfectly illustrative of the positive cycle of empowerment - newly empowered women have confidently altered the present direction and service of our bank.

Smart Cards

Throughout our existence, Mann Deshi Mahila has struggled to find innovative ways to aid women in their desire to save. Early in our development, we heard that other banks found success by providing female clients with 'savings boxes.' These porcelain boxes emblazoned with attractive designs allow a woman to deposit money regularly, in the convenience of her own home. We thought that our women would very much like these savings boxes, and we decided to introduce them as a savings product. When the women saw these boxes they rejected them on the spot. Numerous clients informed us that when their husbands saw this box, they would break it and promptly take the money for their own use. The women would much prefer to save in the safety of the bank.

Women traditionally record savings and loan account information in a paper passbook, much like a checkbook register. Unfortunately, this written information is subject to unwanted inquiries and alterations. The women must make a conscious and continual effort to keep the passbooks hidden from relatives and spouses, or risk losing the hard-earned money. Women often counter this threat by keeping the passbooks in the bank. Our bank was uncomfortable with this practice, as it invites fraud.

In response to this problem, the bank has currently undertaken an initiative to put cutting edge technology into the hands of these rural female clients. Mann Deshi Mahila Bank will be the first rural bank in India to utilize SMART card technology for all of its banking operations. A plastic 'credit card,' equipped with the SIM card technology, will ultimately replace all of Mann Deshi Mahila's paper client passbooks.The card will allow both field agent and client to instantaneously view savings account balance, loan account status, and repayment history. Female field agents will be equipped with complimentary handheld devices that transmit updated data back to the branch office via the mobile phone or wireless Bluetooth card.

Prior to making the SMART card decision, we held numerous meetings with our clients and self-help group leaders. The women are tremendously excited about this new program. The SMART card is both discreet and secure. It will allow our women to keep their account information with them at all times, thereby maintaining absolute control of the information. Additionally, women will be able to more quickly obtain loan approval. For our many female entrepreneurs, decreasing loan turnaround time means increasing business and livelihood.

Smart Cards and Expenditures

Mann Deshi Mahila is also utilizing the SMART card technology to empower its clients in another pioneering way. While a woman's control of savings is a prominent matter in any microfinance discussion, control of expenditures is an often-neglected subject. We believe that control of expenditures is equally critical to any empowerment initiative. Our experience has shown that when women are in control of expenditures, more money is spent on those items that benefit the entire family. Whereas men in our villages often spend savings on alcohol, women tend to spend on household goods and enterprise related items.

A unique feature of Mann Deshi's incorporation of the SMART card system will be its credit-linkage with the Mann Deshi Mahila Mobile Hat. The newest innovation of the Mann Deshi operations, this mobile center is designed to bring products and services to clients in the most remote and rural areas of Maharashtra. Due to our customer's location, many consumption and enterprise-related items are either not available to them, or are exorbitantly expensive.

By utilizing the SMART card technology, representatives of the Mobile Hat can instantly access a client's fiscal information, current loan status, and repayment history. After reviewing and assessing this information, a bank officer may then grant a woman 'credit,' or a loan, to purchase an item from the Mobile Hat. By allowing a woman to use the loan to purchase an item on the spot, we have empowered her with the complete control of her funds. Reducing the need for a large cash transaction removes a barrier of fear for the woman – she can be confident that the money will be spent where she intends to spend it.

We have been conducting a series of meetings with our clients and self-help groups to garner feedback on which items the women are interested in purchasing. The Pise sisters are two of the many newly inspired women who now plan to start a business. After hearing our presentation, the sisters immediately reported inadequate copying facilities in the village of Mhaswad. They plan to take a loan from Mann Deshi Mahila for a Xerox machine and supplies, and to obtain the necessary equipment from the Mobile Hat. Sixty-five year-old Sumantai was equally motivated.

I live near a temple that regularly receives large groups of religious pilgrims and have noticed that these groups have nowhere to buy tea. I have often thought of starting a temple side tea stand but have never had access to both money and equipment. Now, I will take a loan from the bank and order an industrial size tea set and supplies from the Mobile Hat.

The unique offering of credit and product, enabled by technology, is enormously empowering to women. We are finding that this type of 'credit card' also stands to be enormously helpful to our self-help groups. Self-help groups are primarily formed and associated by industry, thereby creating a natural platform for the use of a group loan for enterprise related product. Many agricultural sector women have shown interest in the bulk purchasing of fertilizer, pesticides, and specialized feeds from the Mobile Hat. By allowing self-help groups to take SMART card group loans at the Mobile Hat, women are controlling not only their savings, but also their expenditures.

Empowerment and Development

Unlike the empowerment of men, the empowerment of women is rarely an individual phenomenon. Our experience has shown that a woman continually thinks first of her family. This is occurrence is both a positive, and a negative. From a banking standpoint, we often wish that a woman would use her loan solely to finance her enterprise. However, from a 'woman's' perspective, we understand that women are often both businessperson and caretaker. When a woman becomes empowered, the entire family becomes empowered. As a result, we believe that empowering women, will empower India.

In seeking this empowerment, technology should not be overlooked. Even in rural settings, technology can be used in surprisingly innovative ways to improve lives. The benefits of technology use are twofold - lives are improved and women gain the confidence and skills to take a more active role in society.

Conclusions

It is apparent that women are increasingly becoming technologically and financially savy. We find that when women are given both the tools and the opportunity, they seldom fail to capitalize. Despite progress and our optimistic outlook, we received a disturbing letter recently from the Reserve Bank of India. Currently, women comprise only 1.25% of the entire Indian banking sector's lending portfolio. The Bank has recently set a benchmark to provide 4% of all lending services to women. This target is embarrassingly low, and we believe that it represents a poverty of vision. Microfinance institutions report an average repayment rate of 98% and beyond for female clients. Women have proved their innovation, desire, and dependability. Now, it is vital that policy makers widen their visions to create space for the empowerment of all women.

11

Women's Empowerment: Budget as a Tool to Deal with the Gender Gap

Prashant Raymus

Gender equality refers to that stage of human social development at which "the rights, responsibilities and opportunities of individuals will not be determined by the fact of being born male or female," in other words, a stage when both men and women realize their full potential.

In recognition of the importance of establishing gender equality around the world, the United Nations Development Fund for Women (UNIFEM) was established as a separate fund within the United Nations Development Programme (UNDP) in 1984. At that time, the General Assembly instructed it to "ensure women's involvement with mainstream activities." The Platform of Action resulting from the 1995 Beijing World Conference on Women expanded this concept, calling it "gender mainstreaming"—i.e., the application of gender perspectives to all legal and social norms and standards, to all policy development, research, planning, advocacy, development, implementation and monitoring—as a mandate for all member states. In this way, the gender factor is no longer to be only a supplement to development but central to the practice of development. As a result of the Beijing conference—and the many years of work leading up to it—more than 100 countries announced new initiatives to improve the status of women. In 2000, the follow-up Beijing +5 conference further strengthened the application of the mainstreaming concept, and used it to highlight the need for more progress in reaching equality worldwide.

The Platform for Action at Beijing (1995) had identified 12 critical areas for action; amongst these, the more important ones were, poverty eradication, removal of gender gaps in education and health and establishing women's equal access to labour markets and to property rights.

World Economic Forum in its gender gap study covering 58 nations has ranked India a lowly 53. (Business standard) The report measures the gap between women and men in five critical areas like **economic participation, economic opportunity, political empowerment, educational attainment, and health and well-being**. These five categories identify concrete measures of the gender gap and provide an unambiguous framework for future policy-making. By quantifying the size of the gap in each of five key categories, this will highlight the priority areas for reform.

The ***economic participation*** of women—their presence in the workforce in quantitative terms—is important not only for lowering the disproportionate levels of poverty among women, but also as an important step toward raising household income and encouraging economic development. Economic participation concerns not only the actual numbers of women participating in the labour force, but also their remuneration on an equal basis.

In India, 67 per cent of currently married women in reproductive ages are not employed. 5 percentages are employed at home, and 27 per cent work outside the home. Among those who work outside the home, less than two-thirds work for cash. Women's labour-force participation varies greatly across the different states in India. The proportion of women employed is an appropriate reflection of the acceptability of female employment.

Table 1
Percent Distribution of Women by Employment Status, NFHS, 1992-93

	Not employed	*Employed at Home*	*Employed outside Home not for cash*	*Employed outside home for cash*
India	67.2	5.1	10.3	17.3
Rajasthan	67.7	4.8	19.6	7.7
Orissa	73.1	3.9	1.2	21.7
Andhra Pradesh	45.7	7.6	11.6	35.0
Karnataka	52.2	6.7	14.1	26.9
Maharashtra	49.7	5.0	17.5	27.7

Source: Sunita Kishore and Sulabha Parasuraman, NFHS subject Reports, No.8, IIPS.

Economic opportunity women are wage-employed in roughly equal numbers with men world-wide, the number of women represented in managerial positions is much smaller. Women have slow and uneven progress in obtaining a share of managerial positions, which, according to 2002 statistics of the ILO, ranged between 20-40% in 48 out cf 63 countries.

Qualitative elements such as the availability of government-provided childcare, the impact of maternity laws on the hiring of women, the duration of maternity leave, the percentage of wages paid during the covered period and wage inequalities between men and women for private sector employment. This information on these factor can be particularly useful in quantifying "ground-level" realities

It is argued that a reduction of gender disparity in access to resources and opportunities lead to an increase in the rate of economic growth, which in turn, is poverty-reducing. This is because greater gender equality enables women to take up income-earning opportunities, and participate in the growth process. Klasen (1999) concludes that gender disparities are very closely associated with poverty levels.(Nayyar, 05)

Rural Poverty Head count Ratio: 15 Major Indian States

Figure 1

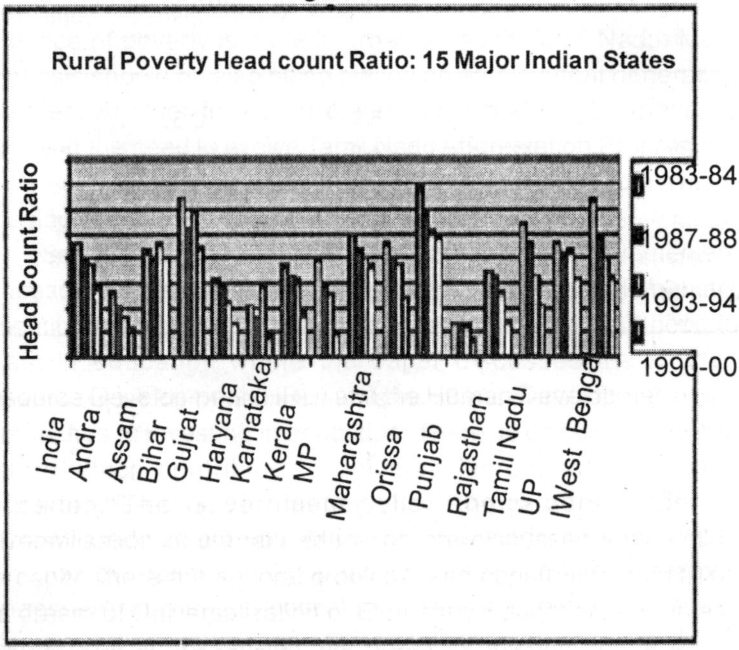

Source: Planning Commission, Government of India.

Political empowerment refers to the equitable representation of women in decision-making structures, both formal and informal, and their voice in the formulation of policies affecting their societies. Women to have a greater say in spending priorities, they would be far more likely to spend family and community resources for improving health, education, community infrastructure and the eradication of poverty, as opposed to the military, alcohol or gambling. In order of spending and development priorities to change, there must be at least a certain proportion of women represented, learning the rules, using the rules and changing the rules of the decision-making "game," and thus having an impact on discourse and decisions at all levels, from the family, to the state and nation.

Educational attainment is the most fundamental prerequisite for empowering women in all spheres of society, for without education of comparable quality and content to that given to boys and men, and relevant to existing knowledge and real needs, women are unable to access well-paid, formal sector jobs, advance within them, participate in, and be represented in government and gain political influence. Empirical work has shown, education and literacy reduce mortality rates of children—including the bias toward female child mortality—and help reduce fertility rates the importance of literacy for women is all the greater, considering that women still constitute half of the India's illiterate population. Gender disparities in educational attainment are captured using data on literacy rates, enrolment rates for primary, secondary and tertiary education and average years of schooling across the population. In this way, we are able to illustrate not only the current levels of women's empowerment through education, but also the potential of future generations of women in a particular nation.

Health and well-being is a concept related to the substantial differences between women and men in their access to sufficient nutrition, healthcare and reproductive facilities, and to issues of fundamental safety and integrity of person.

In India women (15-45 yrs) and children (<15 yrs) constitute 60% of the total population in India (NFHS-2). They comprise the vulnerable fraction of the population due to the risks connected to child-bearing in case of women; and growth, development and survival in case of infants and children. Reduction of child mortality and improvement in maternal health are the major goals in Millennium Declaration, to which India is a signatory. Another important goal is promotion of gender equality and empowerment

Table 2

Gender Inequalities can be strongly seen in the Sex ratio disparities, Access to services, Health outcome, Nutritional Status

				Delivery			*Nutritional Status*	
States	*Birth Rate*	*Death Rate*	*IMR*	*% of safe delivery among births*	*% of institutional delivery*	*% of Women Anaemia**	*Child (underWt.)*	*Women (% with BMI below 18.5 kg/m2)*
Orrissa	23.2	9.8	87.0	32.7	23.4	63.0	54.4	48.4
Jharkhand	26.4	7.9	51.0	20.6	13.7		-	-
W. Bengal	20.5	6.7	49.0	45.6	38.9	62.7	48.7	44.4
Chhattisgarh	25.0	8.7	73.0	22.4	13.0	-	-	-
Andhra Pradesh	20.7	8.1	62.0	59.8	50.6	62.7	37.7	37.7
India	**25.0**	**8.1**	**63.0**	**40.2**	**34.0**	**51.8**	**47.0**	**36.2**

- ever married women age 15-49

Sources: NFHS-2 and Review of health care in India,Cehat
Orissa Human Development Report 2005.

Fig. 1.2
Human Devlopment Index for Major States of India

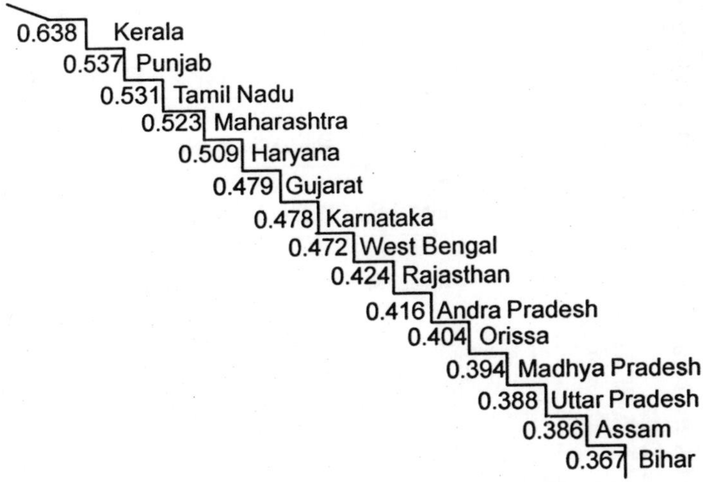

of women that have a direct impact on MCH (Maternal and Child Health). Thus MCH becomes a priority area for the policy makers, planners and various professionals.

Women's particular vulnerability to violence is perhaps the most obvious aspect of reduced physical security and integrity of person, but one which is perhaps the least amenable to accurate statistics. The complexity of the social and cultural issues, combined with the stigma and fear of disclosure lead to a situation where only a small proportion of the crimes of sexual assault, child abuse, wife battering and gun-related violence are ever reported. It is difficult to measure the true extent of violence against women as most incidences of domestic violence and sexual assault go unreported.

(Kishor and Gupta,04)

Finally, reproductive health data, such as the percentage of births attended by skilled health staff, and maternal and infant mortality ratios, under weights babies are the key indicator of poor access to health care and reproductive health care. Since these health outcomes are particularly affected by the level of poverty in a given state.

Table 15: States in Alphabetical Order According to Their Rankings on Variables That Measures Different Aspects of Women's Empowerment and Their Overall Rank on Women's Empowerment Derived from NFHS-2 Data

	Ranks on Variables Measuring Evidence(EE) of Empowrment						*Ranks on Variables Measuresing Sources(Eso) of Empowerment*				*Ranks on Variables Measuring Setting (Ese) for Empowerment*						*Total Empow erment Rank*
						Total EE Rank				*Total Eso Rank*						*Total Ese Rank*	
States	*EE1*	*EE2*	*EE3*	*EE4*	*EE5*		*ESo1*	*ESo2*	*ESo3*		*ESe1*	*ESe2*	*ESe3*	*ESe4*	*ESe5*		
Andhra Pradesh	16	20	22	19	10	18	21	10	11	17	22	18	18	20	21	24	20
Arunachal Pradesh	5	5	12	7	5	3	18	17	15	18	10	5	20	19	22	15	13
Assam	17	25	16	14	13	19	17	22	21	14	15	16	26	14	10	18	19
Bihar	21	17	8	25	24	23	25	26	24	25	25	23	12	26	23	26	25
Delhi	11	6	1	4	11	7	2	1	4	1	9	9	1	2	9	1	2
Goa	9	1	13	9	7	5	3	2	5	3	1	11	10	4	12	3	3
Gujarat	8	4	6	22	21	9	12	15	19	15	16	15	2	12	2	7	10
Haryana	6	15	6	11	22	10	16	14	20	16	18	14	5	9	8	9	12
Himachal Pradesh	1	13	4	6	17	2	6	4	22	12	12	13	7	6	1	5	6
Jammu and Kashmir	15	26	21	15	15	20	19	12	23	21	14	20	13	21	19	20	21
Karnataka	23	11	10	13	14	16	12	9	13	9	19	21	24	14	18	23	16
Kerala	10	7	15	2	2	8	1	3	7	2	4	24	17	1	3	9	4
Madhya Pradesh	25	18	18	24	25	26	22	21	15	22	26	19	10	23	17	22	23

Contd.

Contd. Table15

	Ranks on Variables Measuring Evidence(EE) of Empowerment						*Ranks on Variables Measuresing Sources(Eso) of Empowerment*				*Ranks on Variables Measuring Setting (Ese) for Empowerment*						*Total Empowerment Rank*
						Total EE Rank				*Total Eso Rank*						*Total Ese Rank*	
Maharashtra	22	9	20	21	10	21	14	13	9	14	21	22	14	10	13	17	17
Manipur	12	14	25	5	6	13	6	5	1	5	5	8	8	7	15	6	7
Meghalaya	4	7	24	8	3	6	8	20	11	12	8	2	16	17	25	14	9
Mizoram	3	1	23	1	1	1	4	11	2	4	2	6	9	5	16	3	1
Nagaland	6	21	26	16	16	14	11	18	7	11	5	1	22	10	14	9	14
Orissa	18	21	9	20	20	22	23	24	15	23	17	12	21	18	24	21	22
Punjab	2	11	2	10	18	4	5	6	14	7	6	17	3	3	8	2	5
Rajasthan	24	19	11	26	26	24	26	25	25	26	22	26	4	25	4	18	24
Sikkim	11	10	17	3	8	11	8	8	3	6	7	7	19	22	5	12	8
Tamil Nadu	13	1	19	18	12	12	15	7	5	8	10	3	15	13	26	13	11
Tripura	18	16	7	17	9	15	10	15	9	10	13	4	25	8	7	11	15
Uttar Pradesh	25	24	14	23	23	25	24	23	26	24	24	25	6	24	20	21	26
West Bengal	20	23	3	12	4	16	19	19	15	20	19	10	23	16	11	16	18

Contd.

Contd. Table15

Notes : Sates have been ranked on the following:

Evidence of epowerment indicators. EE1: Percentage of women who participate in each of the household decisions with the lowest rank going to the state where women are most likely to participate in each of the decisions: EE2: Percentage of women who do not need per mission to go to the market and to go to visit friends and relatives with the lowest rank given to the state where the combined rank on both indicators is the lowest. EE3: Perentage of women who agree with atleast one reason justifying a husband beating his wife, wth the lowest rank given to the state where this proportion is the lowest: EE4: Percentage who say boys and girls should be given the same amount of education with the state with the highest percentage receiving the lowest rank: EE5: Ratio of the percentage of women who are using contraception and have only two daughters (no sons) and the percentage of women who are using contraception and have two sons only (no daughters) with the lowest rank going to the state where this ratio is the highest.

Source of empowerment indicators: ESo 1: This indicator is a composite of the percentage of females age 6 and above who are literate, the percentage of females age 20 and above who have completed at least high school, and the ratio of the percentages of females to males age 20 and above who have completed high school. With the lowest overall rank on this indicator going to the state that has the lowest combined rank on each of the three component indicators: ESo2: Pecentage of women regularly exposed to radio, television or cinema/theatre, with the lowest rank going to the state where this proportion is the highest: ESo3: This indicator is a composite of three indicators: the percentage of women who are employed the ratio of women who are earning cash to those who are employed and the percentage of women employed in professional, managerial, occupations wth the lowest rank going to the state with the lowest combined rank on the three component indicators.

Setting for empowerment indicators: ESe1: Median age of mariage with the state with the highest median age at marriage

(*Contd.*)

(Contd.)

getting the lowest rank: ESe2: Percentage of women living in nuclear families wth the lowest rank going to the state where women are most likely loreside in a nuclear family: ESe3: Percentage of women who are at least 10 years younger thantheir husbands with the lowest rank going to the state with the lowest percentage of women in this category: ESe4: Percentage of couples in which both husband and wife have been to school and both have the same number of years of education, with the lowest rank going to the state with the highest proportion of such couples: ESe5: Percentage of women who have ever experienced violece since age 15. with the lowest rank being given to the state where this percentage is the least.

State Rankings on empowerment Indicators - for each state in India empowerment of women are measured by groups of indicators/13 indicators. Lower the ranks reveal higher empowerment

No matter how empowerment is measured, be it in terms of the indicators of the evidence, sources or setting for empowerment the average woman in India is disempowered absolutely as well as relative to men, and there has been little change in this status over time *(Kishor and Gupta, EPW,2004)*

Budget as a Tool

Globalization has dramatically changed the conditions under which the struggle for gender equality must be carried out, especially in developing countries. One of the important tools of gender mainstreaming, aimed principally at poverty reduction, has been the concept of "gender budgeting," i.e. focusing attention in the process of budget formulation in order to assess whether a particular fiscal measure will increase or decrease gender equality, or leave it unchanged.

Gender budget initiatives (GBIs) not only identify targeted expenditures, or allocate more money to women, but also aim to "break down and identify the differentiated impact and incidence ofgeneral public revenue and expenditure on women and men...[and] significantly contribute to overall objectives like equity, equality, efficiency, transparency, the realization of social, economic and cultural rights, and good governance," thus **offering a practical way of evaluating government action** (or inaction). Close monitoring and analysis of gender effects has become a mechanism for holding policy-makers increasingly accountable for the impact of policies on the lives of both women and men, so that the large percentage of women who participate economically in the informal sector can be taken into account in the economic adjustment measures which might directly affect their welfare.

Gendered budget analysis can help to focus on these neglected aspects; it provides women with the vital information regarding the contents and focus of existing government policies.

Armed with that, women can confront policy-makers and demand changes in policies as per their needs and choices. The process is for greater transparency and for deepening of democracy. **Gender budgeting exercises are meant to verify from actual schemes and allotments included in the budget how far these intentions are actually being translated into concrete policies**. Do these exercises serve any purpose? The answer depends on what we mean by purpose. If **our efforts to scan budgets** for gender sensitivity really result in a positive approach to promoting gender equality, we would have indeed won the battle. if we demystify budgets, and people and especially women learn more about them, that alone **would make it a legitimate exercise (Banerjee and Krishnaraj, 04)** Every one should now become better acquainted with the technical jargon of budget documents

Union Budget 2005: Gender budgeting introduced for the first time

> Although the inclusion of gender budgeting has received a positive response from women's groups, concerns are being raised about the inadequacy of funds allocated for various schemes

The introduction, for the first time, of the concept of 'gender-budgeting' in India's Budget 2005 has evoked positive reactions from women's groups, although many feel that more needs to be done.

Budget proposals this year include a separate statement on gender sensitivities regarding budgetary allocations under 10 demands for grants (Expenditure Budget Vol. 1 2005-06 ,statement 19). The finance minister revealed that, henceforth, all government departments would be required to present gender budgets.

According to available data, only 8%, or one-sixth of this year's total budgetary support, is for women's schemes or for the women's component in general schemes.

The National council of Women (NCW) had earlier submitted a 10-point charter of demands to the finance minister, of which tapping water resources, health and education were given substantial allocations. The major boost was in the field of reproductive and child health where allocations have been increased from Rs. 710 crore to 1,380 crore.

"A total allocation of Rs. 14,378 crore has been made as part of gender budgeting. However the budget should have included girls not only from minorities but also other disadvantaged social groups in special education schemes," says NCW chairperson Girija Vyas. She admitted that the budget had left women's share in the rural employment guarantee scheme untouched.

Education

Union's Budget 2005-2006, allocates Rs. 18,337 crore towards education — the largest amount given in the social sector — underlining that, besides rural development, education is a major focus for development this year. With this, Sarva Shiksha Abhiyan, the Integrated Child Development Scheme (ICDS) and the Mid-day Meals Scheme have all received a considerable boost. Of the Rs. 18,337 crore set aside for education, the department of elementary education and literacy gets Rs. 12,536.53 crore and the department of secondary and higher education Rs. 5,800.50 crore. Budget estimates for the Sarva Shiksha Abhiyan (SSA) programme — the cornerstone of the government's intervention in basic education for all children — have been raised from Rs. 3,057 crore in 2004-2005 to Rs. 4,754 crore this year.

The overall allocation made by the Union Government on education, at constant (1993-94) prices, has increased from Rs. 1927 crore during 1994-95 to Rs. 6412.5 crore during 2004-05 (RE). This year, it is budgeted at Rs. 7538 crore (at 1993-94 prices). One may view this as a positive step towards recognising education as a crucial sector. However, in no way the increase in allocation is significant when one considers the glaring educational backwardness of India and the level of expenditure the sector deserves.

- The real capital allocation on education is Rs. 36.18 crore for the fiscal 2005-06. This is grossly inadequate to meet the requirements of capacity creation in the educational sector in India. It is almost one sixth of the actual real capital expenditure incurred (Rs. 197.59 crore) on education during 1994-95.

- Allocation for different sectors of education as a proportion of total budgetary allocation shows a clear positive tilt of Government's emphasis towards elementary education. However, over the years the Governments have been apathetic towards secondary and higher education and the present Budget is no exception to it. The share of secondary, higher and technical education in total budgetary allocation for the year 2005-06 is much less than that during the years ruled by the previous NDA coalition.

- While increase in the share of the social sector in total budgetary allocation has been significant in the Budget 2005-06, the increase in the share of education has not been that significant. In the last fiscal year, the Government had introduced a (2 per cent cess) cess on all kinds of taxes to be earmarked exclusively for education. As the proceeds from this cess, the estimated revenue generated is around Rs. 5010 crore during 2004-05 (RE) and the same is expected to be Rs. 6975 crore during 2005-06. These amount to around Rs.12,000 crore in total, earmarked for universalisation of education.

Over the period of two years, 2004-05 and 2005-06, the entire amount of Rs. 12,000 Crore should be spent on education, in excess of the prevailing level of Union Government spending on education. In the last year's Budget, the Government did not raise the total allocation on education even by a single rupee compared to the Interim Budget of February 2004. This year, the Government has increased the allocation on education only by around Rs.

Receipts from Education Cess (Rs. in crores)

	2004-05 RE	*2005-06 BE*
Corpn Tax	1535	2169
Income other than Corpn tax	994	1234
Customs	760	1046
Excise	1556	2198
Services tax	165	328
Total	5010	6975

RE –Revised Estimates, BE Budget Estimates

4264 crore over last year's Budget. Where has the balance Rs.7721 crore gone? It is quite unfortunate that the Government despite collecting a substantial amount of money from the common public for raising the expenditure on education is not putting all of that money towards increasing the allocations for education.

- Since 1999-00, the Union Government has till now allocated around Rs. 16,467 crore for Sarva Shiksha Abhiyan (SSA), the only comprehensive scheme for universalisation of elementary education.

Rural Employment

In keeping with the focus of the govt. on rural employment, the allocation to National Food for Work Programme shows a substantial hike from Rs. 1818 crores in RE 2004-05 to Rs. 5400 crores BE 2005-06 this is noteable in the demand for Grant by the department of Rural Development, But there is reduced allocation to the other exisiting rural employment programme such as Swarna Jayanti Gram Swarozgar Yojana , Sampoorna Gramin Rozgar Yojana.

Rural Employment Programmes (Rs. in Crores)

	2004-05 RE	*2005-06 BE*
Swarna Jayanti Gram Swarozgar Yojana	900	862.24 (-37.76)
Sampoorna Gramin Rozgar Yojana	4590	3600 (-990)
National Food For Work Prog.	1818	5400 (3582)
Net increase in rural employt. Prog.	6408	9000 (2592)
Rural Housing	2602	2492 (-109.19)
Other rural development prog.	354.53	340.43 (-14.1

Sources: Budget 2005-06, Demand for Grants, FM, GOI.

When looked into the Introduced Gender Budgetting Demand no. 79 Department of Rural Development for the year 2004-05 RE 360 crores and for the year 2005-06 BE 344 crores i.e., 40 per cent of Swarna Jayanti Gram Swarozgar Yojana and 30 percent for Sampoorna Gramin Rozgar Yojana is allocated.

Health

Unfortunately the only mention of the NRHM is in the Finance Minister's speech, "The National Rural Health Mission (NRHM) will be launched in the next fiscal. Its focus will be strengthening primary health care through grass root level public health interventions based on community ownership. The total allocation for the Department of Health and the Department of Family Welfare will increase from Rs. 8,420 crore in the current year to Rs.10,280 crore in the next year. The increase will finance the NRHM and its components like training of health volunteers, providing more medicines and strengthening the primary and community health centre system." When we look at the expenditure budgets and demand for grants of Budget 2005-06 we find that there is no mention of NRHM as an item of expenditure. (Ravi Duggal, 2004) The Finance Minister says that the increase (Rs. 1860 crores) over the previous budget will finance the NRHM component. We have to wait and watch. The overall budget of the Ministry of Health and Family Welfare is outlined below:

Demand for Grants of Ministry of Health and Family Welfare (Rs. Crores)

Category	*Budget 2004-05*	*Budget 2005-06*
Medical and Public Health	3103.12	4253.84
AYUSH	225.73	405.98
Family Welfare	6696.37	7769.01
Gross Total Health	10025.22	12428.83
Grants to States and UTs	4663.00	5158.00
Total Health Central govt.	5362.22	7270.83
Less recoveries	(-)1587.10	(-)1741.72
Net Health Central govt.	3775.12	5529.11

Source: Budget 2005-06, Demand for Grants, Demand Nos. 47, 48, 49, Ministry of Finance, GOI, New Delhi, 2005

In order to popularize the Indian systems of medicine and homoeopathy, AYUSH wings have been opened in District Hospitals. Eight specialty clinics/polyclinics were established and essential drugs were supplied to 8,152 Ayurveda, Sidha, Unani and Homoeopathic Dispensaries in Rural and backward areas. Plan allocation for AYUSH has been doubled. As a part of the proposed National Rural Health Mission and the ongoing programmes, AYUSH services have been mainstreamed. Income-tax exemption was granted for Medical expenses of patients undergoing treatment in Ayurvedic hospitals. About 120 medical institutions of Ayurveda, Siddha, Unani and Homoeopathy were extended support to improve their infrastructure. Integrated North Eastern Institute of ISM&H is planned to be set up at Pasighat in Arunachal Pradesh to ensure reach of AYUSH services in the North Eastern Areas. The State Drug Testing Laboratories and the State Pharmacies have been strengthened to ensure quality control of ISM&H medicines. The Medicinal Plant Board has been made functional in 32 States/UTs to coordinate the development of Medicinal Plant Sector and about 65000 Acre area has been covered under captive cultivation of medicinal plants. Permission has been granted for setting up of 14 new colleges of AYUSH systems including two National Institutes for Siddha and Unani Medicine.

The major boost was in the field of reproductive and child health where allocations have been increased from Rs 710 crore to 1,380 crore.

Conclusion

Appreciating the initiatives being taken for the empowerment of women–Gender budgeting , but we expect that note of the same come in the Economic Survey of India. Concerted efforts must be made to ensure proper , efficient and judicious utilization of the funds allocated for women's component. Schemes and Programmes for the women must be advertised widely through communication media. Capacity building workshops on 'Gendering budgets" must be organized for elected representatives, different ministries at state and central government level. Beneficiary impact analysis of gender budget is a need of an hour.

References

Banerjee N and Krishnaraj M: Sieving Budgets for Gender, Economic and Political Weekly, Oct 30,2004

Bridge, 2003, Gender and Budgets, BRIDGE Cutting Edge Pack, Brighton: Institute of Development Studies, Retrieved May 16,2005 from http://www.ids.ac.uk/bridge/reports_gend_CEP.html

Bussiness Standard, May 17,05.

Center for Budget and Governance accountability 2005, "Response to Union Budget 2002-06 State Intervention in Favour of the Poor: Decisive or Disappointing?'

Duggal Ravi: Where is the Health Agenda: Express Healthcare Management, Vol. 6, No.5, March 16-31,2005.

Government of Orissa 2005. Human Development Report Orissa 2005, Government of Orissa, Bhubaneswar.

Gurav Nayyar: Growth and poverty in rural India-An analysis of inter-state difference, Economic and Political Weekly, April 16, 2005.

IIPS and ORC Marc (2000): National Family Health Survey (NFHS-2) 1998-99: India, IIPS, Mumbai.

Patel, Vibhuti 2003, 'Gender audit of Budgets' Working paper, Deparnment of Economics, University of Mumbai.

Sunita K and K Gupta: Women's empowerment in India and its States-evidence from NFHS, Economic and Political Weekly, Feb.14, 2004.

12

Gender Equality and Millennium Development Goals (MDGs)

Kamayani Bali Mahabal

The Millennium Development Goals are a derivative of the Millennium Declaration of September 2000, which spells out the following values: freedom, equality, solidarity, tolerance, respect for nature, and shared responsibility. They are a clarion call of 189 governments, on behalf of their citizens, to "free our fellow men, women and children from the abject and dehumanizing conditions of extreme poverty, to which more than a billion of them are currently subjected. We are committed to making the right to development a reality for everyone and to freeing the entire human race from want."(Millennium Declaration). These measures, collectively known as the *Millennium Development Goals* (MDGs), have become a prime focus of development work throughout the globe — a gold standard to which programs aspire, and by which they measure their work.

The MDGs, be achieved between 1990 and 2015, include:

- Halving extreme poverty and hunger
- Achieving universal primary education
- Promoting gender equality
- Reducing under-five mortality by two-thirds
- Reducing maternal mortality by three-quarters

- Reversing the spread of HIV/AIDS, malaria and TB
- Ensuring environmental sustainability
- Developing a global partnership for development, with targets for aid, trade and debt relief

The MDGs explicitly acknowledge that gender — what a given society believes about the appropriate roles and activities of men and women, and the behaviours that result from these beliefs — can have a major impact on development, helping to promote it in some cases while seriously retarding it in others. MDG number 3 (out of 8) is specifically about gender, calling for an end to disparities between boys and girls at all levels of education. There is general agreement that education is vital to development, and ensuring that girls as well as boys have full opportunities for schooling will help improve lives in countless ways. Nevertheless, it would be wrong to conclude — as a casual reader of the MDGs might —. Not surprisingly, then, the rules that regulate the behaviours and values of men that the relevance of gender to development is confined to the educational sphere. Men and women, both, participate in nearly every aspect of life in communities throughout the world and women in a given society — that is, its gender system — have the potential to impact nearly every aspect of life. Therefore, while only one of the MDGs is specifically about gender, addressing gender is of critical importance to every MDG.

Women throughout the world play critical roles in economic growth and development, and their contributions have an impact on households, communities and national economies. Over the past three decades, significant improvements have been made in women's status, especially in health and education. In the health sector, greater investment in reproductive health services has led to significant reductions in infant and maternal mortality and declines in fertility rates, reducing women's burdens associated with childbirth and child rearing. In some countries, women's life expectancy has increased by up to a decade over that of just 30 years ago. These improvements mark important progress in women's well-being and their capacity to participate fully in society. They also have contributed to reducing inequalities between women and men. However, progress has not been uniform and continues to lag in many countries. In many developing countries women and girls are still the poorest, least educated, most unhealthy, and most marginalized segments of the population. Of the world's 876 million people 15 years and older who cannot read or write, nearly two-thirds are women according to UNESCO estimates (UNESCO 1999). Although the gender gap in primary and secondary school enrollment rates is closing in many regions, girls still lag behind boys in many countries in sub-Saharan Africa and South Asia. Opportunities for paid employment for women relative to men have also increased, but the quality of employment for women has not increased in the same way and may even have deteriorated. The gender gap in earnings persists and women's jobs tend to enjoy less social protection and employment rights than do men's jobs. In the majority of countries in Latin America and Asia, 50 per cent or more of the female non-agricultural labor force are in the informal sector, where earnings and social protection are far less secure (United Nations 2000). Violence against women continues to be a serious violation of women's rights. According to Heise and Ellsberg (1999), around the world at least one woman in every three has been beaten, coerced into sex, or otherwise abused in her lifetime. And despite the gains mentioned earlier, maternal mortality remains staggeringly high: over half a million women die each year from pregnancy and childbirth-related causes (WHO 2002), 99 percent of which occur in the developing world. The HIV/AIDS pandemic presents an especially urgent challenge because, worldwide, rates of infection among women are rapidly increasing; among those 15-24 years of age, females now constitute the majority of new infections (UNICEF/UNAIDS/WHO 2002). Women's economic vulnerability and low social status contributes significantly to their increased risk of HIV/AIDS. For all of these reasons, Goal #3 is important in its own right and is salient to all the other MDG goals.

I: Definition of Gender Equality and Empowerment

Like race and ethnicity, gender is a social construct. It defines and differentiates the roles, rights, responsibilities and obligations of women and men. The innate biological differences between females and males are interpreted by society to create a set of social expectations that define the behaviors that are appropriate for women and men and that determine women's and men's differential access to rights, resources, and power in society. Although the specific nature and degree of these differences vary from one society to the next, they typically favor men, creating an imbalance in power and a gender inequality that exists in most societies worldwide.

Definition of Gender Equality

According to the UN (2002), "equality is the cornerstone of every democratic society that aspires to social justice and human rights." The term gender equality has been defined in multiple ways in the development literature and has been the subject of great debate in the U.N. It often means women having the same opportunities in life as men, for instance equality of access to education and employment, which does not necessarily lead to equality of outcomes. Several experts have proposed conceptual frameworks for understanding gender equality. The United Nations Human Development Report (1995) refers to gender equality in terms of capabilities (education, health, and nutrition) and opportunities (economic and decision-making). Similarly, the World Bank defines gender equality in terms of equality under the law, equality of opportunity (including equality of rewards for work and equality in access to human capital and other productive resources that enable opportunity), and equality of voice (the ability to influence and contribute to the development process).

Three primary domains of equality between men and women emerge from both of these frameworks: capabilities, access to resources and opportunities, and agency or the ability to influence and contribute to outcomes. The capabilities domain refers to basic human abilities as measured through education, health, and nutrition. It is the most fundamental of all the three domains and is necessary for achieving equality in the other two domains. Access to resources and opportunities, the second domain, refers primarily to equality in the opportunity to use or apply basic capabilities through access to economic assets (such as land and property) and resources (such as income and employment). The third domain, agency, is the defining element of the concept of empowerment (see below) and refers to the ability to make choices and decisions that can alter outcomes. Gender equality in this domain can only result from an equalizing in the balance of power between women and men in the household and societal institutions.

These three domains of equality are inter-related. Progress in any one domain to the exclusion of the others is insufficient to meet the goal of gender equality. While they are inter-related, the three domains are not necessarily dependent on each other. So, for instance, illiterate women may organize, thereby building their agency to influence outcomes for themselves and their households. Not surprisingly, women then use that agency to demand capability (better health or education) and opportunity (access to decent work). Similarly, women with capabilities (as measured by education) may have no economic opportunity, as is evidenced in many Middle Eastern countries.

Gender inequalities exist because of discrimination in the family and societal institutions, and social, cultural, and religious norms that perpetuate stereotypes, practices and beliefs that are detrimental to women. Human rights conventions provide redress for discrimination. Among these, the Convention to Eliminate All Forms of Discrimination Against Women (CEDAW), adopted by the U.N. General Assembly in 1979, is the most universally accepted instrument for realizing gender equality and influencing cultural and traditional definitions of gender roles and family relations. The treaty has been ratified by 170 countries, including every nation in the Western Hemisphere except the United States, but its impact is dependent on political will and resources

Economic institutions and policy can exacerbate existing gender inequalities instead of mitigating them. There is a strong tendency to see the market as a liberating force for women. While modern markets can and do undermine some of the pre-existing forms of culturally-determined gender inequality, they also incorporate and transform pre-existing inequalities into new ones (Elson and Pearson 1997). Similarly, laws and policies play a significant role in determining the extent of gender inequality that exists in a society. They can serve to protect women's rights or to reduce them. For example, in many countries, women still lack the legal right to inherit or own property and, in many others, violence against women is not considered a criminal offense. Without transformations in economic relations or the implementation and enforcement of legal rights and protection, gender equality and the empowerment of women can remain an elusive goal.

Definition of Empowerment

The concept of empowerment is related to gender equality but distinct from it. Based on a review of literature on the definition and measurement of women's empowerment, Malhotra, Schuler and Boender (2002) conclude that empowerment is a process that marks change over a period of time and requires that the individual being empowered is involved as a significant agent in that change process. Several experts agree that an empowered woman is one who has the agency to formulate strategic choices and to control resources and decisions that affect important life outcomes (Kabeer 1999). The core of the concept of empowerment lies in the ability of the woman to control her own destiny. This implies that to be empowered women must not only have equal capabilities (such as education and health) and access to resources and opportunities (such as land and employment), they must also have the agency to use those rights, capabilities, resources, and opportunities to make strategic choices and decisions (such as is provided through leadership opportunities and participation in political institutions). Table 1 illustrates various dimensions of women's empowerment that are important at the household, community, and national levels.

Table 1
Commonly used dimensions of empowerment and potential operationalization in the household, community, and arenas

Dimension 1.	*Household* 2.	*Community* 3.	*Broader Arenas* 4.
Economic	Women's control over income; relative contribution to family support; access to and control of family resources	Women's access to employment; ownership of assets and land; access to credit; involvement and/or representation in local trade associations; access to markets	Women's representation in high paying jobs; women CEO's representation of women's economic interests in macro-economic policies, state and federal budgets
Socio-Cultural	Women's freedom of movement; lack of discrimination against daughters; commitment to educating daughters	Women's visibility in and access to social spaces; access to modern transportation; participation in extra-familial groups and social networks; shift in	Women's literacy and access to a broad range of educational options; Positive media images of women, their roles and contributions

(Contd.)

(Contd. Table 1.)

1.	2.	3.	4.
		patriarchal norms (such as son preferences); symbolic representaion of the female in myth and ritual	
Familial/ Interpersonal	Participation in domestic decision-making; control over sexual relations; ability to make childbearing decisions, use contraception, access abortions; control over spouse selection and marriage timing; freedom from domestic violence	Shifts in marriage and kinship systems indicating greater value and autonomy for women (e.g. later marriages, self selection of spouses, reduction in the practice of dowry; acceptability of divorce); local campaigns against domestic violence	Regional/national trends in timing of marriage, options for divorce; political, legal, religious support for (or lack of active opposition to) such shifts; systems providing easy access to contraception, safe abortion, reproductive health services
Legal	Knowledge of legal rights; domestic support for exercising rights	Community mobilization for rights; campaigns for rights awareness; effective local enforcement of legal rights	Laws supporting women's rights, access to resources and options; Advocacy for rights and legislation; use of judicial system to redress rights violations

(Contd.)

(Contd. Table 1.)

1.	2.	3.	4.
Political	Knowledge of political system and means of access to it; domestic support for political engagement; exercising the rights to vote	Womens's involvement or mobilization in the local political system/ campaigns; support for specific candidates or legislation; representation in local bodies of government	Women's representation in regional and national bodies of government; strength as a voting bloc; representation of women's interestes in effective lobbies and interests groups
Psychological	Self-esteem; self-efficacy; psychological well-being mobilization	Collective awareness of injustice, potential of tance of women's entitlement	Women's sense of inclusion and entitlement; systemic accep- and inclusion

Source: A. Malhotra, S. Schuler, and C. Boender, 2002

The Costs and Consequences of Gender Inequality

A recent analysis conducted by the World Bank (2001) establishes that women bear the largest and most direct cost of gender inequality and lack of empowerment. These costs are individual, societal, and inter-generational. For example, women's economic dependency on men reduces their ability to leverage safer sex options to protect themselves against unwanted pregnancies and HIV infection (Gupta and Weiss 1994). And violence against women which is a gross infringement of women's rights has severe health and economic consequences for women (Heise and Ellsberg 1999, Panda 2002). Several studies have established the benefits of reducing gender inequality. Saito and Spurling (1992), for instance, have estimated that giving women farmers in Kenya the same level of agricultural inputs and education as male farmers could increase yields obtained by women farmers by more than 20 per cent. Hill and King (1995) show that, all else being equal, countries in which the ratio of female-to-male enrollment in primary and secondary school is less than . 75 can expect levels of GNP that are roughly 25 per cent lower than in countries in which there is less gender disparity in education. Finally, research on gender inequality in the labor market shows that eliminating gender discrimination in occupation and pay could increase not only women's income, but also national income. If gender inequality in the labor market in Latin America were to be eliminated, not only could women's wages rise by about 50 per cent, but national output could rise by more than 5 per cent (Psacharopoulous and Tzannatos 1992).

(II) .Historical Development and Characteristics of Goal #3

The MDG goal to achieve gender equality and empowerment of women recognizes the costs to society of continued female disadvantage. As compared to the other goals in the MDGs, the goal to reduce gender disparities is unique because it is not specific to any one sector or issue, such as health, education, or access to water. Instead, it cuts across all the sectors and issues addressed in the MDGs and its success depends on the extent to which it is addressed within each of the other sector-specific goals. Moreover, the goal of gender equality is pre-eminent among the MDGs because if it is not achieved, none of the other goals can be fully met. Despite the instrumental value of gender equality for the full success of the other goals, singling it out within the MDGs as an independent goal serves to underscore its value in and of itself, rooted in the principles of social justice, rights, and non-discrimination. The articulation of this goal and its inclusion in the MDGs marks the culmination of many years of discussions and debates and is related most directly to the discussions and promises made in four particular UN conferences held in three consecutive years in the mid-1990s: the World Conference on Human Rights, held in Vienna in 1993; the International Conference on Population and Development, held in Cairo in 1994; the World Summit on Social Development held in Copenhagen and the Fourth World Conference on Women, held in Beijing, both of which occurred in 1995. Together, the declarations and agreements made at these conferences underscored the importance of women's rights and freedoms, persuaded governments to recognize the gendered consequences of population, social, and macroeconomic policies, and emphasized the importance of mainstreaming gender into all development policies and practice. In addition, at each of these conferences governments agreed to a number of time-bound targets, with 1990 as the base year, to serve as benchmarks of progress (Box 1). While most of these targets focus on education and health, the Beijing Platform for Action includes a target for increasing the representation of women in positions of power and decision-making. Targets for decreasing women's poverty or increasing women's economic equality are notable by their absence. Although poverty and women's economic rights were key themes at both the Copenhagen and Beijing conferences, governments' commitment to addressing these issues did not result in the formulation of specific targets.

Box 1 History of Goal 3*

Commitment	*Target*	*By the Year*	*Conference*
Women in decision-making	30%	1995 ECOSOC	(Reiterated at FWCW, 1995, Beijing)
Gender equality for girls in primary education	Parity: ratio=1	2000	FWCE, 1995, Beijing
Close gender gap in primary and secondary education	Parity: ratio=1	2005	ICPD, 1994, Cairo; WSSD, 1995, Copenhegan, FWCW, 1995, Beijing
Achieve equivalent levels of ediucation for girls and boys	Parity: ratio=1	2015	ICPD, 1994, Caioo

* This box lists only selected commitments made by governments. The full list can be seen in UNIFEM 2000.

III: Review of the #3 Target and Indicators for Goal

The target selected to represent the goal of gender equality and the empowerment of women reflects this history. The target is restricted to education — eliminating gender disparity in primary and secondary education by 2005 and in all levels of education no later than by 2015. Two of the four suggested indicators to measure progress toward this target also reflect this emphasis on education.

The focus on education is fully justified in light of the ever-increasing research evidence that investing in girls' education yields high returns for girls themselves, as well as for households and communities (Shultz 2001). Ensuring that women do not suffer the disadvantage of illiteracy and lack of education is critical for building women's capabilities, a first step in the empowerment process. It is also an essential ingredient for ensuring child health and welfare, reducing maternal mortality, and breaking the cycle of intergenerational poverty. Moreover, by setting an ambitious target for eliminating gender disparities in primary and secondary education – less than a decade — the MDGs send a clear message that gender inequality in education in this, the 21st century, is unconscionable and must be rectified.

Critique of the Target

Equality in education as a target for measuring progress towards gender equality and the empowerment of women is more than justified, but it is not sufficient to measure the achievement of gender equality and the empowerment of women. One problem with the target is that achieving parity in educational outcomes is not the same as ensuring that all girls are properly educated and can fully develop their capabilities. Second, even though education provides women with an essential capability and has intrinsic value, gender equality and the empowerment of women can remain elusive goals without the opportunity to fully use that capability, for example, in employment, or by participating in decision making in the political arena. Because countries adopted only one target for Goal 3, it is important that, at a minimum, all countries achieve that target.

The three proposed targets nevertheless leave out critical aspects of women's lives and the range of inequalities that women experience. Glaring by their absence are targets to measure progress to reduce gender inequalities in each of the other Millennium Development Goals. Gender is highly relevant to achieving all the MDGS, be it protecting the environment, achieving sustainable development, enabling universal access to health care and education, combating HIV/AIDS, or reducing poverty and hunger. The Task Forces for these other MDGs must, therefore, monitor and address gender inequalities as a central component of their work. Ensuring that this happens will be an important task for the Millennium Project Secretariat and the Task Force on Gender Equality.

The overall structure of the MDGs fails to acknowledge gender as a crosscutting determinant of inequity and health, and the goals that do address gender only scratch the surface. Although MDG 3 recognizes the importance of women's health in the wider struggle to reduce poverty and promote development, but the indicators chosen to measure progress against this goal—for example, the ratio of girls to boys attending school, the proportion of births attended by skilled personnel, and the proportion of seats held by women in national parliaments—do not reflect the broad and inclusive notion of sexual and reproductive rights agreed to at the ICPD and the FWCW. Since almost all of the UN's health and development initiatives are beginning to be reshaped and designed with the MDGs in mind, the absence of a strong statement on the importance of sexual and reproductive health and rights—as well as the absence of any substantial discussion of the non-disease elements of women's health, such as abortion, contraception, and violence—will have a significant impact on how resources are allocated and programs are designed.

Critique of the Indicators

The United Nations has suggested four indicators to measure Goal #3:

- the ratio of girls to boys in primary, secondary and tertiary education,
- the ratio of literate females to males among 15-24 year olds,
- the share of women in wage employment in the nonagricultural sector, and
- the proportion of seats held by women in national parliaments.

The first two are indicators of capabilities, the third is an indicator of opportunity, and the fourth is an indicator of agency.

Although they represent all three domains of gender equality, they are not without their drawbacks. In addition, there may be other indicators that are better suited to tracking progress toward the MDG gender targets.

Capability Indicators*:* There are both substantive and technical concerns with the two capability indicators. The ratio of girls to boys in school reflects the input side of education, that is, how many girls and boys are enrolled in school, which is where most policy efforts have been directed. Getting girls and boys to school is clearly an important first step. Yet, the more important issue is school completion and student learning outcomes. The completion of 5 to 6 years of schools is necessary for mastery of basic competencies, such as literacy and numeracy. School enrolment ratios, whether on a gross or net basis, are poorly correlated with the rate of primary school completion; moreover, enrolment ratios are consistent with many different patterns of drop-out and retention. Finally, gender differences are brought into sharper contrast in the comparison of enrolment rates against completion rates.

Beyond the substantive issue of what should be the focus of the MDG goal, there are other concerns with the proposed capability indicators. The ratio of girls to boys in school simply depicts the number of girls relative to boys in school. Enrolment rates, by contrast, give a picture of the number of students, boys or girls, enrolled in a given level of education relative to the population of the age group which should be enrolled at that level. Net enrolment rates, which take into consideration the appropriate age for each grade, are a good indicator of access to education, but they are not available for many countries. Gross enrolment rates are more widely available, but they include repeat students in the calculation and so will be higher than net enrolment rates. There are also concerns about the literacy indicator. This indicator was chosen to reflect the performance of the national education system, as well as the quality of the human resources within a country in relation to their potential for growth, contribution to development, and quality of life. Yet, the quality of the literacy data is suspect. Some countries collect literacy information using sophisticated and comprehensive techniques while others are not able to even provide the most basic information. In addition, because literacy is not a simple concept with a single universally accepted meaning, different countries measure literacy differently. The UNESCO definition ("A person is literate if s/he has completed five or more years of schooling") has been widely criticized partly because it assumes that people can be easily categorized as "literate" or "illiterate" or because adults with five or more years of schooling may still be functionally illiterate, while those with less than four years of schooling may have acquired literacy skills by non-formal means. Despite these limitations, this indicator is the best that exists across countries and over time.

Opportunity Indicators: The choice of indicator in the MDGs to measure progress in economic opportunity is the female share of non-agricultural wage employment. As noted in UNIFEM's Progress of the World's Women 2000, this is an indicator of the extent to which women have equal access to paid jobs in areas of expanding employment. As stated in the report, "Wage employment in industry and services usually puts some money directly into the hands of women themselves, unlike employment as an unpaid family worker on a family farm. Moreover, the pay is likely to be higher than the average pay for self-employment." The drawback of using this indicator is that it could be interpreted to also mean equality in income. A second drawback is that an increase in women's share of paid employment adds to women's total workload such that what women may gain in terms of cash they lose in terms of time (UNIFEM 2000). Third, as Anker (2002) notes, this indicator only measures the presence or absence of work, and not the "decency" of work itself or the disadvantages women face – in access to employment (measured by unemployment rates), in returns to their labor (earnings or wages), in the types of jobs they hold (occupational segregation), and in security of employment (social protection). Finally, in grouping together all non-agricultural employment, the indicator can't distinguish between work which is formal or informal, full time or part time, and permanent or seasonal. There is ample evidence that women's participation in informal employment is as high as 80 percent in some countries such as India, Uganda, Indonesia, among others (Charmes 2000), and that women are more likely to predominate in part-time and seasonal jobs.

The ILO has proposed a series of indicators for equality in access to and fair treatment in employment as part of the ILO's decent work initiative (Anker 2002). These indicators include gender-disaggregated unemployment rates, the female to male wages or earnings ratio (divided by years of school which controls for human capital), and occupational segregation by sex (the percent of non-agricultural employment in male-dominated and female-dominated occupations and the index of dissimilarity), among others.

These indicators show a sobering picture of women's status in employment. For instance, in 1997 female unemployment rates were higher than male unemployment rates in all regions of the world for which data were available, although the gap narrowed in some regions (United Nations 2000). Similarly, in no country for which data are available do women earn as much as men. For instance, in the manufacturing sector in 13 out of 39 countries, women earned up to 20 percent less than men; in the other countries, the pay differential was even greater (ibid). Approximately half of all workers in the world are in gender-dominated occupations where at least 80 percent of workers are of the same sex, a form of labor market rigidity that reduces employment opportunity and impairs economic efficiency (Anker 2002). Occupational segregation is also associated with lower wage rates for women, as typical women's occupations tend to have lower pay, lower status and fewer possibilities for advancement than do male occupations.

Because of multiple data and other problems, it is difficult to recommend one global indicator to measure progress toward eliminating gender inequalities in access to assets and employment. Unemployment rates, for instance, are an important indicator of labor market performance in industrialized countries, but are of much more limited significance in low-income economies where the majority of the population engages in some form of economic activity – usually informal employment or self-employment. Occupational segregation indicators may not cover informal employment, and in some countries, they may not be correlated with other indicators of labor market disadvantage. And finally, data on the gender earnings gap – in both paid and self-employment — are currently not available for many countries. Of these three indicators, the gender earnings gap is probably the best marker of gender equality in the labor market.

Agency Indicators: The United Nations has recommended that progress toward women's empowerment be tracked by the female share of seats in national parliaments. Currently, this is the only indicator that can be tracked on a global scale. It is an imperfect proxy for tracking aggregate levels of female empowerment because it says nothing about whether women have power in parliament to make decisions or whether or not they are sensitive to gender issues and can promote a gender equality legislative agenda. It has also been observed that greater progress has been made in municipal and local level elections than in national elections, so it would therefore be very useful to track progress that women are making at the local level. The International Union of Local Authcrities has scattered data on municipal level institutions but aims to construct a global database on women in local government. At the individual level, indicators could include control over fertility and sexuality. Again, however, there is a paucity of such information for most countries. One barrier that stands in the way of women being able to use their capabilities, exploit opportunities, and exercise agency is violence. Worldwide, it has been estimated that violence against women is as serious a cause of death and incapacity among women of reproductive age as cancer, and is a greater cause of ill-health than traffic accidents and malaria combined. Therefore, another indicator of women's agency, albeit in a negative way, is the prevalence of physical violence in the past year experienced by women aged 15-49 at the hands of an intimate partner.

Measuring the true prevalence of gender-based violence presents several challenges. To accurately measure true prevalence of physical violence, the questions used to gather data must disaggregate specific acts of physical violence such as kicking, beating, hitting and slapping, information which can be hard to obtain because of its sensitive nature. Statistics available through the police, hospitals, women's centers, and other formal institutions often underestimate the levels of violence because of under-reporting. The WHO's World Report on Violence and Health, which presents data from 48 population-based surveys conducted in 35 developed and developing countries, and WHO's recent multi-country study on women's health and domestic violence lay a strong foundation for larger-scale data collection initiatives. Thus, although prevalence rates are a good indicator, they can't be used to track progress toward the goal since data are not currently available for a large number of countries.

General limitations of all indicators

Beyond the specific issues associated with each indicator described above, there are a number of more general issues. First, the paucity of data on some indicators automatically restricts their use, despite the fact that there may be more valid indicators than the ones for which there is more data. Second, good ratios are not good enough because they say nothing about the absolute levels achieved. Third, national averages mask regional variation. Finally, few indicators exist that measure *quality* of progress toward the goal instead of just *quantity* of progress. The dearth of data and lack of standardization across countries limit a complete and accurate measurement of gender equality and empowerment. There are data gaps across all domains – capabilities, opportunity, and agency — but gaps are particularly prevalent in the domain of opportunity. For example, most of Sub-Saharan Africa and South Asia are missing data on the share of women in wage employment in the non-agricultural sector. As noted earlier, even fewer have information on women's relative earnings. Lack of time-series data is an additional hindrance. Finally, data are often missing for countries that experienced violent conflict during the decade.

Meeting the Goal of Empowering Women: Other Actions

Meeting the three targets will lay the foundation for women's empowerment because gaining power in society is dependent upon having capability, opportunity and influence over key decisions that affect life outcomes. However, achieving the goal of women's empowerment is not only about the content of interventions but about the process. The process of empowerment varies from culture to culture, but there are several types of changes that are considered to be central across cultures. Some of these changes include increased participation in decision-making, more equitable status of women in the family and community, increased political power and exercise of rights, and increased self-esteem.

Women can be empowered through development interventions. Some of the clearest evidence comes from evaluations of well-designed micro credit programs (Hashemi, Schuler, and Riley 1996). In addition to gaining greater respect and legitimacy in the broader community – particularly from male members – because of their access to credit, the opportunity to have control over decisions about loan size, use of the loan, and so forth has been found to be empowering for women. Women borrowers have also gained experience and confidence as leaders of their Trust Banks (in the Philippines) and have gone on to be elected within their barangays in the Philippines and Mayor in Honduras (Cheston 2002). A significant barrier to women's empowerment is gender-based violence. As mentioned earlier, the prevalence of violence against women can serve as an indicator of the level of empowerment of women in any given country. The lack of data currently makes this difficult to operationalise in the MDG context, but it does not reduce the urgency to address this problem.

At the country level, most initiatives to address violence have been legislative. Although the legislation varies, it typically includes a combination of protective or restraining orders and penalties for offenders. As with property rights, a formidable challenge are often the enforcement of existing laws. Procedural barriers and traditional attitudes of law enforcement and judicial officials undermine the effectiveness of existing anti-violence laws. Training programs for judicial and law enforcement personnel often go a long way to change such attitudes. Beyond training programs, the establishment of female-staffed police stations has been effective in making them more accessible to women. For the women who have experienced violence, a range of medical, psychological, legal, educational, and other support services is necessary.

Finally, to prevent violence, improving women's education levels and economic opportunities has been found to be a protective factor (Duvvury 2002; Panda 2002). The interventions noted above to improve women's economic opportunities thus become even more important. Ultimately, however, the threshold of acceptability of violence against women needs to be shifted upwards. To do that requires a massive media and public education campaign.

Conclusion

Overall, the Convention to Eliminate All Forms of Discrimination Against Women (CEDAW) provides a useful international mechanism to hold countries accountable for meeting Goal #3. All nation states that have ratified the convention are obligated to take all necessary measures at the national level to implement the provisions within it, including providing legal protection against discrimination of women. In order to monitor progress made by nation states in advancing the agenda of CEDAW, each nation state is required to report to the Committee on the Elimination of Discrimination Against Women on specific measures that they have taken to advance the Convention's agenda. Each country is required to report within one year of acceding to the Convention and at least every four years thereafter, including whenever the Committee so requests. The Committee annually reports to the UN General Assembly and makes recommendations to nation states based on an evaluation of the country reports. A recent study of the impact of CEDAW has shown that it provides a powerful instrument at the national and international level for defining norms for constitutional guarantees of women's rights, for interpreting laws, mandating proactive, pro-women policies, and for dismantling discrimination overall (McPhedran et al. 2000). For CEDAW to be used effectively requires action at many levels and by many actors. Among the many factors identified by the study as being key to the effective utilization of CEDAW were the following: widespread awareness and knowledge of CEDAW; constructive dialogue between government representatives, CEDAW Committee members, and NGOs; governments recognizing how policy goals can be adapted to implement their stated commitment to CEDAW; and the systematic use of gender-specific indicators to assess the impact of governmental policies, laws, and budgets. The CEDAW mechanism be used to monitor progress toward the MDGs and to hold nation's accountable.

It is important that the women organizations advocating for sexual and reproductive rights develop ways to achieve progress on a range of issues within the framework established by the MDGs. They should ensure that a rights based approach be applied to development , both within the UN system and at the country level, that prioritizes equity, profound social changes, and sustainability, rather than simply the achievement of narrow quantitative targets.

The MDG campaign offers an opportunity to attend to the unfinished business of development by fulfilling the promises made by world leaders to reduce poverty, end hunger, improve health and eliminate illiteracy. Gender inequality fuels many of these ubiquitous challenges and is exacerbated by them. Conversely, gender equality and the empowerment of women can secure the future of women themselves, their households, and the communities in which they live. Relative to the past, current international development rhetoric places gender inequality high among the list of development priorities. Having an independent MDG goal on gender equality is a reflection of this new emphasis. The Millennium Development Goals are a derivative of the Millennium Declaration of September 2000, which spells out the following values: freedom, equality, solidarity, tolerance, respect for nature, and shared responsibility. They are a clarion call of 189 governments, on behalf of their citizens

References

Anker, R. 1998. *Gender and Jobs: Sex Segregation of Occupations in the World.* Geneva: ILO.

Anker, R., I. Chernyshev, P. Egger, F. Mehran, and J. Ritter. 2002. "Measuring Decent Work with Statistical Indicators." Policy Integration Paper No. 1. Geneva: ILO.

Charmes, J. 2000. "Informal Sector, Poverty and Gender: A Review of Empirical Evidence." Background Paper for the World Development Report 2001. Washington, D.C. World Bank.

Cheston, S., and L. Kuhn. 2002. "Empowering Women Through Microfinance." New York: UNIFEM.

Commission on Human Rights. 2003. Preliminary Study on the impact of international economic and financial issues on the enjoyment of human rights submitted to working group on the right to development, February 3-14, 2003, Geneva.

Duvvury, N., and K. Allendorf. 2001. "Domestic Violence in India: The Roles of Education and Employment." Paper presented at the Sixth Women's Policy Research Conference, The Status of Women: Facing the Facts, Forging the Future, June 8-9, 2001, Washington, DC.

Elson, D., and R. Pearson. 1997. "The Subordination of Women and the Internationalization of Factory Production." in Visvanathan, J., L. Duggan, L. Nisonoff, N. Wiegersman, eds. *The Women, Gender & Development Reader*. London: Zed Press.

Gupta, G., and E. Weiss. 1994. "Bridging the Gap: Addressing Gender and Sexuality in HIV Prevention. Washington, DC: ICRW.

Hashemi, S., S. Schuler, and A. Riley. 1996. "Rural Credit Programs and Women's Empowerment in Bangladesh." *World Development*. 24(4). Oxford: Elsevier Science Ltd. Heintz, J. 2002. "Global Labor Standards: Their Impact and Implementation." Working Paper Series No. 46. Amherst, MA: Political Economy Research Institute, University of Massachusetts, Amherst.

Heise, L., and M. Ellsberg. 1999. "Ending Violence Against Women." *Population Reports*, Vol. XXVII (4). Baltimore, MD, USA: Johns Hopkins University School of Public Health, Population Information Program.

Hill, A., and E. King. 1995. "Women's Education and Economic Well-being." *Feminist Economics* 1(2): 1-26.

ICRW (International Center for Research on Women). 2000. "Domestic Violence in India. A Summary Report of a Multi-Site Household Survey." Washington, D.C.:

Kabeer, N. 2000. *The Power to Choose: Bangladeshi Women and Labour Market Decisions in London and Dhaka*. London and New York: Verso.

Malhotra, A., S. Schuler, and C. Boender. 2002 "Measuring Women's Empowerment as a Variable in International Development." http://www.icrw.org/docs MeasuringEmpowerment _ workingpaper_802.doc

McPhedran, M., S. Bazilli, M. Erickson, and A. Byrnes. 2000. "The First CEDAW Impact Study. Final Report." Toronto: Centre for Feminist Research, York University and the International Women's Rights Project.

Panda, P. 2002. "Rights-Based Strategies in the Prevention of Domestic Violence." Washington, D.C.: ICRW.

Psacharopoulos, G., and Z. Tzannatos, eds. 1992. *Case Studies on Women's Employment and Pay in Latin America.* Washington D.C.: World Bank.

Saito, K. and D. Spurling. 1992. "Developing Agricultural Extension for Women Farmers." Discussion Paper No. 156. Washington, D.C.: World Bank SAS Institute, Inc. 1985. *SAS User's Guide: Statistics.* Version 5 edition. Cary, NC, USA

Schultz, T. P. 2002. "Why Governments Should Invest More to Educate Girls." *World Development.* 30(2): 207-225. Oxford: Elsevier Science Ltd.

UNAIDS. 2002. "Report on the Global HIV/AIDS Epidemic." Geneva. www.unaids.org/barcelona/presskit/report.html

UNDAW (United Nations Division for the Advancement of Women), ECLAC. 1998. "National Machineries for Gender Equality." Presented at the Expert Group Meeting August 31 – September 4, 1998, Santiago, Chile. http://www.un.org/womenwatch/daw/news/natlmach.htm

UNDP (United Nations Development Programme). 2002. *Human Development Report 2002.* New York and Oxford: Oxford University Press. http://hdr.undp.org/reports/global/2002/en/

UNDP (United Nations Development Programme). 1995. *Human Development Report 1995.* New York and Oxford: Oxford University Press. UNESCO (United Nations Educational, Scientific and Cultural Organization). 2002. "Education for All. Is the World on Track?" Paris. http://www.unesco.org/education/efa/monitoring/monitoring_2002.shtml_____.

UNESCO Statistical Yearbook. 1999, 1996. Paris.

UNICEF, UNAIDS, WHO. 2002. "Young People and HIV/AIDS: Opportunity in Crisis. New York and Geneva. UNIFEM (United Nations Development Fund for Women).

UNIFEM Biennial Report. New York. http://www.unifem.org/progressww/2000/ _____. 1998. *Bringing Equality Home. Implementing the Convention on the Elimination of All Forms of Discrimination Against Women (CEDAW).* http://www.unifem.undp.org/resources/cedaw/

WHO (World Health Organization). 2002a. "WHO Multi-Country Study on Women's Health and Domestic Violence Against Women." Geneva.

"World Report on Violence and Health." Geneva. http://www5.who.int/violence_injury_prevention/main.cfm?p=0000000117

World Bank. 2001. *Engendering Development: Through Gender Equality in Rights, Resources and Voice.* Policy Research Report. Oxford: Oxford University Press.

13

'Women's Empowerment Through Micro-credit '

(With special reference to Nanded District)

G.S.YELNE

Introduction

The Government of India has been undertaking various measures to improve the credit worthiness of the weaker section especially, women those live in rural areas. In a country like India where the moneylenders exploit the poor by way of mortgaging their little assets and charging high rates of interest, steps to provide alternative credit facilities is a welcome move. Also, it has been argued that poverty in India cannot be alleviated through wage employment alone and therefore, generations of opportunities for self-employment are indispensable. It is, in this context, the credit inputs become highly vital. In the process of development, the credit inputs in the form of living conditions of the poor. The programmes like IRDP, DWCRA, SFDA and so on though, humble in their objectives, could not accomplish the expected results due to various factors. The prominent one being the negligence of thrift and saving habits among the beneficiaries.

Lack of emphasis on thrift and savings in the poverty alleviation programmes is attributed to the very assumption of these programmes that the poor are unable to save, as they don't have surplus cash. Such a perception on the part of the planners and administrators perhaps, discouraged the attitudes of the beneficiaries towards the saving and thrift. The recent experience illustrates that even the poor can save whatever the little they can afford.

In the majority of our development programmes, gender dimension has been acquiring special importance. Among the poor, women are the most disadvantaged and underprivileged group. They contribute substantially to the household economy especially, in agriculture families and hardly been rewarded for their labour. They neither own assets nor have access to the income that has been generated by them. Interventions are therefore, needed to improve the status of women in rural areas. Maharashtra Rural Credit Project (MRCP) *Mahila Arthik Vikas Mahamandal Ltd. (MAVIM)* has been conceived to meet the credit needs of the rural poor. The specific objectives of this project are:

* To improve the provision of credit services to the rural poor in the project area by the commercial banks:
* To organise self-help groups and to mobilise savings as the basis for lending to the poor in the project area: and
* To promote people's participation by developing formal credit services, encouraging informal savings and credit and ensuring institutional support.

The project has been initiated by International Fund for Agriculture Development (IFAD) in consultation with the Government of India for a period of seven years (1994-2000). The project targets at the people below poverty line. This would encompass small and marginal farmers, landless labourers, artisans, tribes and women headed households. The project intends to assist 91,250 borrowers of which 50,90 would be women. Neatly, fifty per cent of the women beneficiaries would be assisted through Self-Help Groups and to achieve this 3,260 SHG's are proposed to be formed. The project will be implemented in eight districts of Maharashtra State in two phases of which Nanded is one. The total cost of the project is US$48.3 millions.

Self-Help Groups have emerged as a popular method of working with Women for their empowerment in the recent years. Power to the people signifies a new social movement, which has probably been born out of the realization that society's traditional arrangements for solving their problems are inadequate. This movement stems from the people's desire to meet their needs and determine their own destinies through the principle of "by the people, for the people, and of the people". Ordinarily self-help refers to provision of aid to self, but here self –help is also taken to mean internal. Self-help emphasises self-determination, self-reliance, self-production, and self-empowerment by mobilising internal resources of the persons, the group, or the community.

Thus, collectives of individuals, usually small groups of persons, are formed into "Self-Help Groups" that provide mutual aid to each other around common problems and operate under such concepts as self-determination and joint responsibility. They work together to achieve specific behavior attitudinal or cognitive goals. The group is the central component and everyone. Works with others for the group's further development, and individual needs are met in the process. It is against this backdrop that women's empowerment through Self-Help Group can be examined and analysed.

Statement of Objectives and Methodology

The study intends to address the following set of four objectives;

(a) To examine the effectiveness of SHGs in promoting thrift and savings among women of lower strata of the society;

(b) To understand the dynamics of SHGs in the process of eliciting women's participation;

(c) To assess the implications of women's participation in SHGs on their overall Socio-Economic status; and

(d) To know the extent, the SHGs have facilitated to bring about awareness and empowerment.

Methods of Data Collection

Data has been collected both from primary and secondary sources. Primary data is collected by using structured interview schedules consisting of sixty-five questions by using participant observation .The major themes covered in the interview schedule are personal and family profile of SHG members, information regarding saving habits prior to membership and after membership to SHG, some question on internal lending system and loan received by the members from SHG and economic activities started by the members which shows economic empowerment amongst them. The interview schedules consist a set of question pertaining to social, economic and political empowerment. Lastly it includes some questions aimed at assessing impact of SHG membership and training provided by MAVIM.

Sampling Coverage

As of now, 284 SHGs have been formed representing 71 villages in the district, according to the data available this covers 4330 women who are the members of various SHGs. The progress of *Mahila Arthika Vikas Mahamandal* (the agency implementing the programme).

A list of SELP-HELP GROUPS (SHGs) established by MAVIM in the district was obtained. From the list so obtained, "A" grade SHGs were selected on the basis of their performance (indicators set by MAVIM to measure the performance), appropriate sample was drawn to add up to 300 SHG members using purposive sampling method.

Research Area

The research has been carried out in Nanded district of Marathwada region of Maharastra. Since the district has a rich diversity of socio-economic development at the block level, all eleven blocks of Nanded district were choosen for operationalisation of the research.viz. Nanded, Kandhar, Loha,

Mukhed, Degloor, Biloli, Kinwat, Hadgaon, Umari, Ardhapur and Mahur based on the status of SHGs activities over there.

Analysis of Data

The independent variables considered for analysis are age, qualification, caste, economic status, saving habit. Each variable has been interpreted in the form of tables and in the graph, wherever necessary. The prominent dependent variable considered for analyses were related to various bases to measure empowerment of women through SHG.

Scope of the Study

"*Women's empowerment* "is the central issue that has been parading the empowerment debate after 80s improving the status of the women and empowering them would go long way in accomplishing egalitarian gender relations in the society. Women who are hitherto constrained by the social structure for their self-expression constitute the target of most of the development programmes, which aim at bringing women into mainstream of development process. Giving women access to credit would be a step forward in empowering them. From this viewpoint the study has brought out various situational factors that influence the women to participate in the Self-Help Groups and to control the savings (money) saved by them. The findings of the study would provide with rich insights to the planners, administrators and NGOs who have been working with women for their empowerment.

Findings, Conclusion and Suggestions

The researcher summaries the main findings and conclusion of the present research on "Women's Empowerment through micro-credit with special reference to Nanded District", in a more orderly manner and attempts to derive conclusion on various aspect covered in the study. And includes some suggestions for the policy makers and NGOs.

Quantitative findings and observations

Personal Information

(1) It is found that, majority of the respondents of the SHGs was in the age group of 21 to 45 years. And average mean age of respondents was 30 years.

(2) It is found that, majority of the members of SHGs was having very little educational background. The participation of women in SHGs education is not prerequisite, and if anything is required, it is their willingness.

(3) It is found from the present study that, majority of the respondents of SHG is married.

(4) The very important finding of the present study is that, The SHGs have provided a platform to women from different castes and religious groups to come and work together. From this we can say that SHGs are now becoming important medium to bring communal harmony in rural India.

(5) It is found from the present study that, more than half respondent, are engaged in wage labour in various sectors like agriculture, construction work, collection of forest products, stone cutting etc.

(6) Present study reveals that majority of the respondents involved in SHGs were representing nuclear family.

(7) It is found from the present study that, majority of the members comes from below poverty line category. Annual income of respondent's families was between Rs. 1000/- to Rs.10, 000/-.

Saving and Thrieft

(8) It is found from the present study that, majority members of SHG received information about SHG from MAVIM *Sahayogini*.

(9) As per as objectives joining of SHG is concern this study shows that, majority respondent join the SHG keeping in mind that to save the money.

(10) The study shows that, out of the 300 respondents, only 46 members faced resistance from their family members while seeking SHG membership.

(11) Recorded attendance in the study shows that, majorities of the respondent are regular in attending the meeting of the SHG and almost all members are conscious and committed to the cause of SHG. Whereas, very few respondents were found irregular in attending the meetings of SHGs and reasons behind this irregularity are due to pregnancy, agricultural work, timings of the meetings is not suitable and other reasons like mood of husband, emergencies in the house , marriages of relatives etc.

Social Empowerment

(12) It is found from the present study that, majority respondents are enjoying better status in the family, some of them fell better status in the community / society and some of them feel respected after joining the SHG. On basis of this one can say that, SHGs are working as a change agent now-a-days in the society.

(13) The study shows that, majority respondents are now able to enjoy their rights in terms of participation in decision making process like purchase or disposal of property, education for children, decision regarding marriage of children etc. due to active participation in the SHGs.

(14) The present study shows that, members of the SHGs now a days discuss issues like conflicts of the villagers, health problems, violence against women and social problems like Dowry, Darubandi and education of girls and discuss above all issues as per requirement or the need of time.

Economic Empowerment

(15) the study shows that, respondents were not habitual of saving prior to shg membership, only few 27 % respondents

preferred post office to deposit their money, some of them saved money at home, few of them were engaged in the activity like B.C.

(16) Majorities of respondents were saving an amount of Rs.30 per month, as their monthly share and had save upto an amount of Rs. 2000 to Rs. 4000 on their name.

(17) The very important finding of the present study is that, the loan received by respondents is varying from Rs. 500 to more than Rs.5000. This type of facility is known as micro credit and such a small amount of loan is not available to the rural poor women's by the Banking system, or any other affordable system of this kind.

(18) The study shows that, as regards to savings, loan availability and utilisation, though the amounts are insignificant by the standards of conventional banking, This loans have enabled them to build dry houses, to purchase medicine, to invest and reinvest in small entrepreneurship like goat keeping, poultry trading, to provide their children education, marriage, to meet consumption needs.

(19) A notable significance of SHG reveals that there is no defaulter in repayment, which indicates the spirit of SHG programme, responsibility and commitment of the members.

(20) Majority of the respondents were found satisfied, as there need of loan was fulfilled at the proper time and adequate.

(21) The present study shows that, respondents availed loan from one time to more than five times. The total attempts of loan show continuous repayment of loan and utilisation of group funds for the development of their own.

(22) It is also found that, majority respondents paying monthly rate of interest equal to Bank rate of interest to the SHG, in between 1 % to 2 %, most important thing is that women of these groups getting this loan without involving in the hassles of long documentation which is involved in the formal banking system.

(23) As far as performance of repayment is concerned it is found that, majority of the respondents are very particular about

timely repayments of their loan and some of them doing early repayments.

(24) As for as economic changes is concerned it is found that, majority respondents says that their economic condition is now better off than before, some of them have purchased a land after joining the SHG and remaining feel that now they do not have need to go to money-lender for money in the emergency like health problem, pregnancy, and small amount of loan is available within short period without going to bank and without documentation.

(25) It is also found that, majority respondents have right to use their saving and they feel that this is possible due to SHG membership.

(26) It is also found that, respondents feel that they were financially self-reliant after becoming a member of SHGs.

Political Empowerment

(27) It is also found that, SHGs are now playing important role in the village level politics, in the traditional village power structure, there was no scope for women, but now due to SHG movement women are exposed to out side world, they are taking interest in the rural politics, majority 66% of women reported that SHGs have helped them to get involved in the village level politics. Which was a great move towards redistribution of power according to Bataliwala's definition.

(28) It is also found that, out of 300 respondents 237 respondents were motivated to participate in rural politics due to SHGs and received following kind of help such as inspiration, motivational support, financial as well as moral support. Majority respondents reported that it was possible for them to get elected only because of SHG support, which is very important in the context of women empowerment.

(29) It is also found that, 111 out of 300 respondents got elected and out of these 111 elected members 6 respondents were working as a Sarpanch, 23 Upsarpanch and 82 were

members in the Village Panchayat (Local Self Govt.). This could be possible because of SHGs.

(30) It is also found that, because of SHG activity majority of the respondents from rural area entered in to panchayat election for the first time.

(31) It is also found that, majority of the respondents do not belong to any political party and enter in to the election as a individual.

(32) It is found that, respondents elected first time started implementation of various developmental programme like Dalit Wasti Sudhar Yojana, efforts to solve the problem of drinking water, construction of *Samaj Mandir*, and other programme like Smoke less *Chulha, Shramadan, Gramswachhata Abhiyan* etc. But majority of the respondents are with a feeling that still they are not able to do concrete work.

(33) It is also found that, due to membership in the SHGs women started getting recognition in village community and now they were started getting membership in the village development committee's work. Thus the participation of SHG members to this extent in the developmental work explains the importance of SHGs, which is very important move towards the empowerment of women.

Impact of Training Programme

(34) It is found that, majority of the respondents covered under study has participated in various training programmes organised by (MAVIM) such as the management of kits of SHGs training programme, Entrepreneurship Development Programme, Village Development Council Training Programme, Entrepreneurship Awareness Programme, Leadership Development Training Programme, and some of the respondents participated in the above all training programmes, which reflects the empowerment of them.

(35) It is also found that, the training programmes has played very vital role in the nurturing of these women of SHGs, and

benefited in terms of awareness about economic activities, knowledge of management of kits, managerial skills, leadership qualities, increase in self-confidence, self-confidence building also increased the articulation and enhanced communication skills among the respondents of SHGs.

Observations

The emergence of SHGs has had a great impact on the lives of the local people, particularly the women in Nanded District some of the observations are;

The women have gained a great deal of self-confidence and self -esteem is being elevated.

The women, who felt helpless, now realised that they are secure not only in terms of credit support but also in terms of "feeling as members of the group" which shows that group's solidarity.

The economic activities started by respondents' shows economic development among the respondents.

The SHGs do not touch common savings for any purposes other than lénding, which shows that enormous collective strength among the womenfolk.

Qualitative Findings and Observations

Chapter number five, which dealt qualitative side of the present research, concludes with following findings and observations.

It is found that, all the SHGs have a membership size of minimum 15 to maximum 20 members.

It is found that, majority of the members of SHGs was having very little educational background.

It is found that, majority of the members comes from below poverty line category. And income of respondent's families was between Rs. 1000/- to Rs.10, 000/-, and majority of the members of SHG was working as wage earners.

It is found that, due to SHG activities the members developed a habit of saving, which was, absent prior to becoming SHG members.

It is found that, SHGs have started the internal credit activity on the basis of their mutual understanding. And Banks have started advancing credit to the SHGs on the basis of their saving and performance.

It is found that, SHGs have adopted a strategy to disburse loan to the members only on nèed basis. This has ensured recovery of loan among the members.

The important find of this research is, the amount of internal loan received from SHG by the members has been utilised for the entrepreneurial activities like, purchase of Buffaloes, Goat rearing, Tailoring, vegetable selling and agricultural activities as well as other income generating activities.

It is found that, the average size of loan utilised by SHG members was around minimum Rs. 500/- and maximum Rs. 10,000/- and mostly it was need based. And The SHG members do not face any difficulty in the repayments of internal loan. Also repayment from members to SHG and SHG to Bank was regular and cent per cent. This is because of group pressure and mutual understanding developed among them by way of continuous meetings.

It is found that, participation of SHG members in the monthly meetings was regular and issues being discussed are savings, credit, social problems, health and Politics of the village.

It is found that, majority members of SHGs feel that their status in the family has improved and have a sense of financial security after joining the SHG.

It is found that, women started participating in the Panchayat level elections, and women of SHGs started sending women to participate in local level election. Also women members of SHGs are participating actively in the election campaigns.

It is found that, willingness of women members to go outside (mobility), is increasing in rural areas.

It is found that, the members who participated in training were benefited in terms of awareness about economic activities, knowledge about management of kits and managerial skills and leadership qualities. The content of training includes how to maintain the accounts of SHGs, Entrepreneurship Development Training, and also awareness building. One of the objectives of this training was to facilitate the trainees to understand various aspects of managing the SHGs and it was expected that these trainees later on, disseminate the knowledge to the rest of the members of SHGs. It has been seen during our fieldwork that the knowledge acquired through the training has been passed on from 1st member to the last member of SHGs.

The level of self-confidence was so high among members of SHGs, also the process of self-confidence building was in progress in The SHGs members. The training also increased the articulation and enhanced communication skills among the members of SHGs.

It is found that, all the SHG members showed interest in solving personal and family dispute or social affairs likes Gram Swachhata Abhiyan.

Observations

It has been noted the social, economic and cultural aspects of society influence the participation, the present study also comes up with some interesting observation in this regard. Factors like caste structure, economy of the village, role of Government agencies saving habits, mobility of the women outside the village have played a vital role, in increasing better participation of members in SHGs.

Conclusion

The Self-Help Groups of women (SHGs) for credit and thrift activities have been proliferated with the efforts of Mahila Arthik Vikas Mahamandal (MAVIM) in some districts of Maharashtra. Nanded is one such district where MAVIM started its activities in rural areas in 1995. According to a report of the Nanded district Implementation unit since 1995 to 2001 MAVIM has formed SHGs in 86 villages. There are 449 Self Help Groups spread in different villages with 8130 members. As already highlighted the SHGs are formed on women who belong to families below poverty line. These small thrift and credit groups are mostly informal, where these women pool their savings and re-lend in groups on rotational basis. Lending is mainly based on mutual need and trust with the minimum documentation and without any tangible security.

Economic transactions apart the periodical meetings of women in these villages become a *raison d'être* for the mobilisation. Despite skepticism and apprehensions expressed about micro-credit as a tool for social transformation many see a massive mobilisation of women world wide . What needs to be underlined here is that, in the periodical meetings of different groups in the villages, the women are also expected to involve in discussions related to rural socio-economic problems apart from economic transaction. This component of group meeting may take a novel turn engendering group action, which was rather unanticipated. In the villages under study the women are basically found to discuss 'personal problems'; these personal problems are many a times the issues which become the concern of all members. Many of the group members identify with the narratives of a particular member and they intensely feel to do something about it.

Sahyoginis or animators whose work is to facilitate group formation and provide leadership until such time as the local leadership emerges and takes over the organisation, are a vital agent who infuse the issue of gender sensitivity in the group discussion with their limited understanding of feminist vocabularies and agendas. The *Sahyoginis* are recruited from the local villages and they are imparted certain training in mobilising women to from SHG and to facilitate credit and thrift business among (poor) rural women. The component of gender sensitisation is integral to these training programmes attended by *Sahyoginis*. In a discussion with these *Sahyoginis* it was found that they have partially imbibed feminist vocabularies and language. The *Sahyoginis* work in some ways as catalytic agents whose presence definitely energises the group. The group in turn has provided space to its members to discuss, share and articulate their (oppressive) experiences both within and outside the domestic boundary.

Women in general perceive a change in their life situation after joining and actively participating in SHGs for over three four years. This change can not be reduced to or expressed through mere "economic empowerment". The group is more than a source of credit and one can gauge the importance of the institution called SHG and what it means to many women in these villages, if not all, in their own terminology. Being asked how SHG is useful and beneficial to them, they say in Marathi—*dhistpana aala, himmat wadhali aani pratishtha wadhli*—which means that these women have learnt to become obdurate, unyielding and recalcitrant. "They are courageous now and not always taken for granted in the village". They have some prestige conferred upon by the family members as they have some savings at their disposal and they can arrange some money through credit. They refer to SHG and compare it with their natal home as they have received protection and shelter during various crises.

It is concluded that a process of SHG has brought change among the women to some extent, as they have started to organise themselves in a social group, which is known as SHGs, which was, absent prior to the initiation of SHGs in these selected villages. It shows the increased participation of women at community level in the direction of empowerment of women.

Suggestions

The policy markers need to provide support, exposure and training to the SHG members on under mentioned issues:

(1) Establishing savings and credit systems including frequency and amount of saving norms of credit disbursed and recovery and training of the SHG members and represent who are working for the same.

(2) Training on maintenance of account, sharing periodical financial performance with members, and periodic external audits.

(3) Promoting group based ownership of resources democratic functioning and decision making and transparency in operations ;

(4) At the time of establishment of SHG, the implementing agencies of the scheme should try to favour the most poor sections amongst the backward classes the more backward class should get a due share in the scheme to make it more meaningful and purposeful.

(5) It is interesting to know that after discussion with member of SHG, that loan procedure adopted by bank for linkage of SHG to bank is so complicated, and because of illiteracy women members have been facing more problem for the compilation of documents, bonds and writing procedure. So procedure of getting loan and linkages with bank to be simplify and accessible.

(6) NGOs can help to SHG for nurturing and can link the SHG with concern area banks so that they can avail credit from bank for economic development activities.

Limitations of the Study

As every study has its limitations, this study also have some limitations like, the findings of this study are based on information given by the respondents, which may have its own limitation. Possibility of hiding certain facts on the part of the respondents cannot be completely ruled out although every possible efforts has been made to elicit authentic information.

The scope of this research is limited to the women of rural area who were participating in Self-Help Groups of Nanded district only. So, conclusions based on this study have their own limitations and can be made applicable elsewhere, with certain precautions.

SECTION IV

Reduction of Child Mortality, Improvement of Maternal Health, Combat HIV/AIDS, Malaria, T.B.

14

Macroeconomics, Public Health and MDGs

Ravi Duggal

Background

India is knocking at global markets. Since the mid-eighties India has rapidly integrated with the world economy and now faces not only the ups but also the downs as protection of the internal economy has become a thing of the past. The globalisation of India was speeded up under the Structural Adjustment Program designed by the World Bank to reform India's economy. A large part of the middle class has certainly benefited from the SAP and related initiatives but overall poverty has not declined - if at all it has added to the misery of the already impoverished masses.

Health sector reforms did not stay far behind. But the question is, were they reforms in the positive or progressive sense? In the name of reforms, again under the aegis of the World Bank, and other bilateral and multilateral agencies like USAID, DIFID, WHO, UNICEF etc. public health investment became even more selective and targeted at selected populations. Thus family planning and immunisation services, and selective disease programs like HIV-AIDS, acquired an even more central position in public health care and other concerns like curative services, hospital care, malaria, tuberculosis, maternity services, etc. lost further ground. The new priorities were not priorities determined by those who needed health care but by global agents of change who were in the business of adjusting India to the world economy

Economic reforms towards liberalisation began in the early eighties. This is important to note because most often there is a tendency to look only at the post-1991 period. Data available up to now clearly shows that economic performance of the eighties far outweighs that in the nineties. And the underlying fact about this is that in the eighties there was no structural adjustment or World Bank dictat. The classical 'Hindu' rate of growth in the eighties had doubled from 3% to 6%, without much inflation and with declining levels of poverty. Thus we were already liberalising our economy and speeding up growth without the World Bank running the show.

Infact, the post-1991 reform period slowed down growth, increased poverty and inflation, and reversed many trends of the eighties. No doubt it caught up towards the mid-nineties, but it has not yet surpassed the achievements of the eighties. Thus, in the eighties India was developing rapidly with a gradual globalisation process and with the advantage of its inner strength which insulated it from global shocks. In the nineties there was rapid globalisation which exposed India to global fluctuations; if India survived the Asian shock which destroyed Indonesia and other South East Asian economies it was because of its sheer size and the strengths of its own local markets.

Another fact to contend with is the as yet dependence of over two-thirds of the population on agriculture and 70% of the population living in rural areas. Since the larger impact of macro-economic reforms is on the urban-industrial sector, which integrates globally with much ease, the rural population in a sense still has relative protection from global impacts. Further, it is the consistent good performance of agriculture that has helped ward off the severities of SAP, which many other countries have faced. In addition, India's strong investments in the past in rural development, especially employment guarantee programs and agricultural subsidies aided in reducing the adverse impact of SAP.

And this is not likely to change thanks to the strong farm lobby that is in fact demanding greater investments and subsidies for the rural economy.

Thus, at one level India is much more exposed to the global market with increasing vulnerability. But at another level it continues to enjoy an inner strength and autonomy because of its sheer size, its large rural-agricultural population and a large local market of its own, despite the fact that politically the situation is very fluid. This background is important for understanding the impact and changes in the health sector.

Poverty is the real context of India. Three-fourths of people live below or at subsistence levels. This means 70-90% of their incomes go to food and other survival consumption. In such a context social security support for health, education, housing etc. becomes critical. Ironically India has one of the largest private health sectors in the world with over 80% of ambulatory care being supported through out-of-pocket expenses. The health care market in India, as elsewhere in the world, is based on a supply-induced demand and keeps growing geometrically, especially in the context of new technologies. Thus India has a large and dominant private health sector and a weak public health sector despite its poverty, with the former having curative monopoly and the latter carrying the burden of preventive services.

The public health services are very inadequate. The public curative and hospital services are mostly in the cities where only 25% of the over one billion population resides. Rural areas have mostly preventive and promotive services like family planning and immunisation. The private sector has virtual monopoly of ambulatory curative services in both rural and urban areas and over half of hospital care. Further, a very large proportion of private providers are not qualified to provide modern health care because they are trained in other systems of medicine (traditional Indian systems like ayurveda, unani and siddha, and homoeopathy) or worse still have no training whatsoever, and because of lack of regulation they are also using modern medicine to treat patients. This adds to the risk faced by the already impoverished population.

The State's insufficient commitment to provide health care for its citizens is reflected not only in the inadequacy of the health infrastructure and low levels of financing but also in declining support to various health care demands of the people, and especially since mid-nineteen eighties from when began the process of liberalisation and opening up of the Indian economy to the world markets. Under structural adjustment since 1991 there has been further compression in government spending in its efforts to bring down the fiscal deficit to the level as desired by the World Bank. The impact of new economics unleashed on people comes via income and prices and affects people through final consumption and / or employment, and for the poorest sections the development expenditures like IRDP, JRY, health care, education, housing and other welfare programmes are crucial in the context of the existing overall life chances available to such sections. There is clear evidence that expenditures on such social programs are declining in real terms and its benefits are accruing to fewer people. For instance the GOI budget expenditures have declined from 19.8% of the GDP in 1990-91 to 16.58% in 1993-94 and the central health sector has been even more severely affected.[1] The states share in health expenditure has increased and that of the Centre declined drastically, and especially so for the centrally sponsored disease control and other national programs which are mostly of a preventive nature. If the states do not pick up the added burden of allocating additional resources for these programs then tuberculosis, malaria, AIDS, leprosy etc. would be plaguing the Indian people more severely.

The Healthcare System

The political economy of health care services in India has various dimensions. Multiple systems, various types of ownership patterns and different kinds of delivery structures make up a complex plurality that makes the development of an organised system difficult.

Allopathy, ayurveda, homoeopathy, unani, siddha, among others, are different systems of medicine available in the country. However, allopathy is the dominant system of medicine. Its domineering influence is evidenced by the fact that practitioners of the other systems of medicine also primarily practice allopathy. National surveys done by NSSO and NCAER and other small-scale studies clearly bring this out.

As regards ownership, while the broad characterisation could be made as public and private, there are various intricacies involved. The public sector ownership is divided between central and state governments, and municipal and panchayat local governments. The facilities include teaching hospitals, secondary level hospitals, first level referral hospitals (CHCs or rural hospitals), dispensaries, PHCs and sub centres, and health posts. Apart from this there are public facilities for selected occupational groups like ESIS, defense, CHGS, railways, post and telegraph, mines etc. These are usually hospitals of various capacities and dispensaries or clinics.

Private ownership is of two kinds, for-profit and not-for-profit. The former could be self-employed or individual ownership or various other forms of ownership like partnership, cooperative or corporate. The not-for-profit is usually a Trust or a Society, many of these also being called NGOs. These again could be teaching hospitals, hospitals and nursing homes of various sizes and kinds of care, clinics and dispensaries, and diagnostic facilities.

Public health facilities appear to be organised into some sort of a system. They are even allocated on the basis of population-based norms and/or on basis of specific geographic units. Thus for primary care there are dispensaries and health centres which provide largely ambulatory care. Rural areas have mostly health centres like Primary Health Centres and sub centres through which preventive and promotive care is provided, largely through paramedics. Presently there are about 24,000 PHCs and 140,000 sub centres in the country catering to about 700 million rural population. In addition in the public sector there are about 4000 rural dispensaries and about 2950 rural hospitals, which provide medical care and first level referral care. In urban areas public health services are largely of a curative nature being provided through dispensaries and hospitals of varying sizes and types of facilities. Taluka and other small towns usually have only dispensaries and a basic hospital. The district towns and larger towns and cities have dispensaries and one or more secondary level hospitals depending on their population size and these may be owned by either state and/or local governments; some of them may even have a teaching hospital and/or special hospitals. Compared to rural areas the urban areas are much better endowed with public health facilities (see Annex 1). Another special feature of public health services is that there are mass health care programs, largely of a preventive and promotive nature, like selected disease control programs (malaria, tuberculosis, leprosy, AIDS etc..), family planning and maternal and child health programs (contraception, immunisation, ante-natal care, etc.).

Private health care is much larger and more widespread than public health services. Individual practitioners in their clinics provide ambulatory care, which may often be within their residence. Data on the private sector is a major problem. For practitioners the only information available is the registration data from the various medical councils but this data has various limitations. The actual practitioners are much more than the registered numbers because due to lack of regulation all kinds of persons set up medical practice on one hand and different kinds of practitioners indulge in large-scale cross-practice across different systems of medicine. The number of registered practitioners is estimated to be about 14 lakhs across the country with large concentrations in states like Maharashtra, Gujarat and the southern states. Eighty percent are in the private sector. The allopathic doctors constitute about 45 per cent of total registered practitioners and are located mostly in urban areas, whereas the non-allopaths are mostly located in the smaller towns and rural areas. With regard to private hospitals the data gaps are similar. There is no proper registration process for private hospitals and hence the data available is a gross underestimate as revealed by surveys in Maharashtra and Andhra Pradesh[2]. The latest estimate reveals that nearly 70% of all hospitals and 40% of all hospital beds in the country are in the private sector with over 80% of them being in urban areas. A peculiar characteristic of private health services is that unlike the public health sector they provide almost entirely only curative care.

Current Scenario

Communicable diseases not only continue to be the single largest cause of mortality but prevalence of many diseases like tuberculosis and malaria has increased and diseases like AIDS, leptospirosis, dengue, encephalitis, etc. have got added to the list. And apart from this the burden of non-communicable and lifestyle diseases is also very high making for a double burden, unlike the developed countries who no longer have the burden of communicable diseases.

Public investment in the health sector since SAP has declined and this is reflected in drastically reduced capital expenditures and no further expansion in the public health infrastructure. Further revenue expenditures on health have declined both as a proportion to the GDP as well as percent of total public spending, and within this reduced expenditure allocative inefficiencies have increased especially after the 5th Pay Commission.

The above has further reduced the credibility and acceptability of the public health system and one sees declining utilisation rates of public health facilities. On the other hand the dominance of the private health sector is increasing but with absolutely no regulation and minimum standards being followed. The medical profession pays no heed to self-regulation, ethics and has never looked at the possibility of an organised system of healthcare. Infact the profession is losing control to the corporate sector, which is now looking beyond the hospital sector at not only diagnostics but also consultant services and general practice. Such a scenario is bound to impact on costs and increases the burden of the patients. Such a situation is not good for 70% of the country's population that lives in poverty or at subsistence level.

The health status indicators amply testify to the poor state of health and healthcare in India. Our trajectory has been worse than the low-income country average over the years and we reached that level only in the nineties and we are stagnating at that level. Infant and child mortality rates which had shown substantial improvements in the eighties with stepped up public health investment under the MNP, especially in the rural areas, are presently not only stagnating but the rural – urban gap which was narrowing down is again getting wider (see Graphs 1 and 2). Apart from the rural-urban divide, there are issues in health and healthcare related to various vulnerable sections of the population and these are not only related to poverty and class concerns but also social concerns. Both access and health outcomes for women, dalits, adivasis, and other minority communities, show clear differentials in terms of adversities in health and healthcare (see Tables 1 and 2). NFHS-2 and NSSO 52nd Round data provide strong evidence for this.

The tables and graphs at the end of the text based on data from NFHS 2, clearly point out those vulnerable groups like Scheduled castes and tribes and those from lower socio-economic groups have health and nutritional outcomes which are two to four times worse for the lowest groups as compared to the highest groups. This is evidence of the reality that equity is grossly absent within our healthcare system. Further NSSO data on utilization of public and private healthcare facilities across classes and social groups also highlight the adversities in access the vulnerable groups have to face[3] .

Another growing concern in current times is the environment of conflict and hate in various parts of the country. The violence that we witness creates severe health impacts not only for the victims and survivors of the violence but also for the healthcare system, which often ends up discriminating against the vulnerable groups. This has happened across the northeastern states, in Kashmir, and in Mumbai and Gujarat during the recent communal riots in these places. The impact of communal hate during the Gujarat carnage is fairly well documented.[4]

Impact of the Changing Political Economy

While the existing situation is very dismal, the changing political economy does not show too much promise of change for the betterment of health and healthcare; unless of course there is a radical transformation in the political commitment. For this to take place the support of civil society pressures and demands for a transformation of the healthcare dispensation will be needed.

The changing political economy demands reduced state participation in the economic sphere both in terms of policy and intervention. But at the same time the new political economy has failed to strengthen the welfare role of the state. Under SAP and other related measures, the states intervention in the economy declined but so have Tax:GDP ratios and consequently investments, expenditures and interests in the social sectors. This trajectory of growth has worsened the situation for the poor and subsistent population of the country.

One very clear impact is declining state investments in the health sector. With rising debt burdens of the state, the social sectors are the first to receive the axe. There has been a declining trend since 1991 in social sector expenditures, especially by the Central government and this is best reflected in compression of grants to the states for social sector expenditures. Health care expenditures too have been affected both in quantitative terms (declining reai expenditures) and qualitative terms (increasing proportion of establishment costs and declining proportion on medicines, equipment, maintenance and new investments)[5].

Another very striking impact is the rapidly rising cost of medicines. With a large dependence on the private health sector even by the poor this has meant extreme hardship. With the drug price control virtually on its way out and with India having signed the WTO treaty on IPR we are moving closer to international prices of drugs. The combined effect of the above facts makes a deadly mixture that results in reduced access of the poor to health care. We have seen above the historical dominance of the private health care sector in India in provision of ambulatory care and rising costs could spell disaster for the poor given the fact that the State is gradually reducing its responsibilities in provision of health care. Since the poor too have been active users of private health care their dependence on it makes the case for "right to health care" becoming a political agenda a distant dream.

At the global level World Bank is propagating selective care for selected (targeted) populations under the public domain. The

WHO too has dropped its Health For All commitment and fallen in line with the World Bank thinking. This global pressure on the Indian State is evident through its policies of focusing on selective services, for instance RCH and AIDS receive overriding support over primary health care or basic referral services.

Another trend that further reduces access is the increased corporate control of health care. New medical technologies have helped complete the commodification of health care and this has attracted increased interest of the corporate sector, which has jumped into the health care business in a very big way. The State has nurtured the private sector over the years and corporatisation is only a logical progression of the State's vision of health care provision. Some examples:

- medical education is almost wholly state financed (though in the last decade private medical education has expanded rapidly) and its major beneficiary is the doctor who sets up private practice after his/her training.
- the government has provided concessions and subsidies to private medical professionals and hospitals to set up private practice and hospitals. It provided incentives, tax holidays, and subsidies to private pharmaceutical and medical equipment industry. It manufactured and supplied raw materials (bulk drugs) to private formulation units at subsidised rate/low cost. It allowed exemptions in taxes and duties in importing medical equipment and drugs, especially the highly expensive new medical technologies.
- the government has allowed the highly profitable private hospital sector to function as trusts which are exempt from taxes. Hence they don't contribute to the state exchequer even when they charge patients exorbitantly.
- construction of public hospitals and health centres are generally contracted out to the private sector. The latter makes a lot of money but a large part of the infrastructure thus created, especially in rural areas is inadequately provided hence cannot meet the health care demands of the people.

- medical and pharmaceutical research and development is largely carried out in public institutions but the major beneficiary is the private sector. Development of drugs, medical and surgical techniques etc. are pioneered in public institutions but commercialisation, marketing and profit appropriation is left with the private sector. Many private practitioners are also given honorary positions in public hospitals which they use openly to promote their personal interests.

In the late seventies and the first half of the eighties the Central government supported a massive expansion of the rural health infrastructure through the Minimum Needs Program. This helped states mainstream modern health care in the rural areas. Since then the Central government has abdicated its responsibility. Their only interest remains supporting medical care in Delhi and some union territories and promoting aggressively family planning in the rest of the country, especially the villages. The little support it gives for public health programs like tuberculosis, AIDS, leprosy, blindness control etc. are increasingly coming from international borrowings[6] and serving the agenda of international agencies like World Bank and the USAID. Capital expenditures have almost disappeared and grant in aid to states, which largely supports preventive care programs like the National Disease Control Programs, is also declining as a ratio within the Central health budget. This is clearly an indication that the Central government is cutting back expenditures in the health sector.

The situation of the state governments is not very different from that of the central government. One sees the same declining trends. The state government's expenditures too are mostly on urban health care – teaching hospitals, district hospitals and health administration – and on family planning in the rural areas. One sees a drastic decline of expenditures by state governments on medical care, part of which is absorbed by family planning. Capital expenditures, which were low in the seventies and eighties when the big rural infrastructure expansion took place under the Minimum Needs Program (largely supported by the Centre), also show a declining trend. The fifth pay commission has put a further strain on resources and further worsened the allocative inefficiencies[7].

Given the bad shape in which the public health sector is "health sector reforms" is the new keyword. At one level the World Bank is pushing processes based on the idea referred to earlier (selective care for selected groups) and at another level the existing health care situation in the country is crying for reforms of various kinds.

The various reforms underway presently, largely under the tutoring of World Bank and its allies, are not reforming the system in the sense of bringing about structural changes but only tampering with it and pushing through ideas like user charges, privatisation, and new public management systems etc. Further, other global initiatives like the Millennium Development Goals (MDGs) also serve the same purpose of selective and targeted programming which is a clear move away from the spirit of other progressive international initiatives like International Covenant for Economic Social and Cultural Rights, Health for All, Agenda 21, ICPD Program of Action, Beijing Platform etc.

At another level a number of macro changes, like opening up of the insurance sector to private capital and allowing MNCs to set up health care facilities, promoting 'medical tourism' will bring about its own impact by integrating India's health care services with the world market, and this would spell further disaster for the poor, what with the State too reducing its role in the provision of health care. In this context the MDGs have become a route for the Indian state to move away form a comprehensive and universal approach to health and healthcare and hence the MDGs need to be reviewed within that context.

The MDG Health Goals and Health Inequity

In September 2000, 189 nations ratified the *United Nations Millennium Declaration*[8], an ambitious document affirming the right of every human being to development and laying out a path toward freedom from want for every woman, man, and child. To ensure that progress towards this end be measurable, representatives of

UN agencies and other international organizations defined a set of goals, targets, and indicators for combating poverty, hunger, disease, illiteracy, environmental degradation and discrimination against women. These measures, collectively known as the *Millennium Development Goals* (MDGs), have become a prime focus of development work throughout the globe — a gold standard to which programs aspire, and by which they measure their work[9].

This targeted approach adopted by the UN may have provided a focus to deal with the very pressing issues listed out in the MDGs but the latter has also helped shift the focus away from the Alma Ata Declaration and the ICESCR provisions. This change in focus is critical because it implies a paradigm shift in the UN agenda and strategy. If the UN is not able to stand by HFA and ICESCR then for the developing countries, including India, it becomes even more difficult to sustain the rights based approach. This must be viewed in the context of the right to health and healthcare campaign both globally and in India steered by the Peoples' Health Movement (Jan Swasthya Abhiyan in India). If the State abdicates its commitment to ICESCR and HFA and only focuses on MDGs (see Box 1) then there is every likelihood that not only the poor and underprivileged but also the middle classes will have further difficulties in accessing healthcare.

Box 1: MDG Health Goals, Targets and Indicators

Targets 1.	*Indicators for Monitoring Progress* 2.
Goal 4: Rduce child mortality	
Target 5: Reduce by two-thirds, between 1990 and 2015, the under five mortality rate	13. Under-five mortality rate 14. Infant mortality rate 15. Proportion of 1 year-old children against measles
Goal 5: Improve maternal health	
Target 6: Reduce by three-quarters,	16. Maternal mortality ratio

(Cond)

(Contd. Box 1)

1.	*2.*
between 1990 and 2015, the maternal mortality ratio.	17. Proportion of births attended by skilled health personnel
Goal 6: Combat HIV / AIDS, malaria and other diseases	
Target 7: Have halted by 2015 and begun to reverse the spread of HIV / AIDS	18. HIV prevalence among 15-24 year old pregnant women 19. Condom use rate of the contraceptive prevalence rate(a) 20. Number of children orphaned by HIV / AIDS (b)
Target 8: Have halted by 2015 and begun to reversee the incidence of malaria and other major diseases	21. Prevalence and death rates associated with malaria 22. Proportion of population in malaria risk areas using effective malaria prevention and treatment measures (c) 23. Prevalence and death rates associated with tuberculosis directly observed treatment short course (DOTS) 24. Proportion of tuberculosis cases detected and cured under

(a) Amongst contraceptive methods, only condoms are effective in preventing HIV transmission. The contraceptive prevalence rate is also useful in tracking progress in other health, gender and poverty goals. Because the condom use rate is only measured amongst women in union, it will be supplemented by an indicator on condom use in high risk situations. These indicators will be augmented with an indicator of knowledge and misconceptions regarding HIV/ AIDS by 15-24 year-olds (UNICEF – WHO).

(b) To be measured by the ratio of proportion of orphans to non-orphans aged 10-14 who are attending school.

(c) Prevention to be measured by the % of under 5s sleeping under insecticide treated bednets; treatment to be measured by % of under 5s who are appropriately treated.

Source: WHO, 2003: *op. cit.*

The Health MDGs are very narrow, focusing only on maternal and child health, contraception and selective disease surveillance and their monitoring indicators are largely demographic. And what is intriguing is the fact that these are precisely the goals of India's primary health program, especially for rural areas. So the focus on MDGS is old hat for India's health policy makers and planners. Thus for the Ministries of Health in India the MDGs are godsend as they coincide with their 2002 National Health Policy (NHP) of limiting the State's role in healthcare, providing them an opportunity to debunk the goals of the 1982 NHP of comprehensive universal primary healthcare. This is very clear evidence that India follows the global agenda set in Washington or Geneva – post 1978/1979, that is HFA and ICESCR, India adopted a NHP which emphasized comprehensive universal primary healthcare and post 2000 MDGs India adopts a NHP that follows the diluted agenda of MDGs!

It's been five years since the MDGs but we have miserably failed to make any significant improvements in the goals mandated under the MDGs. Whether it is child mortality, maternal mortality or diseases like malaria, tuberculosis, HIV/AIDS or for that matter diarrhoeal diseases or vaccine preventable diseases, we have not made significant improvements even when compared to the early nineties. The goals of the 1982 NHP on many of these indicators that were to be achieved by the year 2000 are still unachieved - IMR was to be brought down to under 60, MMR to under 200 and births attended by skilled persons and antenatal care to universal coverage[10]. The Indian State has undertaken too much target practice and yet is far away from the bulls-eye! There is all probability that the MDG targets will meet the same fate. Below we review the current status of the Health MDGs:

1. *Infant and child mortality rates*: India's infant and under-5 mortality rates are amongst the highest in the world. India's child

mortality rate of 87 is higher than even its poor neighbours Bangladesh (69), Bhutan (85) and Nepal (82)[11]. Infant mortality rates too are more adverse for India. Further, it is observed that the decline of IMR and U-5 had peaked 25% and 35%, respectively, (see Graph 2) for the decade 1981-1991 when with NHP-1982 in place India's public health investments and expenditures also peaked to 1.4% of GDP[12]. Subsequently, with economic reforms and SAP we see a major slowing down in decline of IMR and U-5 mortality.

Further the comparative picture of IMR trends over the last 40 years (see Graph 1) shows that India continues to remain in the bottom quartile of low income countries even at the turn of the millennium, with urban India also showing stagnation as reflected in the reducing gap of urban India with low income countries' average. Within India the differentials in child mortality due to regional, gender, class and social groups continue to be wide (see Table 1). IMR, U-5 and NNMR all show large variance across different groups thus providing evidence that disparities are widespread and the MDG strategy is not working.

2.Access to Maternal and Child Health Services: As part of the primary healthcare program in India maternal and child health services are an important feature and these are linked intimately with the Health MDGs. Since they form the core of the primary healthcare program one would have expected that access to these services would be nearly universal. But recent national data from the NFHS 2nd Round shows that there are significant variances in access depending on social geography, gender, class and social groups (dalits. adivasis, OBC etc.). Given this situation it is no surprise that India's maternal mortality rate got worse between the two rounds of NFHS increasing from 424 per 100,000 live births in 1992-93 (rural 434 and urban 385) to 540 in 1998-99 (rural 619 and urban 267)[13]. And the most recent estimates put MMR in India at 408 with India accounting for one-fifth of all maternal deaths in the world and this places India in the bottom quartile in the world[14].

Maternal health services include antenatal check ups, tetanus- toxoid and iron-folic acid prophylaxis, safe delivery (institutional or attended by health professional), nutritional supplementation and contraception. This package of services is mandated by health policy and the RCH and ICDS programs and now also having the support of the MDGs but yet we find (see Table 1 and 2) that all these services suffer widespread disparities in access due to regional, class or social status. Thus scheduled castes, adivasis, low standard of living and rural populations have grossly low levels of access as compared to better off sections and urban population.

The situation of child health services like immunization for vaccine preventable diseases and access to nutritional supplements, and their nutritional status suffers a similar fate with severe disparities across caste groups, gender, classes and regions. (see Table 1 and 2)

3. *HIV/AIDS, Malaria, Tuberculosis etc.:* While these diseases are extremely important and contribute to very high morbidity and mortality in India, the approach through vertical programs to fight these and other diseases has miserably failed. Tuberculosis and Malaria are only getting worse. We have not been able to control even diarrhoeal diseases. NFHS–2 data in Graph 3 shows that class disparities with respect to some selected diseases are huge. This disease specific strategy has not worked for the last 55 years and there is no reason why under MDGs it will work. The approach to HIV/AIDS follows the same trajectory wherein the focus is on prevention and the curative dimension is completely ignored. Healthcare has to adopt a comprehensive and universal access approach if the MDG goals have to be achieved. The experience of all countries that achieved the MDG targets in the seventies and eighties and some in the nineties is very clear – near universal access to comprehensive basic health services, larger role of public financing in healthcare and a regulated healthcare delivery system.

Thus what emerges clearly from assessment of this data is that this focused approach of selected goals under the MDG strategy is not going to work until we make the transition from policy mandate to healthcare as a right.

Conclusions

The foregoing analysis gives ample evidence of the failure of public health in India and if we continue in the same breath then we will soon see the end of public health and equity. How do we remedy this scenario? The political economy of health in India is increasingly following the market route with very rapid expansion of the private health sector in India as well as privatization through user fees and other indirect means of the little public health sector which remains. Even highly developed market economies like Europe, Canada, Japan, Australia and some of the emerging economies like South Korea, Malaysia, Brazil etc. have healthcare systems which are predominantly publicly financed and the market plays a very limited role in healthcare in these countries. Their health systems are organized and regulated and supported through pooling of resources via tax revenues, social or national insurance and payroll deductions for social security. This is the only route to universal access for healthcare and to achieve the goals which MDGs have set. And these issues are primarily governance issues. We have no choice but to restructure the political economy of health in India.

India has an opportunity to shift gears. First there is the decentralization mandate via Panchayat Raj. The constitution of India has made health care services largely a responsibility of state governments but has left enough maneuverability for the Centre since a large number of items are listed in the concurrent list. And this the Centre has used adequately to expand its sphere of control over the health sector. In recent years efforts to decentralize governance has resulted in many functions being transferred to the district level under the Panchayat Raj Acts in various states. Under the health sector a very large domain has been suggested for local authorities to take over. However it must be noted that as yet the implementation of these various provisions is very poor, especially since fiscal decentralization has not taken place.

Provision of healthcare services is indeed amenable to decentralization if there is adequate political will and faith in local communities to take their own decisions. To do this we have to move out of the framework of national programs and a program based approach. Instead the approach as suggested by the 1982 National Health Policy of universal comprehensive healthcare is what we need to adopt in provisioning of healthcare services. Today we do have an opportunity to plan differently. The Central government is in the process of setting up a National Rural Health Mission and a lot of discussion and debate is taking place. The unfortunate part of this mission approach is that *babus* from the Centre, who are far removed from the grassroots reality, are trying to shape this mission from their perspective rather than that from where the services will be located. So this needs to be changed.

In order to change this, the first thing we need to do when we think "decentralization" is not to romanticize it. Decentralization should not become a holy cow and we go to the other extreme and say that "people's health in peoples hands". This is not decentralization but abdication of responsibility. Provision of healthcare has a logic and scale of its own and hence the basic unit of healthcare provision need not coincide with the administrative / revenue unit. The health district must be independent of the administrative units. Secondly we have to keep in mind that healthcare access, especially ambulatory care has to be in easy local reach. This is a very critical issue for rural areas. Unlike urban areas which have high density of population, rural communities are scattered and hence provision of clinical services at very close distance in most rural areas becomes problematic and hence innovative approaches are needed. It is here that the community health model has a role to play but again we must be pragmatic and not romanticize community health as it is unfortunately being done. Community health workers within compact habitats are important first contact persons for health promotion and limited curative care. They are critical link workers within communities where access to the first clinical or epidemiological unit is relatively remote.

In terms of scale of operations a clinical unit at 5000 population level and an epidemiological unit at 10,000 population level seems the best option in planning decentralized health services. This means that a PHC at 10,000 population level with two doctors (for clinical services, and not necessarily employed by the state) and one Public Health Nurse (for the epidemiological unit) along with the required paramedical and support staff becomes the primary unit for health planning and provisioning. Five to ten such units, depending on population density, would form the health district (between 50,000- 100,000 population) which would have the equivalent of the Community Health Centre and this should be governed by a committee (Standing Health Committee) of the Panchayat members of that population unit, who should employ/contract the providers and monitor and regulate them. This committee, with secretarial/technical support from the providers, would be the planning unit for the health district and control the health resources which should be allocated to them on a per capita basis by the state government from their health budget. This comprehensive decentralized unit if optimally provided should take care of 90% of healthcare needs of the population and this would in turn help decongest the district and tertiary hospitals which would become primarily referral centres. The community under each such unit would have to be enrolled (like the NHS in Britain) with the unit and it would be the unit's responsibility to look after their members' healthcare needs, including referral demands for higher level care. This would then become a rights based entitlement for the community and the unit would be accountable to it to deliver, failing which it would be violation of their rights. Of course this system will have to be mandated by legislation and provided adequate resources which estimates show would not exceed the commitment of 2 to 3% of GDP as promised in the Common Minimum Program of the present coalition government at the Centre.

Such a decentralization strategy cannot be done by political (policy) action alone but requires concerted effort at reorienting and organizing the present unregulated healthcare system into an organized entity which is governed by a well defined regulatory mechanism as well as is socially audited. Such a strategy will also require fiscal and planning autonomy to local governments who should be given the resources on a per capita basis and be left alone to decide how the resources are best used for their community's welfare.

The second opportunity is a larger public interest in healthcare as a right as is evidenced through the increasing influence of the *Jan Swasthya Abhiyan* (Peoples Health Movement). The JSA since the last two years has been campaigning for the right to health and healthcare and has increasingly involved public agencies like the National Human Rights Commission (NHRC) in facilitating processes that help move closer towards the goal of right to healthcare. Similarly the JSA has decided to monitor the implementation of the NHRM and use it as an opportunity to steer it towards a rights based direction.

To conclude it is important to reemphasize that healthcare is a public or social good and cannot be left to the vagaries of the market. To realize its social or public value it has to be organized and regulated using both public and private resources for social benefit. Further, healthcare cannot be planned at the central or state level but has to be decentralized at an appropriate community level as discussed above. The role of the centre and state is to strategize such actions, mobilize and disburse resources and monitor its outcomes. The planning and provision functions are best left to local governance under community vigilance. Such is the global experience where healthcare is universally accessible with equity. Why should it be different in India?

Graph 1: IMR Trends in India and Low-income Countries 1960-1995

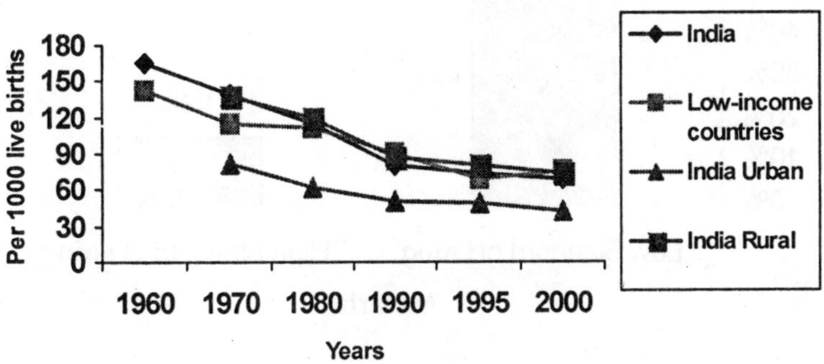

Graph 2: Decline in Rate of IMR and U-5 Mortality 1971-2001

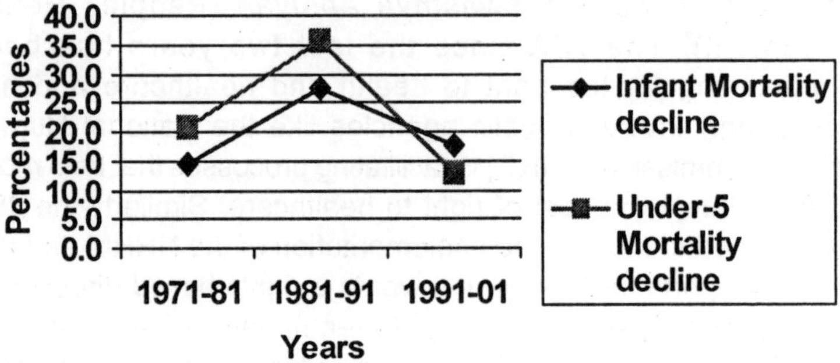

Source for Graphs 1 and 2: SRS Bulletins and UNDP HDRs

Graph 3: Prevalence of Malaria and Tuberculosis across Classes

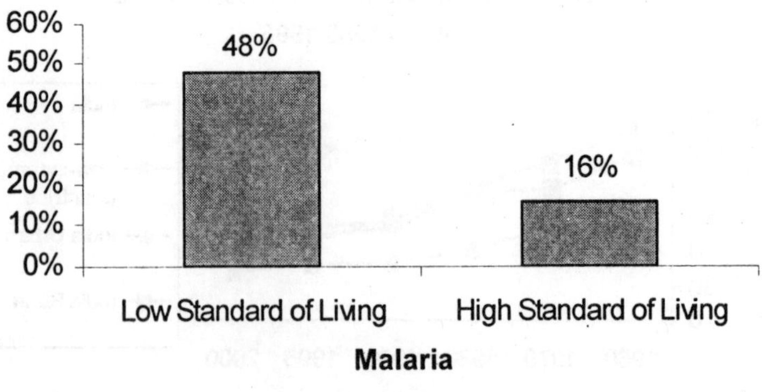

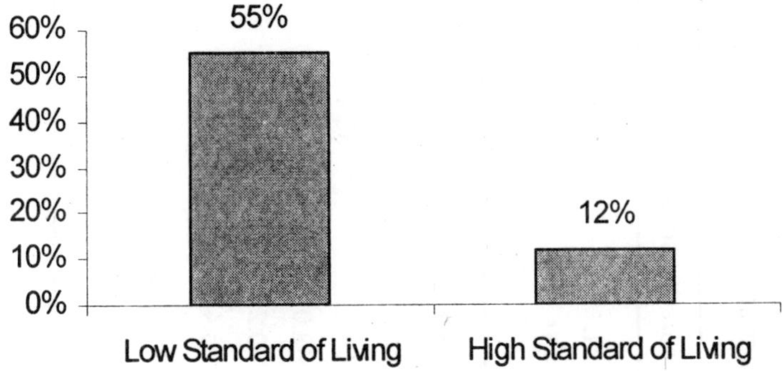

Tuberculosis

Source for Graph3: NFHS-1998, 2000: *op.cit.*

Table 1
Selected Health Outcomes Across Social Classes

Social Group	*No*	*TFR ANC*	*IMR*	*U-5 Mortality V*	*Completed Immunisat n*	*Delivery by Doctor*
Low	45.1	3.37	88.8	130.0	30.4	15.8
Medium	32.8	2.85	70.3	94.6	43.2	31.1
High	12.4	2.10	42.7	51.5	64.7	60.9
All	34.0	2.85	73.0	101.4	42.0	30.3
SC	38.2	3.15	83.0	119.3	40.2	23.5
ST	43.1	3.06	84.2	126.6	26.4	14.5
OBC	34.8	2.83	76.0	103.1	43.0	31.8
Other	27.9	2.66	61.8	82.6	46.8	37.3

Source: NFHS-1998, 2000: *op.cit.*

Table 2

Selected Nutritional Outcomes Across Social Classes

	Percent Women 15-49			*Children< 3 years % below-3SD*		
Social Group	Below 145	Below BMI 18.5 kg/m ^{2}	Any Anemia	Wt. For Age	Ht. For Age	Wt. For Height
Low	45.1	3.37	88.8	130.0	30.4	15.8
Medium	32.8	2.85	70.3	94.6	43.2	31.1
High	12.4	2.10	42.7	51.5	64.7	60.9
All	34.0	2.85	73.0	101.4	42.0	30.3
SC	38.2	3.15	83.0	119.3	40.2	23.5
ST	43.1	3.06	84.2	126.6	26.4	14.5
OBC	34.8	2.83	76.0	103.1	43.0	31.8
Other	27.9	2.66	61.8	82.6	46.8	37.3

Source: NFHS-1998, 2000: op.cit.

Annex 1
Healthcare Development in India 1951-2004

		1951	*1961*	*1971*	*1981*	*1991*	*1996*	*1997*	*2001-02*	*Latest**
1. 2.	3.	4.	5.	6.	7.	8.	9.	10.	11.	12.
1. Hospitals*	Total	2694	3054	3862	6805	11174	15170	15188	18436	22000
	%Rural	39	34	32	27		34	34	30	30
	%Private				43	57	68	68	62	75
2. Hospital& dispensary beds*	Total	11700	229634	348655	504538	806409	892738	896767	914543	1500000
	% Rural	23	22	21	17		23	23	21	21
	% Private				28	32	37	37	35	50
3. Dispensaries*		6600	9406	12180	16745	27431	25653	25670	22291	
	% Rural	79	80	78	69		41	40	50	
	% Private				13	60	57	56	54	
4. PHCs		725	2695	5131	5568	22243	21917	22446	22842	23500
5. Sub-centres				27929	51192	131098	134931	136379	137311	140000

(Contd.)

(Contd. Annex 1)

1. 2.	3.	4.	5.	6.	7.	8.	9.	10.	11.	12.
6. Doctors	Allopaths	60840	83070	153000	266140	393640	462745	496941	605840	660000
	All systems	156000	184606	450000	665340	920000		1080173	1297310	1430000
7. Nurses		16550	35584	80620	150399	311235	565700	607376	805827	880000
8. Medical colleges	Allopathy	30	60	98	111	128	165	165	189	195
9. Out turn	Graduates	1600	3400	10400	12170	13934				20000
	Postgraduates		397	1396	3833	3139		3656		6000
10. Pharmaceutical Production	Rs. in billion	0.2	0.8	3	14.3	38.4	91.3	104.9	220	280
11. Health outcomes	IMR/000	134	146	138	110	80	72	71	66	65
	CBR/000	41.7	41.2	37.2	33.9	29.5	27	27	25	24
	CDR/000	22.8	19	15	12.5	9.8	9	8.9	8.1	8

(Contd.)

(Contd. Annex 1)

1. 2.	3.	4.	5.	6.	7.	8.	9.	10.	11.	12.
Life Expectancy	years	32.08	41.22	45.55	54.4	59.4	62.4	63.5	64.8	65
Births attended by Trained Practitioners	Percent				18.5	21.9	28.5			
12. Health Expenditure Rs. Billion	Public CSO Private	0.22	1.08 2.05	3.35 6.18	12.86 29.70	50.78 82.61	101.65 329.00	113.13 373.41	211 1100	249 1464
Health Expenditure as percent of GDP	Public Private CSO	0.25	0.71 1.34	0.84 1.56	1.05 2.43	0.92 1.73	0.91 2.95	0.88 3.00	0.89 5.32	0.91 5.40
Health Expenditute as % to Govt Total	Public	2.69	5.13	3.84	3.29	2.88	2.98	2.94	2.72	2.60

*Data on hospitals, dispensaries and beds pertaining to the private sector is grossly under reported and figures for 2001-02 for public facilities also suffers from under-reporting as a number of states do not send uptodate information. Thus the actual figures should be much higher, and especially so for the private sector

**Latest years – rounded figures are estimates by author and figures pertain to years 2003/2004

Sources : Health Statistics / Information of India, CBHI, GOI, various years; Census of India Economic Tables, 1961, 1971, 1981, GOI; OPPI Bulletins and Annual reports of Min. of Chemicals and Fertilisers for data on Pharmaceutical Production; Finance Accounts of Central and State Governments, various years for public expenditures; National Accounts Statistics, CSO, GOI, various years for private expenditures; Statistical Abstract of India, GOI, various years; Sample Registration System - Statistical Reports, various years.

Note: This paper is a modified version of an earlier paper titled **"Health MDGs – End of Public Health and Equity"** prepared as a background paper for the "Wada Na Todo" Campaign in India

Refereces

1.Tulasidhar V, 1993: Structural Adjustment Program - Its Impact on the Health Sector, NIPFP, Delhi.

2.See Nandraj, Sunil and Ravi Duggal, 1996 : Physical Standards in the Private Health Sector, Radical Journal of Health (New Series) II-2/3

3.NSSO (1998): Report No 441 on Morbidity and Treatment of Ailments

4.Medico Friend Circle, 2002: Carnage in Gujarat – A Public Health Crisis, mfc, Mumbai.

5.Duggal, Ravi, 2005: Public Health Expenditures, Investment and Financing Under the Shadow of a Growing Private Sector, in Gangolli, Leena, Ravi Duggal and Abhay Shukla (eds): Review of Healthcare in India, CEHAT, Mumbai

6.Gupta, D and A Gumber, 2002: External Assistance to the Health Sector and its Contributions – Problems and Prognosis, ICRIER, New Delhi

7 Duggal, Ravi, 2005 :*op. cit.*

8.www.un.org/documents/ga/res/55/a55r002.pdf

9.WHO, 2003: Engendering the MDGs on Health, Department of Gender and Women's Health,World Health Organization, Geneva

10.MoHFW, 1983 : National Health Policy, Govt. of India, Ministry of Health & Family Welfare, New Delhi

11. http://www.who.int/whr/2005/annex/annexe1_en.pdf accessed July 15th 2005

12.Duggal, Ravi, 2005: *op. cit.*

13.NFHS-1998, 2000: National Family Health Survey –2: India, IIPS, Mumbai

14.http://www.who.int/whr/2005/annex/annexe1_en.pdf accessed July 15th 2005

15

A Need to Re-emphasize the Role of Public Healthcare in India

Manisha Karne

Introduction

A single factor that will play an important role in achieving the Millennium Development Goals no doubt is infrastructure[1]. Accessibility of better infrastructure facilities creates an environment conducive for achieving this MDGs. Public intervention in health, education and nutrition is crucial for increasing life expectancy and reducing infant mortality. This paper concentrates on public health infrastructure.

The health agenda is very much evidence in the Millennium Development Goals (henceforth MDGs) as it is explicit in three of the eight goals. Improved health contributes to poverty alleviation and at the same time sustainable improvement of health mainly depends on successful poverty alleviation. The MDGs 4 and 5 aims at Maternal and Child health. The health of mothers and children is a priority that emerged long before the 1990s but in the last decade the health of mothers and children was transformed from a purely domestic concern into a public health priority with corresponding responsibilities for the state and there has been global focus on the Millennium Development Goals.

The nature of the priority status of maternal and child health (henceforth MCH) has changed overtime. Mothers and children were previously thought of as targets for well- intentioned programmes, they now increasingly claim the right to access quality care as an entitled guaranteed by the state. In doing so, they have transformed maternal and child health from a technical concern into a moral and political imperative. (World Health report, 2005)

At the global level it was stressed that mothers and children are vulnerable groups and therefore priority targets for public health action[2]. The notion of mothers and children as vulnerable groups was also central to the primary health care movement launched at Alma- Ata (now Almaty, Kazakhstan) in 1978. This paper examines important issues of health infrastructure in India with a focus on its impact on important health indicators relevant to Millennium development goals four and five.

Some Issues of Healthcare Services in India

Universal access to safe drinking water, health and education are must for any society to progress, which can also be considered as the basic requirements of the people.But even after five and half decades of development planning, India have been unable to ensure a decent living for a large number of people in this country. Despite various development plans, lack of or inadequate basic infrastructure, both social and physical, continues to remain a major constraint to progress in numerous parts of our country.

Traditionally, State intervention has occurred within a centralized framework especially in regard to infrastructure provision in sectors such as transport, power, health etc. The traditional approach to infrastructure has been based on detailed government intervention in the sector, apparently to protect public interest. In other words, direct state provision has been the norm and state ownership and state monopolies always seem to have played a dominant role in the provision of infrastructure and services. The arguments for active state intervention and participation have been as follows

- The recognition of the role of infrastructure in the larger social context.

- The experience with problems relating to supply technology which often require a highly activist response by Government, and
- A belief that markets may fail to provide the services on efficiency and equity grounds.

On the above arguments Public health is considered as a public good where everybody benefits from it but no body is individually ready to pay. Government is believed to be in the best position to finance (through tax) and conduct public health programme through primary network. With the help of a network of primary and community health care centers (PHCs and CHCs), spread all over the country, India has been able to provide some access to health services to the poor in Urban as well as rural areas. Though there has been some success in this sector the health status in India is not very satisfactory which is indicated in the following table.

Table1
Selected Healthcare Indicators in India

Health Facilities	
(a) Population per hospital	61881
(b) Population per bed	1498
(c) Registered doctors per lakh population	51.8
Fertility and Mortality indicators	
(a) Crude Birth Rate	24.8
(b) Total Fertility Rate[3]	2.85
(c) Crude Death rate	9.7
(d) Infant Mortality rate[4]	67.6
Life expectancy at birth	
Males	60.1
Females	61.4

Source: Human Development report, 2002

Though we have made progress towards the MDGs in maternal and child health, success is over shadowed by the persistence of an unacceptably high mortality rate as compared to the developed countries, increasing inequality in maternal and child health and access to health care in especially in the rural areas. There are failures in many areas. For instance, compared to other developing countries government health care in India is low. This can be seen in the following table.

Table 2
Government Health Care as % of GDP

Country	%
Brazil	3.2
Korea	1.8
Thailand	1.2
China	0.7
India	0.9

Source: World Health Report, 2005.

The public component of health care funding is focused on improving health care besides providing health care for most of the country's population. It is this index that reflects the commitment that a nation has to the improvement in the health of the people. In developed countries such as Canada, France, Australia, Denmark and Japan the health expenditure as % of GDP is 8 to 10%. Taking the health expenditure as a % of GDP, India has the smallest commitment to the health of its people, it was 1.3% of GDP in 1993 and has increased to 6.1% of GDP. This can be seen in the following table 3.

On current trends, most regions in India will fall short of the health related goals, including reduced child and maternal mortality. As it can be seen in the above table the general Govt. Expenditure on Health as % of total Govt. Expenditure has declined where as the out- of –pocket expenditure as a % of private expenditure on health is substantial. This indicates there is an increasing dependence on the private health care facilities. Decline in public spending can have adverse consequences on health care services in India. Though funding is a necessary but not a sufficient condition for delivery of health services to the poor, against the background of large-scale poverty in the country, it is believed that public sector has to play a crucial role in provision and delivery of health infrastructure.

Table 3
Measured Levels of Expenditure on Health, 1998-2002

Description	*1998*	*1999*	*2000*	*2001*	*2002*
Total Expenditure on Health as % of GDP	5.2	5.7	6.3	6.1	6.1
General Govt. Expenditure on Health as % of Total Expenditure on Health	26.5	23.6	20.9	20.7	21.3
Private Govt. Expenditure on Health as % of Total Govt. Expenditure	73.5	76.4	79.1	79.3	78.7
General Govt. Expenditure on Health as % of Total Govt. Expenditure	5.2	4.8	4.6	4.4	4.4
Social Security Expenditure on Health as % of General Govt. Expenditure on Health	3.8	4.2	4.1	4.1	4.6
Out of Pocket Expenditure as % of private Expenditure on Health	98.4	98.6	98.8	98.5	98.5

Source: World Health Report, 2005

Health care is delivered by public as well as private provider in India the health infrastructure provided by govt. is large but of a low quality especially in rural areas and is suffered from inequitable distribution in rural and urban area. The Private providers in rural as well as urban areas are fragmented and unregulated.

If the healthcare provision as % of total spending (2000-2001) is taken in to consideration, the Government and public employers has 37% share whereas the private providers' share is 63%.[5] About 75% of the health infrastructure is concentrated in the urban areas where just 27% of the population, thus indicating serious problem of regional disparities in distribution of health infrastructure. There is also poor coverage of population by public health infrastructure, which was reflected in the Mckinsey Report. The report indicated poor coverage where two third of health care spending is out of pocket. Lack of access to government facilities is not the only reason for choosing private health care; the reason for this preference is better availability and perceived quality of private care, which make Indians go to private provider for their health care.

Thus, describing the dismal performance in health Srinivasan (2005) said, "We need 7,415 community health centers per 100,000 population. We have less than half the number. Worse, at the healthcare facilities we do have, the basic staff is not in place. Only 38% of our primary health centres have all the required medical personnel. With the public health infrastructure in such a shambles, how can the poor count on government health centers?"

So this is the condition of public health care in India. Even during the last decade of economic reform process, started in 1991, state of infrastructure including health infrastructure has not been able to achieve desired levels of health indicators. There are many areas, e.g.. the social sectors, especially health where the governments' role will clearly have to increase. There are large gaps in the public and private sector and the public sector role needs to be re-emphasized. Private sector cannot be expected to step in significantly and play a major role in provision of health care, as there is a problem of ability to pay for a very large section of the people. Therefore the role of the state remains crucial in promoting these sectors, despite of observed state failures in these sectors.

Health Scenario in Maharashtra

To examine the conditions of public health at the state level this paper takes a case of Maharashtra. Promotion of maternal and child health has been one of the most important objectives of the Family Welfare Programme in India. The current Reproductive and Child Health Programme (RCH) was launched in October 1997. Reduction of maternal mortality is an important goal. The Maternal Health Programme, which is a component of the Reproductive and Child Health Programme, aims at reducing maternal mortality to less than 100 by the 2010. Investment in reproductive health, including family planning and access to contraceptives are crucial components of investments in disease control, which is likely to translate into reduced fertility for women. This paper gives focus on Total Fertility Rate (henceforth TFR) and Infant mortality rate as an indicator of improvement in maternal and child health condition to analyze the health condition in Maharashtra. A comparison of Total Fertility Rate in Maharashtra with other selected States is given in the following table.

Table 4
IMR, Comparison of Selected States (1998— 1999)

States	*TFR*
Maharashtra	2.52
Kerala	1.96
Karnataka	2.13
Tamil Nadu	2.19
Andhra Pradesh	2.25

Source: Human Development Report, Maharashtra 2002.

Table 5
IMR in Maharashtra (1971- 1999)

Year	*Total*	*Rural*	*Urban*
1971*	101	109	81
1981*	75	84	52
1991*	59	67	41
1999	48	58	31
2002(p)	45	52	34

Percent Decline

Year	*Total*	*Rural*	*Urban*
1971-81	25.7	22.9	35.8
1981-91	21.3	20.2	21.2
1991-99	18.6	13.4	24.2
1971-1999	52.5	46.8	61.7

Source: Human Development Report, Maharashtra 2002.

*Based on moving averages of SRS rates of the given year, previous year and the following year.

Both the above tables indicate that the progress achieved by Maharashtra is reasonably good. But as compared to Kerala that has done impressively well, performance of Maharashtra is still to improve as shown in the table. no. 7.

Now we also need to examine the Maharashtra Government's commitment to healthcare with help of following measures. As observed at the national level in the earlier part of this paper, at the state level too there has been declining share of public healthcare facilities. This is indicated in the following table no. 8

Table 7
IMR, A comparison of Maharashtra with selected states (Year 1999)

State	*IMR*
Kerala	14
Maharashtra	48
Tamil Nadu	52
West Bengal	52
Andhra Pradesh	66

Source: Human Development Report, 2002

Table 8
Public Expenditure on Healthcare in Maharashtra (in Rs. Million)

	1980-81	*1985-86*	*1990-91*	*1995-1996*	*1998-99*
Total public health expenditure	1307	4782	4967	9061	11855
Per capita (Rs)	20.99	69.12	63.67	105.46	132.20
Percent to revenue expenditure	6.53	10.65	5.68	5.28	4.62
Percent of NSDP	0.80	1.70	0.80	0.60	0.60

Source: Finance and Revenue Accounts, Government of Maharashtra, various years,

Population and Income data used from Statistical Abstract of India.

Table 9
Utilization of Public and Private Facilities in Rural and Urban Maharashtra (1998-99)

	Impatient Care				*Outpatient Care*			
	Rural		*Urban*		*Rural*		*Urban*	
	Public	*Others*	*Public*	*Others*	*Public*	*Others*	*Public*	*Others*
NSSO 1986-87	43.6	56.4	46.2	53.8	26.7	73.7	25.07	5.0
NCAER 1993	30.5	69.5	58.8	41.2	43.8	56.2	32.5	67.5
NSSO 1995-96	31.2	68.8	31.8	68.2	16.0	82.0	17.0	81.9

Source : NSSO 1992; NSSO 1998a.

As indicated in the table no. 9 though the total public expenditure in absolute terms has increased over the above time period and there has been substantial increase in the per capita expenditure on health. But public expenditure as % of NSDP has declined in the post 90s.in Maharashtra. This is a matter of concern for us. Thus, at the state as well as national level public funding has been unsatisfactory.

Let us now examine the utilization of health care services in Mahararashtra taking in to consideration the public sector and the private sector.

From this analysis one can say that the governments' role is to ensure egalitarian arrangement in the public healthcare, as a large number of people cannot afford to pay for the health facilities. But in urban areas the choice is also determined by a desire for better quality of health facilities that creates a demand for private sector health care. But still the role of the public health care remains dominant.

This argument can be substantiated by quoting the study conducted in Mumbai (Dilip and Duggal, 2004) that indicates 65% respondents depend on public sector health facilities as the "cost is affordable", private hospital is opted by 45% of the respondents as it is the nearest facility that is available and 30% had no other option but to go to private hospitals. This study clearly indicates that if convenient public option were available preference for it would increase further. It is important to realize that a large section of the Indian population that we are concerned with has such low levels of income and standards of living that their ability to pay for healthcare is low. The people cannot afford to pay for the facilities and therefore the state steps in to provide certain goods, which need not necessarily provided by the public sector in the developed countries. So though there are state failures, state cannot withdraw.

The analysis of public healthcare at the national and state level reflects that the expenditure on health is inadequate and the share of public healthcare is a matter of great concern.

Strategies for Future

This analysis indicates state failure in provision of healthcare services to certain extent. As India has a problem of large scale poverty, the state intervention is not only essential, it needs to succeed. The role of state needs to be re-emphasized. We have to think about alternative institutional options under existing framework of state intervention. The most important organizational; reform that deserves to be implemented is to decentralize delivery of government health services. Government should continue to focus on public health with greater decentralization to increase effectiveness of the public healthcare programmes.

Decentralization i.e. the transfer of political and economic power to local levels of Government has been systematically promoted in economic literature. There is adequate literature on the failures arising from such a centralized framework of provision and of the possible replacement by a more decentralized structure[6]. If the arguments in favour of decentralization are examined in the context of infrastructure provision, it is realized that in most cases since benefits accrue mostly locally, decentralization is the most effective way to deliver these infrastructure services. The potential to improve the efficiency of public provision of infrastructure is one of the most important arguments made in support of decentralization. Decentralization is potentially the most important force for improving efficiency and responding to local health conditions and demands. in India the local authorities have been given authority to implement the national progrmmes but there is no financial authority. This kind of centralization of financial power is the major hurdle in making health services more responsive to local needs and local conditions. With passing of 74th Amendment to the Indian constitution, which envisages the involvement of NGOs and other civil societies organization in developmental activities a favourable environment has been already created for decentralization in India. Therefore, decentralization can be implemented for the potential benefits it will bring in healthcare services in India.[7]Thus, decentralization of financial powers, with appropriate audit requirements and performance monitoring can contribute to improving the quality of healthcare and strengthening the accountability of local institutions.

Secondly public health care achievements also depend on the political commitment of the Government. In countries like Thailand, Peru and Malawi this factor has contributed in achieving success in this area. Thus we too need strong and sustained government commitment, favourable policy environment, well targeted resources and more important a decentralized structure in which public health care is provided.

In conclusion, public sector should continue to play a major role, though in a decentralized framework in providing services such as family welfare programme, maternal care and control of infectious diseases which have wide spread positive externalities and thus important for achieving higher levels of important health indicators. However, the role of private sector also needs to be recognized and government has to take an additional responsibility to regulate and monitor the privately provided healthcare services to improve overall health condition in India.

Lastly to re-emphasize the rationale for the existence of state in this sector I would like to Quote (Jalan, 1996) "We must continue to hope that political and social activist will eventually succeed in their efforts to improve the working of our systems, and realize the ideal of Benthamite state which can promote the greatest good of the greatest number".

References

1. Dilip T.R., and Duggal Ravi (2004) : Unmet need for Public Healthcare Services in Mumbai, India, in Asia Pacific Journal, June 2004, Vol. 19(2).

2. Godbole M. (2002): Maharashtra Human Development: Some Issues, EPW October 19-25, 2002, Vol. 37 (42).

3. Government of Maharashtra (2002): Human Development Report, Maharashtra 2002, GOM, Mumbai.

4. Jalan Bimal (1996): India's Economics Policy, Preparing for the Twenty first Century.

5. Karande Alka (2005): City Perspectives in Child Mortality and Maternal Health, 2005, Paper presented at World Mayor's Conference, Cochin.

6. Karne M.A. (2004): Decentralisation of Infrastructural Services, Unpublished Doctoral Dissertation.

7. Mackinsy Report (2002): Health Care in India: The Road Ahead, The Report by CII- Mackinsy Company with support from Indian Health Care Federation.

8. Sen A.K. (1993): Economics of Life and Death, Scientific Americans, may 1993

9. World Bank (1991): Economics for Health Sector Analysis, Concepts and Cases, Economic Development Institute of the World Bank.

10. World Health Organisation (2005) : The World Health Report, 2005, Make Every Mother and Child Count, WHO, Bookwell Publishers.

11. World Health Organisation (2001): Macro Economics and Health: Investing in Health for Economic Development, Report of The Commission and Macro Economics and Health. WHO 2001.

Notes

1. Infrastructure is "the basic facilities, equipment, and installations needed for the functioning of a system" (Websters II, 1984).

2. WHO, 1948

3. Total Fertility Rate is defined as roughly the average number of children per women during her reproductive lifetime, calculated on the basis of the age-specific fertility rates in the country at any one time.

4. Infant mortality rate is the number of deaths under age one per 1000 live births.

5. Mackinsey Report, 2002.

6. Decentralization of Infrastructural services, Unpublished Doctoral dissertation by Manisha karne

7. Such efforts have been taken in Maharashtra and Kerala and these states are certainly performing better than other states in India.

16

Children Infected and Affected with HIV/AIDS

Rita Sonawat

It is very upsetting for a child to be indirectly aware of the presence of HIV/AIDS that doesn't understand at all, but at the same time it is affecting his life tremendously. It is hard to know from the appearance if someone has HIV/AIDS. People with this disease look the same as everyone else. This makes the child very curious to know why has the family environment become so gloomy leads to questioning the parents, but most the times the answers given by parents are unsatisfactory for the child. The reasons for this can be:

1. Parents themselves are not sure about their own problem.
2. How to disclose to the child about their status is not known
3. How much information to he given to the child is not known.
4. Parents are scared of the children's endless "whys".

Since the child's curiosity is not fulfilled at home the child then turns to the next most trusted person who many a times is the teacher, because children consider them as a safe haven for disclosure. This is the point at which the teacher's response is critical. This uninvited question now challenges the teacher to integrate the knowledge of HIV/AIDS Teachers are disturbed for not having correct knowledge, fearful about transmission and uncertain about what to do.

Facts about HIV/AIDS

HIV/AIDS is not just the problem of the individual alone, but also the problem of the entire family and community. It enters the family through one parent or member, thus affecting the health, social, psychological, physical, economic and spiritual well being of others. {Lears, 1995}.

HIV/AIDS is factually India's greatest health problem as well as a potent threat to economic and development prospects. AIDS can affect anyone. It crosses age, sexual, racial, ethnic, socio-economic boundaries. The problem in India is serious because of lack of awareness and knowledge about the killer disease, poverty and social stigma attached to HIV positive individuals. AIDS is a life threatening communicable viral disease that attacks the human immune system, leaving it unable to fight off infections. An increasing number of children are born with AIDS from mothers who have the disease. However, you may not know whether a child in a classroom has AIDS or is HIV (human immuno deficiency virus} positive. The child may not be aware that he or she has the disease. Because of discrimination against such youngsters, many states do not require parents to report this information to schools or childcare programs. AIDS is not passed to others by skin contact, biting, hugging, kissing or sharing the bath room. The greater concern is that a child who is HIV positive may pick up a disease from other children and be unable to fight it off AIDS in children was first described in 1982. By June 1998, 8280 children under the age of 13 had been reported. There are only 3 well defined routes through which HIV can be transmitted. They are:

1. Contact with contaminated blood/blood products and contaminated needles and syringes.
2. From an infected mother to her child during pregnancy and birth.

3. Sexual exposure: All forms of sexual intercourse carry a risk of HIV transmission. The virus can be transmitted by any penetrative sexual act in which infected semen, vaginal cervical secretion or blood is exchanged, but the precise level of risk associated with each type of sexual intercourse is not yet known.

Age Group	*Male*		*Female*		*Total*	
	Dec 2004	*March 2005*	*Dec 2004*	*March 2005*	*Dec 2004*	*March 2005*
0-14 years	2440	2651	1658	1836	4098	4487
15-29 years	19654	20655	12173	13211	31827	33866
30-49 years	420049	45024	12107	13215	54156	58239
>50 years	5416	5690	1481	1575	6897	7265
Total	69559	74020	27419	29837	96978	103857

Source: HIV/AIDS Surveillance in India, December 31, 2004 and March 31 2005, NACO.

Needs of the children: infected and affected

- Medical care
- Alternative care preferably community based
- Education
- Life skills and vocational training
- Protection from discrimination and an exploitative environment, and
- Their psychosocial needs have to be understood and appropriately addressed

Sensitivity towards an infected or affected child's behaviours and queries.

Infected means a person has a virus in his or her body, this causes medical illness and multiple psychosocial problems {emotional, social and educational} for the infected child. Affected means a family member or a friend has the virus or is sick with AIDS; this causes psychosocial problems for affected children, family members and friends. When talking about children's queries; the most important aspect of their queries is "Why:

- -Why me?
- -Why are my parents always i
- -Why don't they work?
- -Why don't we celebrate festivals?
- -Why are my parents not physically active?
- -Why don't they take me out?
- -Why our relatives don't visit us?
- -Why my siblings play when I can't?

An individual has to understand and accept the child as he or she is. One has to acknowledge the child most often than not as a" miniature adult'- a concept of the child which existed in the early 18 century and which was rejected later on, but which seems to be relevant in the context of children with AIDS.

A LOST CHILDHOOD
BECOMES MINIATURE ADULT

Caretaker
Decision maker
Handling finances
Supplement family income
Experience death at close quarter

Awareness of the problems faced by children in different contexts:

The pandemic is a "threat that puts un balance the future of nations" AIDS kills those on whom society realize to grow the crops, work in the mines and factories, nut the schools and hospitals and govern the countries It creates new pockets of poverty when parents and breadwinner's die and children leave school earlier to support remaining children.... Themselves affected and infected by HIV/ADS.

[A] Problems Faced at Home.

-Taking care of Parents
-Going to hospital
-Managing home front
-Managing money
-Ignoring own health
-Managing funeral arrangements
-Stress in caring for their sick parents, and trauma, and grief at their death
-Denial of their inheritance
-Economic hardships

[B] Problems Faced at Health Care Centers:

- Overcrowded hospitals
-Insensitive staff
-Lack of accommodation
-Lack of proper care
-Lack of supply of medicines
-Improper facilities in the hospitals
-Denial of admission and treatment by private hospitals to maintain "brand" image
-Doctors fear for their own health

[C] Problems Faced in Schools

Children who live in families infected and affected by HIV/ AIDS often experience losses, changes in their caretakers, an uncertainty about future; they often become behavior problems in school. Some of the problems they manifest are:
-Absenteeism
-Ridiculed by class mates
-Not spending time with friends

-Lack of interest in studies due to tiredness
-Non participation in extra-curricular activities
-Lack of awareness regarding school activities
-Not able to pay fees on time
-Inability to indulge in physical activities
-No field trips
-Change in altitudes of teaching and non-teaching staff
-Denial of admission leading to lack of educational opportunities

School aged children and youth are kept out of school sometimes by the family if they are needed at home to care for sick family members, or to work on fields or other income generating assignments [including prostitution]. Children drop out of school if their families or sponsors cannot afford school fees due to household income as a result of an AIDS death, or incapacitating HIV- related illness.

But it has to be remembered that everyone deserves compassion, care and kindness. No one deserves to be sick, stigmatized, discriminated against.

[D] Psychosocial Problems

The psychological, social and psychiatric sequelae of AIDS are modified by psychological factors that characterize the child's previous level of psychological adjustment and social support. Presence of a personality disorder is more apt to result in severe psychological symptoms and a maladaptive response to the stresses of illness. The availability of social support is especially crucial, due to need for both physical and social assistance.

AIDS is one of the many stigmatized diseases that result in multiple problems with diagnosis. The first set of difficulties is the physical and emotional problems stemming from the infection. Additionally, trauma often strikes the infected or the affected child when he or she realizes the facts. These attitudes result in discrimination in the varied aspects of the child's life.

Losses from AIDS are hence much more than death events. They profoundly influence the child's sense of identity and include losses of future expectations, personal history, emotional well being, security, self-esteem, hope, interest in life, assumptions about life, privacy etc.

The common psychological symptoms include; anxiety, depression, low—self-esteem, social withdrawal, suicidal thoughts, isolation, anger, suspiciousness of attitudes of others.

To address HIV/AIDS related issues within the community the development of specific guidelines is required. These guidelines will help those who are involved with these children; such as the parent's, teacher's, counselor's to be less disturbed and more competent in dealing with it.

Also it is the responsibility of all those involved with these children to ensure that all children are protected and that their basic needs — Safety, Shelter, Nutrition ,Socio emotional support — are provided for in order to facilitate healthy development.

1. Safety

All those involved in direct care of children with HIV/AIDS should be trained in first aid that includes:

-Bleeding
-Burns
-Poisoning
-Choking
-Shock
-Sprains
-Dental emergencies
-Head injuries
-Allergic reactions
-Eye injuries
-Loss of consciousness
-Electric shock
-Convulsions or non-convulsive seizures
-Injuries including — insect, animal and human bites.

The care takers of the children infected with HIV/AIDS should be ready to respond to an emergency. There should so be a meeting for and consensus on the emergency procedures and first aid. In general the first-aid kit should be available in all the settings where there is a likelihood of these children to be present. The content of the first aid kit should be:

-Disposable non-porous gloves
-Sealed packages of antiseptics
-Flexible roller gauze
-Sterile gauze
-Scissors
-Tweezers
-Thermometer
-Bandage tape
-Safety pins
-Eye dressing
-Pen and note pad
-Cold pack
-standard first aid text
-Insect sting preparation
-Emergency telephone numbers of doctors and hospitals
-Water
-Small plastic or metal splints

One has to understand that although the emergency conditions and the contents of first aid are common for all children irrespective of the presence of AIDS, but the most vital distinction between the two groups is the management

2. Nutrition:

Many of the complications of AIDS affect the child's nutritional status. Malnutrition well documented consequence of AIDS. Weight loss, body cell mass depletion, decreased skin fold thickness are a common occurrence in children with AIDS Deficiencies of micro-nutrients, malabsorption of vitamins and essential fatty acids may also occur. The opportunistic infections of AIDS lead to increased nutritional requirements. Infections from any source causes fever accompanied by increased basal metabolic rate. Therefore the child requires additional calories.

The Factors to be considered in nutritional therapy are:

-Decreased appetite: The child's appetite would-be reduced due to a number of causes such as fever, infections, gastrointestinal symptoms, medication side effects, respiratory illnesses that AIDS brings along Effective management would include:
-Small frequent feedings
-Intake of juices, snacks, milkshakes, eggs, soups
-Altering the timing of drug infusions

-Oral and esophageal pain: This result in oral and esophageal ulcers, sore gums, esophageal inflammation and difficulty in swallowing this could be taken care by:
-Individuals tolerations to foods must be determined.
-Highly seasoned or acidic foods may increase irritation and should be avoided
-Fluids and blenderised foods which minimize chewing and are easier should be given.

-Mechanical problems with eating: These are caused may be due to central nervous system infections, AIDS encephalitis, dementia, impaired motor ability etc. These may result in confusion and dementia, more so in adults. The patient might not remember to eat Management would include:
-Balanced food should be set up for the child.
-Close monitoring and encouraging the child is required
-Special eating utensils caS4pchildren with impaired motor ability

Diarrhea and malabsorption: This would be due to infections that are resistant to treatment such as cytomegalovirus, mycobacterium etc. The management would include:

-A detailed workshop for bacterial, virus and fungal causes of gastrointestinal symptoms should be considered.

-Dietary modifications such as low lactose, low fat diet.

-As malabsorption leads to malnutrition, nutritional status should be maintained. A multivitamin supplement increases the amount of nutrients available for absorption.

Specific or standard nutritional recommendations for the children suffering with AIDS are not possible because of the heterogeneous nature of the secondary complications of the disease. Owing to the fact that manifests itself with different complications in each individual, nutritional treatment plans will vary.

3. Socio-emotional Support:

AIDS unlike most disasters continues to exert an ongoing impact on children as well as adults who are either infected or affected. This contributes to the development of various coping responses, which may be either constructive or destructive. The socio-emotional support available to the child and his family has a major role to play in coping.

Socio-emotional support has been conceptualized as the emotional or tangible aid or assistance that is provided from individuals in one's interpersonal network. This is especially salient in discussions of HIV/AIDS because of the disabling nature of the disease as it progresses and the social isolation commonly see&

Social support refers to the functions performed for an ill/ distressed, by persons in the social network. The existence of socio-emotional aid, which could be in terms of a confidant, reduces or buffers the impact of adverse stress producing events, bolsters self esteem and perceived competence.

4. Shelter:

It is a place where children and families who are either infected or affected are catered to. It is like a home where they can stay. The shelter should provide various services to the individuals such as medical- wherein a visiting doctor would prescribe treatment as deemed necessary. It should have nurses and caretakers round the clock. It would give children and other adults the necessary freedom, such as allow them to spend money for their own use and allowing family members to visit whenever they want to.

Coping Mechanisms

It is defined as an intentional physical or mental action, initiated in response to the consequences of one's 1 status, which is directed towards external circumstances or on internal states. Thus a child who is infected will have a different response than a child who is affected. What is it that enables some of 'these children to cope with the impact of HIV/AIDS in their families and what makes one child more resilient and able to cope than another? Again a number of issues arise:

-Open communication between children and their parents, including preparing for parents death.
-Children's ability to express their emotions.
-A positive goal to live for.
-Memories and records of their own past and of good, loving relationship, usually with their parents.
-An opportunity to help others and thereby gain a source of resourcefulness and self- esteem.

1. Coping Mechanisms are Categorized into Constructive and Destructive.

[A] Construciteve Coping Mechanisms for Children

1. Active Coping: It is the process of taking active five steps to try to ameliorate or circumvent the problems related to HIV/AIDS. It includes initiating direction action, increasing one's efforts and trying to execute a coping attempt in stepwise fashion.
2. Planning: It involves thinking about how to cope with the situation. e.g. coming up with action strategies, what steps to take how best to handle the situation.
3. Seeking social support for Instrumental reasons: It includes advice, assistance, and information regarding HIV/AIDS.
4. Seeking social support for Emotional reasons: It implies getting moral support, sympathy, and understanding from people due to individuals concern.

5. Acceptance: It is functional coping response; person accepts the reality of the stressful situation. Acceptance of the HIV/ AIDS status as real-occurs.
6. Turning to religion; Religion might serve as a source of emotional support, as vehicle for positive reinterpretation and growth.
7. Positive reinterpretation and growth: It is coping aimed at managing distress emotions rather than at dealing with the stressor {HIV/AIDS} per se.
8. Focusing on and venting of emotions; It refers to focusing on whoever distress one is experiencing and to ventilate those feelings.

[B] Destructive Coping Mechanisms

1. Behavioral Disengagement: It is the mechanism of reducing one's effort to deal with the condition, giving up the attempt to attain goals with which the disease is interfering.
2. Mental Disengagement: It can be referred to as indulging in activities that serve to distract a person from thinking about the condition and its future implications.
3 Denial: It is a strategy of' refusing to accept the reality or existing conditions.
4. Alcohol drug Disengagement: It involves indulging in the intake of alcohol, tobacco, drugs to overcome the thoughts.
5. Suppression of activities: It is a way of putting other projects aside, loosing interest in perysal of activities, hobbies or suppressing desires due to one's status or conditions.

2. How Teachers Can Help

The need for helping the children so to alternate stress responses and maintaining reduced risk behaviors. Researchers have shown that psycho-neuron-immunity that is interactions among the psychological processes, the central nervous system and the immune system has a direct impact on HIV/ AIDS is most closely associated with immune functioning, psychosocial factors that affect immune functioning need to be understood and effectively dealt with.

Strategies focused on bolstering social support or improving coping capacities could have positive effects on children and families affected with HIV. The approach, being more realistic could decrease emotional distress and promote well being with distant goal of prolonging survival.

Steps for Supporting Children's Problem:

1. Acknowledge the problem of the child as well as the child's feelings- Children infected and or affected with the disease would be challenged by varied conditions that pose a lot of stress on them. For instance, the child would have to be absent at school due to the parents sickness. This should be recognized by the teacher and dealt with it in a manner that helps the child ease some stresses, atleast those pertaining to the school and home.
2. Encourage the child to describe the problem to you- Once the teacher is aware of the child's problems and acknowledges the feelings related to them, it would be very important/ beneficial if the child is made comfortable to share. Describing problems to an unthreatening person would have a cathartic effect, thus leading to the beginning of healing.
3. Ask the child for idea on solutions to the problem/ brainstorming- Children are individuals who are capable of cognizing situations at their level. Thus if given the right kind of support and environment, they can be motivated to think constructively. Children would think of ideas for solving problem when they are stimulated to do so.
4. Allow enough time for the child to solve the problem independently. Any kind of change or transformation cannot discount time. Time is an important factor, one which cannot be controlled always. Thus the teacher should facilitate and not push the child.
5. When the child is too frustrated or on the verge of abandoning his or her own ideas, offer your help. Well, one

has to keep in mind that although tome cannot be controlled always, our pace can be controlled. Thus when you see that a lot of time has passed out and the child is getting frustrated, you should intervene and help the child with other ideas.

On the Spot Comfort and Support Strategies

1. Do nothing simply wait. Sometimes other adults involved in the situation, understanding and patience with young children's behaviors will handle the situation without your interference.
2. Resist the urge to yell at children or shame the children when they say or do things that are uncomfortable for you. In stead, remain clam, and have matter -of - fact as you address the situation. Understand that people come in all types. This kind of understanding will help you to empathize with children and the kind of situations they are in.
3. Give children information about social rules, in a way that make sense to them. The information given to children should not be too complex, it should be developmentally appropriate.
4. Model more appropriate ways for your child to deal with social situations. A simple, "I am sorry her/his words upset you", may open the door to later conversation with the child.

Helping Children Resolve Issues with Others

1. **Approach the conflict in a calm manner-** Nothing escalates an already difficult situation more, than third people who yells children apart or otherwise add to the existing team.
2. **Stop any hurtful behavior by taking direct action and describing limits to children-** Do this firmly, without judging or blaming the child. Remember that child's differing personalities will create clashes among them, and that their

ability to deal constructively with their strong emotions is just emerging.

3. **Encourage children to talk to one and another about the problem-** Ask for and listen to their explanations of the situation. Again, do so without making judgments. Your job is to maintain neutral and let children know that teacher will listen to all sides. This step will take time and great deal of patience; however it will eventually give children a sense of mastery and independence in difficult situations.
4. **Encourage children to take responsibility for their actions and help them understand that their actions have an impact on the other people-** Young children often see only the immediate things and from their own point of view, which makes the step more difficult to accomplish. However, with adult support, children can learn to solve problems and trust that adults will be available to help them. They will also learn to empathize with and help others.
5. **Offer statements that might more a statements argument along.** However, resist the temptations to simply solve the problem for the children. Try saying, "I can't help, but notice that, while you are arguing, no one is allowed to tease the other child".

17

Combating HIV/AIDS, Tuberculosis and Malaria

Elvis Thomas

In the last decade of the last century, India undertook a change in strategy on the path to development. The ten Finance Minister, Dr. Manmohan Singh (our present Prime Minister) in the government of Mr. P.V. Narasimha Rao, ushered in the New Economic Policy that was supposed to take the country to the heights of prosperity. One of the pillars of this new strategy was 'privatization'. Taken as a mantra for development, subsequent governments have gone on a 'privatization spree'. As with everything the Public Health services too are on the road to privatization. Trying to integrate ourselves into the Global community these measures have become the norm. Earlier, as a signatory to the Alma-Ata Declaration (1978), India adopted the goal of "Health for All by 2000 AD". This goal influenced the basis of the National Health Policy'.

More recently in September 2000, representatives from 189; countries met in New York to adopt the U.N. Millennium Declaration, which are now widely known as "millennium Development Goals". (K. Park, Preventive and Social Medicine, pp.688)

Three of the 8 goals and 18 of the 48 indicators of progress are health related. Prominent among them is the need to combat

HIV/AIDS, malaria and communicable diseases of which T.B. is the most prevalent in India.

'In the year 2001, AIDS, tuberculosis and malaria caused more than six million deaths: three million people died from Aids; two million died from tuberculosis, with nearly 25,000 people per day developing active tuberculosis; and malaria killed at least another one million, over 80% of them children under the age of five.' (Annual Report – The Global Fund – to fight AIDS, Tuberculosis and Malaria, p. 3) The majority of these victims were from poor countries, where health services are inaccessible or inadequate. The unchecked spread of these diseases could bring about social disintegration and political instability.

In India today there are more than 5 million people affected by HIV/AIDS According to National Tuberculosis Institute, Bangalore, T.B. is responsible for 53 deaths per lakh population per year in India. Roughly this means a mortality rate of 70 per 100,000 population.

The tubercularization of population in India is wide-spread; on an average one-third people are Mantoux positive at all times because of high quantum of infection in the environment' (Gupta/ Mahajan- Textbook of Preventive and Social Medicine p. 169).

1976 saw the highest number of positive cases of malaria in the country (6,467,215), 21,17,460 in 1991 and marginally increased to 28,70,082 in 1996.

The Govt. of India began programmes to control and eradicate these diseases.

The National Tuberculosis programme aimed at a systematic reduction of T.B. in the community, with the available resources and in a given timeframe. The programme poured money into training personnel, establishing District Tuberculosis control teams, creating infrastructure for treatment and control, etc. In a nationwide review of the programme it was found that, financial outlay was insufficient, there was poor organizational support, poor outreach, multiplicity of treatment regimens, lack of proper health education etc.

The National Malaria Control Programme (NMCP) was taken up in 1951 and the main strategy was indoor residual spray with

D.D.T. This was an error as various negative outcomes occurred. For eg. Development of DDT resistance in other insects, refusals to DDT spray etc. Even today India remains the only country to use DDT in quantities that are large enough to enter the human digestive system through the food chain.

Through all of the claims being made by the government of action taken (reports even show the declining numbers of cases), one needs to realize that these will have no impact if:

(a) The Privatization trend is not reversed and public health services strengthened.
(b) There is no proper health education imparted to people.
(c) There is a lack of people's participation in not only deciding National Health Policies, but also in setting up and maintaining local health services.

Jan Swasthya Sabha, a National Coordination Committee has outlined the following objectives for betterment of people's health.

- To re-establish health and equitable development as tope priorities in policymaking, with primary health care as the strategy.
- To forge a local, national and global unity of all democratic forces to work towards building long term sustainable solutions to health.
- Reinforce the principle of health as a broad inter-sectoral issue.

The above aspects are important in reaching towards the goal of 'Health for All'. Today, the expansion of health services is taking on the hue of an industry. Private hospitals with five start comfort are becoming the norm. This, white local health services are decaying for want of medical personnel, drugs and infrastructure. Primary health centers in remote areas are constantly closed, creating the need for patients to visit towns and cities for medical care. This may entail long journeys and expenditure.

Often, the government waits till situations get out of hand before acting on them. The recent epidemic in Mumbai is such an example. Short term solutions are found more feasible and no effort is made towards sustainable solutions.

Also, health issues are always looked at in isolation and diseases like T.B. and Malaria have been isolated and are treated only from the biological perspective. HIV/AIDS infection, T.B. and Malaria can be caused as much by life style as by biological factors and most of all be the economic status of people. Ill health has many contributors.

(a) Malnutrition - kills the largest number of people in India and yet we spend more money on treating other diseases that result from malnutrition.

(b) Despite the National Health Policy stating as an objective the need for safe drinking water for all, this remains a pipe dream. Unsafe drinking water and lack of proper sanitation cause havoc with people's health. The recent floods in Mumbai have increased the number of malaria victims.

(c) Poor living conditions and ecological changes have a direct impact on people's health. The levels of pollution in our metro cities are among the highest in the world. In a televised statement, Ganesh Naik, Minister in Maharashtra suggested that to wipe out the debt of the state the State Government should sell off the open spaces in the city for development and use the money to repay debts. What will this do to the number of people suffering from respiratory diseases like T.B?

(d) Poor working conditions also add to the increase in the incidence of Malaria and T.B.

(e) Patriarchy is a hidden cause of ill health among women. This social order is accepted without a murmur, but the effects on the health of the woman and girl child are completely ignored, either consciously or unconsciously.

(f) Stress is a common factor in our lives today due to the breakdown of collective institutions, unemployment, lack of security, etc. More and more people, especially the poor are being displaced in the name of development.

(g) No access to health services is another contributing factor. Remote areas and even villages are bereft of quality health services, even primary health services are hard to come by.

Thus, privatization of health services will not solve the problem only exacerbate it. The State must not move away from it's responsibility of providing health care to the people. It should also like health to other spheres of people's lives, creating a holistic perception.

In conclusion, what is urgently required is capacity building to develop and organize people to decide for themselves.

The emphasis should be on 'improving the quality of existing and future programmes and to increase the scope and quantity of future programmes. A strong emphasis should also be placed on enabling more mutual learning from experience'. (IFCB. Approaches to Capacity Building , p.21). Priority should be given in the areas of planning, organizing and strategic management. Advocacy, research and analysis, gender sensitivity, networking and evaluation are all important skills to be imparted. These should not remain in the realm of jargon but must be operationalised so as to become potent tools in the hands of people.

The tide of HIV/AIDS, Tuberculosis and Malaria my take some time to ebb, but, through collective action, that time span can be shortened.

Bibliography

1. Dr. Surendra Singh and Dr. P.D. Mishra, 2000 — *Health and Diseases-Dyanamics and Dimensions* New Royal Book Company, Lucknow

2. Internation Forum on Capacity Building 1998 — *Approaches to Capacity Building* INTRAC, Oxford

3. Jan Swasthya Sabha 2000 — *Whatever Happened to Health for All by 2000 A.D?*

		National Co-ordination Committee
4.	M.C. Gupta and B.K. Mahajan 2003	*Textbook of Preventive and Social Medicine (Third ED)* Jaypee Brothers Pub. New Delhi.
5.	K. Park 2005	*Preventive and Social Medicine (18th Ed).* M/s. Banarsidas Bhanot Pub. Jabalpur
6.	The World Bank 2004	*World Development Indicators.* The World Bank, U.S.A.
7.	The Global Fund 2002/03	*The Global Fund Annual Report 2002/03* The Global Fund, Geneva

18

Combat HIV/AIDS, the Millennium Development Goal

Vaijayanta Anand

In September 2005 the UN secretary will review the progress that has been made so far towards achieving the Millennium Development Goals. Many people saw the turn of the millennium as a time to look at the world around us, to identify the major problems, which were causing large scale suffering and loss of life, and to apply themselves to solving these problems. The Millennium Development Goals are a list of the eight achievements which were thought to be important on a global scale, and which were thought to be most crucial in making the world a better place for everyone – regardless of their race, religion, or country of origin.

The sixth goal is 'Combating HIV/AIDS, malaria and other diseases'. Specifically, this aims to:

- Halt and begin to reverse the spread of HIV/AIDS
- Halt and begin to reverse the incidence of malaria and other major diseases

All of the 191 United Nations Member States promised to meet these goals by the year 2015, so a third of the time allowed to achieve these goals has now elapsed. It is time now to really look at the situation especially with relation to HIV/AIDS. In December 2004 there were 39.4 million people around the world who were living with HIV/AIDS, and 4.9 million new infections had occurred during 2004.The number of people living with HIV has been rising in every region, compared with two years ago, with the steepest increases occurring in the East Asia, and in Eastern Europe and Central Asia. These numbers show that, at least on a global level, we are not even close to slowing the spread of HIV, let alone reversing the trend.

HIV/AIDS in India

India's socio-economic status, traditional social ills, cultural myths on sex and sexuality and a huge population of marginalized people make it extremely vulnerable to HIV/AIDS epidemic. In fact, the epidemic has become the most serious public health problem faced by the country since Independence.

Since the first case was reported in Chennai, the capital of the South Indian state of Tamil Nadu, HIV has spread rapidly from urban to rural areas and from high risk groups to the general population. Various studies indicate that more and more women attending ante-natal clinics are testing HIV positive thereby increasing the risk of prenatal transmission. About 85 percent of the infection occurs from the sexual route (both heterosexual and homo sexual). About 4 percent through the blood transfusion and another 8 percent through injecting drug use. About 89 percent of the reported cases are occurring in the sexually active and economically productive age of 18-49 years.

Migrants, work place and HIV

One of the major attributable factors for such rapid spread of the epidemic across the country today is labour migration and mobility in search of employment from economically backward to more advance regions, low literacy levels leading to low awareness among the potential high risk groups, gender disparity, Sexually Transmitted Infections and Reproductive Tract Infections both among men and women.

Population mobility seems to be the key factor in the spread of HIV India Limited employment opportunities forces many to move from rural to urban areas from one state to another and from one country to another. There are more than 180 million migrant workers in India, many of whom are single men or who live apart from their families. Their life pattern evolves into transient. Insecure and emotionally turbulent way of living. The mobility factor does not provide opportunities to the migrant in developing long term monogamous relationship. The high risk behaviour pattern adopted by the migrants is part of the survival mechanism however this pushes them to the vulnerable position as far as infections like HIV is considered.

Economic growth has led to rapid urbanization, which in turn has resulted in large slum population and an increase in the categories of unorganized labour such as construction workers, casual landless labourers and child workers. These migrants get absorbed in the ever-growing unorganized sector, which is also known in the world of work as the informal sector. The migrant labour force is characterized as illiterate, or semiliterate, insecure, coming from very low socio-economic strata, mostly landless. Their workplaces in the urban cities are bleak shanties put up temporarily. Majority single men also stay in sheds or rental places together in the groups of 10 to 20. The poor unhygienic working as well as living conditions with no social support system contributes to the adaptation of high-risk behavior rendering them vulnerable to HIV infections.

Among the workforce the situation of women is more vulnerable compared to that of men. The work place is strife with sexually exploitative conditions. Many times lack of employment opportunities or daily source of income force them to enter the sex trade. HIV scenario affects women and men differently in terms of vulnerability and impact. There are biological factors, which make women more vulnerable to infection than men, and structural inequalities in the status of women make it harder for them to take measures to prevent infections, and also intensify the impact on them. Many women especially in the poverty sector experience sexual and economic subordination in their marriage so are unable to negotiate safe sex or refuse unsafe sex. As mentioned earlier, the power imbalance in the workplace exposes women to the threat of sexual exploitation. Poverty also becomes another contributing factor, as it is more likely that a woman is forced to work in the unorganized sector in the exploitative conditions.

Thus while addressing the problem of HIV among economically productive and sexually active sections of population, specific emphasis needs to be given not only to high risk groups like commercial sex workers and injecting drug users, but also to specific groups in general population like youth, migrant workers in urban and rural areas, women and children. Among the working population, long working hours, relative isolation from the family and geographical social mobility foster casual sexual relationships and make them highly vulnerable to STI/HIV.

All these aspects provide an unusual challenge of spread of HIV infection through various routes, which comes with its long period of invisibility, and subsequent manifestation through opportunistic infections. In India with a large population and population density, low literacy levels and consequent low levels of awareness, HIV/AIDS is one of the most challenging public health problems ever faced by the country.

Combating HIV/AIDS

Soon after reporting of the first HIV/AIDS case in the country, the government recognised the seriousness of the problem and took a series of important measures to tackle the problem. The Millennium Development Goals have set the target of reducing prevalence among 15 – 24 years olds by 25 percent by 2005 in the most severely affected countries and 2010 globally. Lots of money is being invested through the international agencies and the government to achieve this target.

Since 1992 the Government has formulated a multisectoral strategy for the prevention and control of AIDS in India. It is implemented through National AIDS Control Organisation at the National Level and State Level AIDS cell at State Levels. The programme has been concentrating on the areas, which conform to the global AIDS prevention and control strategy. The areas covered are

1. Programme Management
2. Surveillance and research
3. Information, Education and Communication including social mobilization through Non government Organisations.
4. Control of Sexually Transmitted Disease
5. Condom Programming
6. Blood Safety
7. Reduction of Impact

The key features of the second five years programme (1999 – 2004) developed through a participatory process are:

Greater ownership by the states through decentralization of responsibility for programme implementation to the state:

Targeted interventions for communities at risk.

Prevention of transmission among the general population such as young people and women.

Provision of low cost home based and community based care and support.

Strengthening of institutional capacity at state level including that of the NGO's

It must be recognized that the epidemic has become a major developmental challenge that will affect the productive population the most and thus affect the economy of the country. The emerging complexity of the epidemic has made it an issue that touches all aspects of human life. And the perspectives are diverse: medical, human rights, ethical, legal, religious, cultural and political. The need to prevent the epidemic and provide care and support to those infected and affected calls for an unprecedented response from all sections of society.

Bibliogragphy

Panda, S.Chatterjee, A.Abdul – Quader, Abu S; Living with HIV/AIDS virus: The epidemic and the response in India, Sage Publications, New Delhi, 2002.

National AIDS control Organisation of India.
www.naco.nic.in/nacppublctn.htm

SECTION V

Ensure Environmental Sustainability and Develop a Global Partnership for Development

19

Ensuring Environmental Sustainability

Veena Devasthali

Introduction

Environmental degradation is one of the most serious threats facing the world at large in the coming years. The development as it is commonly understood is largely based on non-renewable resources. The development strategy has been responsible for the large scale environmental degradation all over the world. There is a pressing need to search for an alternative which will focus on the sustainability as a core issue of the development strategy. The focus in the developed countries is more on the adverse effects of industrialization-urbanization leading to environmental pollution, global warming, acid rains, depletion of ozone layer etc. whereas in developing countries the focus is on the degradation of their natural resource base. It has caused loss of livelihood sources to the large sections of the population that depend on the natural resource base for their subsistence requirements. Integration of the environmental concerns into the developmental strategy is therefore the need of the millennium.

We find this concern expressed in the Millennium Summit of the United Nations (UN) held in September 2000. At this Summit

United Nations adopted series of goals outlining the future thrust areas of the UN. A set of eight goals were adopted which are known as the Millenium Development Goals (MDGs). Focus of the present paper is on MDG – 7 *viz* 'Ensuring Environmental Sustainability'. The components of this goal are -

(a). integrating the principles of sustainable development into country policies and programmes and reverse the loss of environmental resources
(b). reducing by half the proportion of people without sustainable access to safe drinking water and
(c). achieving significant improvement in lives of at least 100 million slum dwellers by 2020.

Each member country will have to incorporate this concern into their respective policies and programmes. Before exploring the way of inclusion of the same into the developmental planning let us first review briefly the developments in this context at the UN level.

The Focus of United Nations

The focus of the UN on the threat to the environment may be traced to 1970s. All over the world there was a growing concern about the sustainability of the development model. The degradation of the natural resource base and the rapid increase in different types of pollution had forced the world to take a note of this phenomenon. UN took initiative and organized a Conference on the Human Environment. It was held at Stockholm in 1972. This is one of the early initiatives on the issue of environmental sustainability. A large number of countries and the non - governmental organizations (NGOs) had participated in the same.

This conference arrived at a Declaration and an Action Plan. The differences in the concerns, approaches etc. between developed and developing countries had surfaced at this conference. Some of the contentious issues were exploitation of natural resources, damage to the environment and the unequal distribution of wealth. In the subsequent years these differences have widened further. However the efforts at the UN level continued further to find ways of incorporating environmental concerns into the developmental planning on the one hand and to find ways of focusing on the special concerns of the developing nations.

Immediately after Stockholm Conference a United Nations Environment Programme was established at Nairobi in Kenya. A decade later in 1983 UN General Assembly established UN Commission on Environment and Development. Dr. Gro Harlem Brundtland - who was the first woman Prime Minister of Norway – was the chairperson of this Commission. After four years in 1987 Commission published a report 'Our Common Future'. This report is one of the most significant and a comprehensive document on environmental sustainability. After the publication of this report the term sustainable development became the focus of policy and action programmes.

In 1992 UN Conference on Environment and Development was held at Rio de Janeiro in Brazil. The heads of the state gathered signed the Convention on Climate Change and Convention on Biological Diversity and adopted Agenda 21 – a plan for achieving sustainable development in 21st century. A Commossion on Sustainable Development was established to monitor and report on the implementation of the Earth Summit Agreements. The Millenium Summit was held in the year 2000. This was followed by the World Summit on Sustainable Development held at Johannesburg in 2002.

Thus, starting from 1972 the focus of UN has continued and has become more prominent and broad over the years. The issues of concern range from environmental pollution to the conservation of biodiversity. One of the important aspects of the MDGs is the expression of the need to incorporate this concern in the policies and programmes of the respective countries. This requirement is necessary since the biodiversity as well as the socio-economic relationships and the historical factors differ from country to country.

Sustainability is a comprehensive and a complex concept. Broadly it means improving the present condition without compromising the needs of the future. The objectives of growth, equity and productivity should go hand in hand along with environmental sustainability. These accompanying objectives are of special importance for developing countries like India. The developmental strategy must focus on the questions like who are the beneficiaries, what will be the impact of various policies and the action programmes on different sections of the population. The planning process must explore the ways of incorporating the requirements and priorities of people as perceived by the people *vis-a vis* their eco-system. The vast knowledge base of the given eco-system available at the local level should be given due scope in the policy matters.

MDG – 7 states that the principles of sustainable development should be integrated into country policies and programmes and that there should be reversal of the loss of environmental resources. It is in this context that the micro level planning assumes special relevance for developing countries. One important development in this context is the watershed based development approach which incorporates the objective of environmental sustainability along with equity, productivity and growth.

Indian Context

Let us take a look at the developments in the context of Indian economy. Though the pace of urbanization in the Indian economy is increasing rapidly still large sections of the population depend on the agricultural sector for their livelihood. Indian agriculture is dependent on monsoon. The environmental degradation taking place rapidly over the years has put severe strain on the agricultural sector. It was during 1970s that the watershed development programme (WDP) was initiated in Indian economy. This programme has tremendous potential to achieve the objective of sustainability and the related and important objectives of equity and productivity.

Indian agriculture is essentially dependent on monsoon. Therefore irrigation policy was one of the important policies in the post independence period. Top priority was given to the agricultural sector (including irrigation and power) in the First Five Year Plan. Agriculture continued to be one of the priority areas in the successive Plans. The irrigation policy focused on the major and medium projects and the minor projects in an integrated manner. After half a century of the developmental planning it is found that despite the huge expenditure incurred on the major and medium projects the area brought under irrigation by way of minor projects is more than that of major and medium projects. Noting the requirements of the rainfed agriculture the watershed development programme was launched in 1970s.

Environmental degradation has already reached alarming levels in India. There is large scale deforestation and ground table levels are also depleting very rapidly. There is an urgent need to adopt a strategy which would lead to conservation of natural resource base. Rainfed agriculture being the source of livelihood for nearly 60% of rural households its development crucially depends on the conservation of natural resource base (Kolavalli and Kerr, 2000).

In various parts of the country local initiatives have emerged to deal with the extreme adverse situation arising out of environmental degradation. The Committee appointed by Ministry of Rural Development (MORD) under the chairmanship of Prof. CHH Rao strongly recommended planning on watershed basis through participation of people at all stages (Rao, 2000). Based on the report of this committee MORD issued guidelines for the implementation of the WDP. These guidelines gave tremendous boost to the spread of this programme in the country.

Watershed Based Strategy

Watershed is a natural geo-hydrological unit of land. It has a hutment area and a command area. The size of this unit varies from region to region. The boundaries of a watershed are marked by natural conditions and social relationships. It is a very intricate relationship among humans, animals and the environment (Paranjape, S. and others 1998).

Basically it is a strategy conceived for protecting the livelihoods of the people inhabiting the fragile ecosystems experiencing soil erosion and moisture stress. The objectives of this strategy are to ensure the availability of drinking water, fuelwood and fodder and to raise the income and employment levels of the farmers through improvements in agricultural production and productivity (Rao, 2000). The programme is essentially based on the conservation and enhancement of the natural resource base of the region.

There have been several local level initiatives in different parts of the country. These initiatives had emerged as a response to the extreme adverse situation existing in those areas. The successful initiatives like Sukhomajari and Ralegan Siddhi now serve as guidelines to the areas suffering from tremendous hardships caused due to environmental degradation.

Case of Maharashtra

The watershed based strategy of development is of special importance for Maharashtra. The prevailing agricultural situation which is discussed below brings out the relevance of the goal of ensuring environmental sustainability as well as the role of people's initiatives in the State in ensuring this goal.

Maharashtra's agriculture is rainfed in nature. Throughout the post independence period in every decade one major drought had occurred in the State. Thousands of villages were affected in each of these droughts. Various committees were appointed by the State government from time to time to review the situation and to suggest a solution to the recurring droughts and to improve the irrigation in the State.

Maharashtra Government had appointed the First Irrigation Commission in 1960. This was immediately after the State had come into existence. It is therefore clear that the government was aware of one of the most pressing problems of the State. Mr. S.G. Barve was the chairperson of this Commission. The Commission was expected to study the conditions prevailing in the state in detail regarding the estimation of water resources, irrigation potential, distribution of wter resources etc. Commission reported that out of the total cultivable area only 30% could be brought under irrigation. It recommended that this potential should be realized by the year 1980 (GOM, 1962).

The pace of realization of this potential was very slow. The environmental degradation continued over the years. The Second Irrigation Commission was appointed by the government in 1995. Mr. M.P. Chitale was the chairperson of this Commission. Later the Commission was called as The Second Water and Irrigation Commission. The Second Commission was expected to make river basin wise assessment of water resources, their utilization, the backlog of irrigation development etc. With the availability of the new techniques at its disposal the Commission reported the ultimate irrigation potential in the state to be 39% of the total cultivable area.

What is significant here is that even after full realization of the irrigation potential in the state nearly 60% of the cultivable area would remain rainfed in nature. This is despite the fact that nearly one third of the total dams constructed in the country happen to be in Maharashtra. The hardships caused due to the environmental degradation continued over the years.

Local Level Initiatives

The solution to such a situation has emerged from local initiatives. These initiatives may be traced to 1970s. They gathered momentum in 1980s and thereafter. These initiatives are very diverse in nature. What follows is a brief review of some of these initiatives which will enable us in understanding their relevance in diverse agro-climatic conditions in ensuring the objectives of sustainability as well as equity and productivity.

Gokul Prakalp Pratishthan is one of the important initiatives in Maharashtra (Menon,2000). It was established in 1978 by Mr. Vasant Gangavane. After working in the country and abroad Mr. Gangavane returned to his native village Pinguli in Sindhudurg district in 1972. It is well known that Konkan region is one of the high rainfall areas in the state and yet suffers from acute scarcity of drinking water during summer months. The initial experiments were carried out in village Vilye on 40 acres of land. Bunds were constructed to block the water which withstood the heavy rainfall in the region.

Indo-German Watershed Development Programme (IGWDP) is another important programmes launched in the State. Fr. Bacher the initiator of IGWDP had long experience of prevailing agro climatic conditions in the state. As early as in 1968 he established a voluntary organization called Social Centre. A coordinating agency of IGWDP *viz* Watershed Organization Trust (WOTR) was established in 1993 at Ahmednagar. More than 150 villages are covered under this programme. One of the important aspects of the programme implemented by IGWDP is the emphasis given to the capacity building of the people. Training forms an essential component of their programme.

Adarsh Gram Yojana (AGY) is an important programme launched by the government of Maharashtra. Based on the experience of Ralegan Siddhi AGY was launched in 300 villages in the State. It is a programme carried out in collaboration with the people, government and the local non governmental agency. This programme has incorporated the sustainability principles like ban on open grazing and on cutting trees. The environmental awareness is spreading rapidly. The response that this programme has received is also partly due to the spread of this awareness. There are several other initiatives e.g. Adgaon, Ralegan Siddhi, Naigaon, Hiware Bazar and so on. Gram Swachchata Abhiyan launched by the state government has also given tremendous boost to the WDP.

Outcome of the Initiatives

The three instances cited above are of different types. They have emerged in different agro climatic zones. These are the initiatives of some prominent individuals from the local area taking major responsibility of launching such an important programme or an organization which is working in the area and the programme launched by the government. These villages have achieved the availability of drinking water throughout the year, security of kharif crop, and possibility of additional crops. The conservation of natural resources by way of progammes like ban on free grazing and an active programme of tree plantation is an integral aspect of the programme. With the stabilization of kharif crop, increase in the crop yields move towards the achievement of objectives of sustainability along with equity and productivity has begun.

Future Thrust

The number of such experiments has increased over the past decade. There is a need to evolve an action plan which will help in spreading this programme at a fast pace over wider area. The objective of sustainability is a complex one. The sustenance of the objective of sustainability will depend upon ensuring sustained local participation in safeguarding their eco-system, a long term programme of capacity building and emphasis on the research on rainfed agriculture.

With the new guidelines issued by the MORD the WDP is spreading rapidly. There is a need to monitor the programme and conduct evaluation studies to find out how the objectives of sustainability, equity and productivity are realized. Such evaluation studies should become an integral part of the programme itself. Capacity building programmes should also incorporate the same. This is important because in a vast country like India there is tremendous diversity in agro-climatic conditions and socio-economic relationships and the success of WDP depends upon the integration of these factors and the technological solutions. The programme has potential to move beyond these objectives. There is a need for streamlining the networking among all these initiatives. WDP is not the end in itself. In fact it is the beginning. It has the potential of being truly a programme of the people who have the primary claim on their eco-system and whose very survival depends on the same. The programme has the potential to transform itself from a mere programme into a movement – a movement towards the achievement of the objective of growth which would be equitable and sustainable.

United Nations has taken a very important initiative in identifying the priorities for the new millennium by way of focusing on Millenium Development Goals. Within the framework outlined by the United Nations for the objectives all concerned countries will have to chalk out their own programmes. Ensuring environmental sustainability is one of the important goals of the UN. In order to achieve this goal all concerned countries need to take into consideration the prevailing agro climatic conditions in their respective countries. The policies and the action programmes should focus on the grass root level conditions. In the Indian context watershed development programme has the potential to take into consideration and accordingly incorporate the diversities that exist in the natural base of different regions. This essentially micro level programme can play a leading role in ensuring environmental sustainability.

References

Asbe, Pratap (2001) : 'Gram Swachchata Abhiyan' *Maharashtra Times*, May 7.

Awasthi, R. and Panmand D. (1994) : *Ralegan Siddhi – A Model for Village Development*, FRCH

Datar, Chhaya (ed.) (1998) : *Nurturing Nature : Women At the Centre of Natural and Social Regeneration*, Earthcare, 1998

Datye, K.R. (1997) : *Banking on Biomass : A New Strategy for Suitable Prosperity Based on Renewable Energy and Dispersed Industrialization*, CEE.

Deshpande, R.S. and Narayan, Moorthy, A. (2001) : 'Issues Before Second Irrigation Commission of Maharashtra' *EPW*, Vol. 36, No. 12.

Dev, Mahendra S. and Mungekar, B.L. (1996) : 'Maharashtra Agricultural Development, A Blue Print', *EPW*, Vol. 31, No.13.

GOI (1994) : *Guidelines for Watershed Development Programmes*, Ministry of Rural Development.

GOM (1962) : *Report of the Irrigation Commission of Maharashtra*, Bombay.

GOM (1999) : *Report of Water and Irrigation Commission of Maharashtra*, Mumbai.

Kolavalli, S.L. and Kerr, John (2002) : 'Mainstreaming Participatory Watershed

Development', *EPW*, Vol.37, No. 3, 2002

Menon, M. (2000) : 'Where Knowledge is Free', *Humanscape*, Vol. 7, No. 2.

Paranjape,S., Joy K.J., Varma, A. and Swaminathan, S. (1998) : *Watershed Based*

Development – A Source Book, Bharat Vigyan Samithi.

Parasuraman, S. and Sengupta, S. (2001) : 'World Commission on Dams',*EPW*,

Vol. 36, No. 21.

Rao, CHH (2000) : 'Watershed Development in India : Present Experience and Emerging

Issues' *EPW*, Vol. 35, No. 45.

Thakkar, U. and Kulkarni, M. (1995) : *Politics in Maharashtra*, Himalaya.

www.un.org/milleniumgoals

www.milleniumcampaign.org

www.unep.org/

www.unhabitat.org/mdg/

20

Environmental Entrepreneurship Programme for Urban Poor Women

Jyoti Mhapsekar, Stree Mukti Sanghatana,

Mumbai, economically rich, prosperous and growing, is a city of almost 12 million people. Who generate considerable amount of waste (around 7000 tons) every day. Growing affluence increases volume of waste. Workers in the informal economy are an invisible part of the urban landscape providing a variety of the services to ever increasing urban population.

"Sustainable human development is development that not only generates economic growth but distributes its benefits equitably; that regenerates the environment rather than destroying it; that empowers people rather than marginalising them. It gives priority to the poor, enlarging their choices and opportunities and providing for their participation in decisions affecting them. It is development that is pro-poor, pro-nature, pro-jobs and pro-women."[Future of the United Nations Development Programme: Initiatives for Change. 1994.]

Waste pickers, though sizeable in numbers, are among the most marginalized and invisible within this category of workers. As per the definition prepared by "SWACHH: Alliance of Wastepickers in India", the term "Waste-pickers" and "Wastepickers organisations" should be included and defined in MSW rules 2000 (Issued by Central pollution Control Board of India) as follows. "Waste pickers are those workers whose livelihood depends on informal collection, segregation and sale of scrap. It does not include poor workers such as domestic workers, watchmen, doorstep waste collectors hired by contractors, municipal workers/ *safai karmacharis*, all of whom may be supplementing their incomes through sale of scrap. The latter category earns salary/wages while the waste pickers do not."

Waste pickers are engaged in various kinds of work like waste picking, segregation, recycling and at the organized level, door to door collection and composting and recycling recovery. The issue of urban poverty is intricately linked with waste. In India lakhs of people find livelihood opportunities in the area of waste. Therefore it is important to understand issues about waste in this context.

Parisar Vikas

An Environmental Entrepreneurship Program for Urban Poor Women

Stree Mukti Sanghatana, Women's Liberation Organisation (***SMS***) established in 1975 has directed its efforts towards the upliftment of women irrespective of caste class, creed, religion, language & nationality; primarily by creating awareness in the society about women's issues and the issues related to equality, peace and development. For last 28 years SMS is working among the men & women to achieve equal status in all spheres of life, i.e. political, economic, social cultural & psychological fields. It is an apolitical, autonomous, voluntary organisation.

Since its inception, ***SMS*** has made the significant contributions to the women's movement in Maharashtra thorough various activities such as ten Counselling Centres for distressed women, Five Day Care Centres Adolescent Sensitisation Program, Large scale awareness campaigns on issues regarding women in various parts of Maharashtra and India using the medium of a Theatre, poster exhibitions, seminars, talks etc., Publication of book and magazines, Production of audio -video cassettes and CDs. . These efforts have now been recognized and appreciated at both the national and international levels. In June 1999 ***SMS*** received the consultative status from ***UNITED NATIONS (ECOSOC).***

SMS started the work for the *Parisar Bhagini* women of Mumbai in 1998. The ***Parisar Vikas*** programme aims at addressing the problems of rag picking women, engaged in the 'menial' tasks of 'cleaning the waste' and also the problem of waste management, engulfing the urban existence.

Background

Studies in Mumbai, Pune and Ahmedabad have effectively documented that,

a. Waste picking is a caste and gender based activity.
b. All Waste pickers belong to the scheduled castes (Dalits)
c. Age group of Waste pickers - 7 to 70 years.
d. In most cities gender division of waste pickers is: women waste pickers – 85%, Men Wastepickers-10% and Children Waste pickers - 5%
e. 90% of all Waste pickers are the primary breadwinners for their families
f. 98% of Waste pickers are illiterate with no alternative skills
g. Most of waste pickers are from drought-prone areas of Maharashtra and other southern states
h. Waste pickers suffer serious health hazards resulting from unhygienic work conditions. Injuries from carelessly thrown glass and metal pieces, acid bottles, needles and dog and vermin bites are common occupational hazards. Most of them suffer from severe Anemia and occurrence of Tuberculosis, Respiratory diseases and backache are very common
i. Their day starts at the dawn and extends to more than 10 hours and entails walking 10-12 km. daily carrying heavy loads of up to 40 kg
j. Harassment by the police and municipal workers and exploitation by scrap traders and money-lenders is a common occurrence

After analyzing the findings of the survey of 2000 women waste pickers, SMS initiated a meaningful dialogue with waste pickers (Parisar Bhaginis). Twenty-five years of experience of working for women's Cause helped SMS to ensure a comprehensive approach towards these problems with proper perspective.

SMS developed a specialized program for Parisar Vikas

i) Survey of 2000 Parisar Bhaginis. Today, almost all of them are members of the organization. With the help of community workers though various awareness, educational and health activities SMS also tries to reach out to their families.

ii) Issuing Identity cards, with the endorsement from MCGM, to Parisar Bhaginis.

iii) Establishing 200 groups with a group leader. 170 groups out of these have already started working as saving groups. Saving groups have already disbursed Rs. Fifty lakhs for its internal lending up to 31st march 2005. Federation of these groups is already registered as an independent organisation 'Parisar Bhagini Vikas Sangh. (PBVS)'

Thus the program developed by SMS is actually a perfect practical application of most of the Millennium Development Goals stated by the United Nations in 2000.

I. Eradication extreme poverty and hunger

SMS efforts of bringing change into this lot of urban poor lead to another important development. The Urban Poverty Eradication Cell of Municipal Corporation of Greater Mumbai has undertaken a number of initiatives and adopted innovative concepts and strategies in the implementation of various components of this program. A novel concept has been adopted in which the 'Waste picker' community has been addressed as a special group as they constitute the 'poorest of the poor' of this city. The concept paper written by CCDO Ms. Jyoti Pandya titled 'People's participation in the critical issue of Solid Waste Management and linkage with U PA program' bore fruit when all components of Suvarna Jayanti Shahari Rojgar Yojana SJSRY were applied in practice to this extremely needy group. Thus started a significant partnership between SJSRY (MCGM), SWM (MCGM) and SMS. Most of the components of Poverty eradication program are being covered under this joint venture.

Access to resources

1. Permission for Issuing of Identity cards jointly signed by SMS president and Deputy Chief Engineer, SWM.
2. House hold Survey of these women for BPL status and their inclusion (100 groups and 1000 women so far) under SJSRY- another 70 groups are in the process.
3. Grant of Rs. 10000/- to each group as a running capital to start their micro enterprises- Out of 200 groups 63 groups with 678 women already received revolving fund of Rs.6,78,000/- disbursed under the 'Thrift and Credit Societies' component of S.J.S.R.Y.
4. Provision of tempo for collection of dry waste and inclusion of Parisar Bhaginis in such schemes in five wards
5. Recognition to SMS as the training Institute
6. Vocational training of 5 batches women under SJSRY
7. Under Infrastructure development of SJSRY, sanction to construct sheds in seven wards for storage of dry waste which will operate on Cooperative basis under the aegis of PBVS (5 such informal sheds are already in use.)
8. Formation of neighborhood committees
9. Approval of design submitted by SMS for the composting of wet waste in the pits of the size 5'x 3'x 2'
10. Sanction of grant to SMS to construct and maintain two NISARGRUNA PLANTS (Producing Bio gas and manure) at Shatabdi Hospital and Deonar abattoir respectively under the guidance of scientists of BARC for MCGM. Today SMS is maintaining five such plants.

Joint efforts are now being made by designing business proposals such as purchase of tempo, establishment of medicinal plant- nursery, sale of manure etc. to establish bank

Linkages for self help groups. Urban Development Department of Government of Maharashtra has noted the importance of this partnership and in its G R of May 2004 has recommended adoption of this approach to all other Municipalities in the state.

II. Universalization of primary education

Making pre-primary education available to the children of the Parisar Bhaginis by starting Balwadis (Kindergartens) in the communities with the help of Pratham, an organization working for Universalisation of Primary Education. 300 girls were given special educational assistance with the help of local donors. Almost 80 % of the children of age group 6-14 attend the formal school. SMS is now trying to organize youth in the community and is also trying to give them orientation in further educational opportunities, professional courses, life skills etc.. *Improvement in health, Combat HIV/AIDS, malaria and other diseases*

III. Reduction in child mortality

IV. Improvement in maternal health

- Holding Health camps for the women and children and provision of counseling facility to the needy families
- Development of special immunization, Anemia detection, cure and prevention program with the help of P.S.M. department of K.E.M. Hospital
- Starting a Crèche (a day-care centre), for the children of Parisar Bhaginis, in the Community Centre next to the Deonar dumping ground.
- Special health workers' Training to community workers with the help of Alert India
- After sustained efforts waste pickers have been covered as special category under Janashree Vima Yojana and Antyodaya Yojana

V. Gender equality and empowerment Of women Social empowerment

SMS has dedicated itself to the Women's Cause. It has developed lot of material using various forms over the years such as theater (its famous play Mulagi Zali Ho or Beti Aayi Hai), songs, CDs. Poster exhibitions etc... on various issues pertaining to women and children. All this was extensively used while conducting various awareness programs in the communities, SMS also used the material developed by other organizations like Pratham, Tathapi, Institute of health management, Pachod etc. for this purpose. SMS is also organizing awareness and leadership development camps (36 Sessions) for the group leaders with many inputs such as Equality, Solid waste Management, Health, Importance of education, work culture, P.D.S., Atrocities, Effective parenting etc.

Economic empowerment

SMS Established two training centres in M-ward (Chembur), for training Parisar Bhaginis in bio composting, vermiculture and gardening. 300 women have been trained in manure and gardening techniques so far. As a result of this 250 women have gained meaningful employment...

As a trainer and facilitator SMS secured work opportunities for Solid Waste Collection and Treatment in major public and private sector housing colonies and office premises viz. Tata Power, T.C.S., R.B.I. Navy, BEST, Pfizer , CIDCO, MCGM, BARC , Somaiya etc.. 250 trained Parisar Bhaginis successfully brought near zero-waste status in these colonies, campuses and also in the small housing complexes spread over 13 wards in Mumbai. In last 2 years work has spread to Navi Mumbai, Kalyan, Dombivili and now in Thane.

At WSF 2004, PBVS took over the contract of collection and disposal of waste and made a sizeable profit.

In November 2004 along with SMS experts, Parisar Bhaginis participated in training the staff, workers and residents of IPCL Township in Nagothane (Dist. Raigad). Today IPCL Nagothane is first Petrochemical Township in India achieving near zero waste status.

SMS as facilitator helped Parisar bhaginis to register six service-cooperatives, 50 women each under the Cooperative act for business entrepreneurship.

SMS is one of the conveners of the following networks

1. **Swachha:** Alliance of Wastepickers in India
2. **AWM**: Alliance on waste management. (National Alliance of organizations working on waste issues)
3. **MMAF:** Maharashtra Microfinance Action Forum (Alliance of organizations working with self help (Micro finance) groups)

VII. Environmental sustainability

The approach adopted by SMS in Parisar Vikas is found to be most sustainable as it imparts the beneficiaries with the knowledge and skills, advocates for their rights and helps them to be organized. It combines Economy, Empowerment and Environment. This will help Parisar Bhaginis to have increased bargaining power, better social organization, increased income and self-sufficiency

To make this model sustainable, SMS Simultaneously developed 5-6 composting models for use with the available space in localities of different Socio-Economic background. SMS also took help of the concept of Advanced Locality Management Groups (Citizens' groups) encouraged by MCGM Authorities. Many of these local groups gave employment opportunity to trained Parisar Bhaginis in their lanes. In turn Parisar Bhaginis brought near Zero waste situation in these areas. Soon SMS received an opportunity to upscale its activities. SMS received maintenance contract for NIsarga Runa (Biomethanation) plant developed by BARC scientists with capacity of treating 5 tons of biodegradable waste every day. Today SMS is maintaining 3 such plants at Anushakti Nagar. SMS has also constructed two such plants for MCGM and maintaining them. One of the plants has successfully produced electricity from the biogas generated.

Three factors - poverty, gender inequality and poor 'quality of life' - pose major challenges to sustainable urbanisation. If good governance can combine adequate powers, resources and operational capacities with community and partner empowerment, local authorities can take a central role in sustainable urbanisation. Mobilisation of local resources, whether private or public or community-centric, is a major challenge. There is a greater participation of voluntary organizations along with Municipal

Corporation in the field Solid waste management now. SMS therefore feels that treatment of waste can become a potential opportunity to increase the people's participation in the whole process and make them aware of their own responsibilities. This initiative can also convert the wet waste into Green Gold and make a considerable difference in the environment. Use of such manure or soil in the cities will stop the relentless exploitation of hills and river basins in the rural area. It will also create better working conditions for the Municipal conservancy workers who struggle day and night to keep the cities clean. It will bring the necessary attitudinal change in the people, which will help in the gradual acceptance of the Parisar Bhaginis by the society as responsible partners of the environmental entrepreneurship program.

VI. Global partnership for development

SMS secured funds from War on Want, a UK-based organization for the purpose of carrying out the above program

Observations

Parisar Vikas is proving to be a learning experience for all the workers and the SMS as an organization. Help from private and public sector is coming in the form of providing solid waste management contracts from residential colonies.

"There is a direct, although non-proportional relationship between population growth and waste generation. According to TERI calculations the population growth 1981-1991 was from 8.2 million to 12.3 million, a growth of about 49%. At the same time, the municipal solid waste (MSW) generated increased from 3,200 tonnes / day to 5,355 tonnes / day, an increase of around 67%. Thus the growth in MSW has clearly outpaced population growth, which is likely to happen in other places as well." (Up scaling people's participation in urban solid waste management Pub. by Toxics Link, New Delhi

Proper function of solid waste management needs involvement of people at every stage. People are not informed on what this solid waste is where it is taken and what happens to it afterwards. The Municipalities in any of the developing countries do not do any recycling recovery on their own. They still view solid waste management from the conservative (traditional) perspective of waste collection, transport and disposal. This needs to be changed to include resource conservation and recycling and get reflected in the solid waste management rules by giving due importance to the formal and informal players in the same. Contribution of waste pickers was not recognised even in the MSW Rules 2000.Their presence needs to be acknowledged, recognized and strengthened in multiple ways so that there is convergence between the livelihood protection and up gradation needs of waste pickers (poverty alleviation) and the statutory obligations of municipalities in respect of management of urban solid waste Poverty Alleviation Program. For developing countries recycling of waste is the most economically viable option available both in terms of employment generation for the urban poor with no skills and investment. Indirectly this also preserves the natural resources going down the drains. Some local governments have taken initiative to burn waste through incineration or gasification for insignificant quantity of electricity generation with astronomical cost and dangerous environmental impacts, which will take away the livelihoods of lakhs of urban poor. In their haste to comply with the Municipal Solid Waste Rules 2000, Urban Local Bodies in certain cities have contracted out door to door collection to private contractors displacing and further marginalizing waste pickers who can no longer access waste. The negative fall out is already seen in Nashik (1000), Nerul, Virar, Pimpri-Chinchwad and Nagpur (2000); Surat (2000) and Ahmedabad in Gujarat. The belief of municipal administrators and citizens that NGOs are small scale, inefficient unprofessional, and unaccountable and therefore incapable of providing such services has little basis in fact. The lack of cooperation, vested interest in waste collection and transportation, lack of coordination and accountability at municipal levels despite their infrastructure and manpower discourages voluntary organizations to upscale their efforts. NGO initiatives and arrangements that do not fit in their conventional contractual framework.

The **Significant Contribution** of waste pickers to the city is

- Reduction in municipal waste handling and transport costs

- Supply of raw material to recycling factories
- Saving space at dumping ground
- Resource recovery in form of valuable compost
- Conservation of environment

SMS therefore feels that the Municipal Authorities should issue identity cards to Wastepickers authorizing them and granting them permission to collect scrap for recycling. The BPL survey to be conducted should take special note of waste pickers under BPL. While out sourcing door to door collection of waste even private contractors, should be asked to employ waste pickers on first priority basis. This should be written into the contract between municipality and Contractor. Wastepickers' organizations should be encouraged, promoted and given preference by municipalities when outsourcing door to door collection of waste as mandated by the MSW rules 2000.

With the full cooperation of IPCL Authorities SMS could achieve 90% zero waste situation in IPCL- Nagothane Residential colony and Factory campus. However due to lack of cooperation by Municipal authorities could not complete B.C.P.T. funded project of Area Adoption in Chembur SMS also participated in the study of B ward undertaken MEDC which shows that first step for decentralisation of waste management is the proper dedicated services to collect the segregated waste of hotels and Markets. This waste then can be sent preferably for Bio methanation in Nisarga Runa Plant and or Bio composting. Second step can be tackling of the waste generated by Public and Private sector residential complexes and their disposal then and there. Separate collection and scientific disposal of Debris (Brick making) and Medical waste (Hydrolysis) can take care of inert material and health hazards. The third step should be providing area wise sheds for dry waste, Encouragement and incentives to citizens for segregation at source and composting and public education can transfer the face of Waste management in Mumbai. In Pune, PMC has taken a policy decision to incorporate waste pickers in house to house collection. It has also warned citizens about Corporation's non ability to collect dry waste. Public- private partnership of this kind can definitely benefit Municipal Corporations and the environment.

Reduce, Recycle and Reuse is the slogan for waste Management R of Responsibility need to be added to this slogan. Because that sustainable waste management requires reducing the waste and controlling the products that do not create undesirable waste. All over the world and in Europe EPR (Extended Producers' Responsibility) is fundamental to the waste policy, while we in India have not looked at this. Manufacturers should be required by law to create Eco-friendly packaging and put proper instructions on the product as to how best to dispose them in an Eco-friendly way. For example, sanitary napkins-which are otherwise biodegradable -should not be using plastic shields and have clear instructions as to how they can be disposed in the paper bags only. Similarly Municipal Corporations should issue clear guidelines to the citizens or industries when they are undertaking the interior designing or civil Work. Recently SMS with help of Tetra Pak has successfully completed pilot project of collection and storage of 6 tons of Tetra Pak, which is multi layered and therefore otherwise would have gone to dumping ground and stayed there.

The main constraints faced by SMS are:

- Management and organizational skills
- Capital and financial management skills
- Technological and design inputs for suitable equipment.
- Interface between voluntary approach and professionalism
- Improvement of productivity, reduction of health hazards
- Marketing and logistic support.

The experience of *Parisar Vikas*, the initiative of involving Waste Pickers in the mainstream of Solid Waste Management system of MCGM, is a lesson on managing such challenges. Above all, it highlights the reality that women from marginalize groups need not be passive victims of poverty and human rights violations; they can successfully participate in the struggle to survive, to gain control over economic, social and political resources and lead a life of dignity.

21

Develop a Global Partnership for Development

Vibhuti Patel

> **"The Millennium Development Goals were adopted five years ago by all the world's Governments as a blueprint for building a better world in the 21st century."**
>
> Kofi Annan

The MDGs represent a global partnership that has grown from the commitments and targets established at the world summits of the 1990s. Responding to the world's main development challenges and to the calls of civil society for poverty reduction and promotion of education, maternal health, gender equality, and for combating child mortality, AIDS, malaria, tuberculosis and other diseases. The MDGs make clear that it is the primary responsibility of poor countries to work towards achieving the first seven Goals. They must do their part to ensure greater accountability to citizens and efficient use of resources. But for poor countries to achieve the first seven Goals, it is absolutely critical that rich countries deliver on their end of the bargain with more and more effective aid, more sustainable debt relief and fairer trade rules, well in advance of 2015.

Set for the year 2015, the MDGs are an agreed set of goals that can be achieved if all actors work together and do their part. Poor countries have pledged to govern better, and invest in their people through health care and education. Rich countries have pledged to support them, through aid, debt relief, and fairer trade. Since the first summit for MDGs in 2000 A.D., organizations across the globe have convened and collaborated on campaigns to raise awareness of the critical importance of the goals, and to compel world leaders to fulfill their promises of additional **quality funding, trade reform** and **debt cancellation** to achieve the Goals.

Important Issues Coming in the Way of Global Partnership:

Trade

- The United Nations estimates that unfair trade rules deny poor countries $700 billion every year. Less than 0.01% of this could save the sight of 30 million people. (Source:ChristianAid, U.K. 2005)
- International trade is worth $10 million a minute. 70% of this is controlled by multinational corporations. (Source: ChristianAid, u.k. 2005)
- The poorest 49 countries make up 10% of the world's population but account for only 0.4% of world trade. Their share has halved since 1980. (Source: ChristianAid, U.K. , 2005)
- World trade robs poor countries of £1.3 billion a day - 14 times what they get in aid. (Source: Catholic Agency for Overseas Development, CAFOD, 2003)
- The prices of many poor countries' key exports are at a 150-year low. (Source: ChristianAid, 2005)
- It's estimated that rich countries are gaining $141.8 billion per year in trade and Africa is $2.6 billion per year worse off. (Source: ChristianAid, 2005)
- Rich countries spend $100 billion a year to protect their markets with tariffs, quotas and subsidies - this is twice as much as they provide in aid for developing countries. (Source: Oxfam, 2005)

- Current trade rules force Mexican farmers who live on a dollar a day to compete with American farmers receiving subsidies of more than US $20,000 a year. (Source: ChristianAid, 2005)
- The average cow in the EU receives more than $2 a day in subsidies, whilst more than 3 billion people in developing countries are struggling to survive on less than this. (Source: Catholic Agency for Overseas Development CAFOD, 2003)
- The EU gives $86.8 billion a year to its farmers in subsidies. Just $5 billion could help give everyone in the world access to safe water and sanitation. (Oxfam, 2005)
- On average, coffee farmers are getting $1 a kilogram while consumers are paying about $15 - a mark up of 1500%. (Source: *Oxfam*, 2005)

Aid

In 1970, 22 of the world's richest countries pledged to spend 0.7% of their national income on aid. 34 years later, only 5 countries have kept that promise. (Source: *Save The Children*, U.K., 2005)

Countries, which are already at or above 0.7% ODA/GNI

- Denmark (2004 actual: 0.85%)
- Luxembourg (2004 actual: 0.83%)
- Netherlands (2004 actual: 0.73%)
- Norway (2004 actual: 0.87%)
- Sweden (2004 actual: 0.78%)

Countries, which have made an 'independent recommitment' to 0.7% ODA/GNI i.e. independent of the EU-15 commitments of May 2005

- Belgium: 0.7% by 2010 – commitment even written into law. (2004 actual: 0.41%)
- France: 0.7% by 2012, 0.5% by 2007. (2004 actual: 0.41%)
- Finland: 0.7% by 2010, 0.4% by 2007. (2004 actual: 0.35%)
- Ireland: 0.7% by 2012, 0.6% by 2010 and 0.5% by 2007. (2004 actual: 0.39%)

- Spain: 0.7% by 2012, with annual targets including 0.5% by 2008. (2004 actual: 0.24%)
- UK: 0.7% by 2013, 0.4% by fiscal year 2005-06. (2004 actual: 0.36%)

Further commitments of 'advanced' European countries

- Luxembourg: 1% by 2005.
- Netherlands: 0.8% average over 2004-07.
- Norway: 1% by 2005.
- Sweden: 1% by 2006.

Other commitments of Non-European and non EU Countries

- Canada: 8% growth in ODA per year between 2002 and 2010, so as to double the budget in nominal terms by 2010 (projection for 2010 is only 0.33%). (2004 actual: 0.27%) >>Read our goal 8 country brief 'What about Canada?'
- Japan: $10 billion total extra ODA expenditure over the period 2005-2009. (2004 actual: 0.19%)
- New Zealand: 0.28% by 2007, 0.27 in 2005 and 2006. (2004 actual: 0.23%)
- Switzerland: 0.4% by 2010. (2004 actual: 0.41%)
- USA: 0.15% by 2006. (2004 actual: 0.17%)

In 2002/3 the UK spent just 0.3% of national income on aid. If the UK met the 0.7% target by 2008, an extra 1.5 million people could beat poverty that year. (Source: Save The Children, U.K., 2004) . To achieve 0.7%, the UK needs to increase its aid budget by £3 billion. It sounds huge, but it is possible - the UK government found £5.5 billion to fund the 'war on terror'. (Source: Guardian, 2005)

Debt

- 7 Million children die each year as a result of the debt crisis. (Source: Jubilee Debt Campaign, 2001)
- For every £1 in grant aid to developing countries, more than £13 comes back in debt repayments. (Source:World Health Report 2000)

- Every year Sub-Saharan Africa, the poorest region of the world, spends $14.5 billion repaying debts to the world's rich countries and international institutions such as the World Bank and International Monetary Fund. (Source: DATA)
- If we are to reach the Millennium Development Goal of halving the number of people living on less than one dollar a day by 2015, we must cancel all the debts of the poorest countries. (Source:Jubilee Debt Campaign, 2005)
- More than 85% of the debt owed by the world's poorest countries has yet to be cancelled. (Source: CAFOD, 2005)
- Debt cancellation needed by the world's poor: US$ 300bn. Debt relief promised by creditors so far: US$ 110bn. Debt cancellation delivered by July 2003: US$ 36bn. (Source:CAFOD, 2005)
- Spread over ten years the cost to the UK taxpayer of cancelling £1.3bn debt is £171m a year or £2.85 per UK citizen per year - the price of a pint. (Source: World Development Movement, WDM)
- Spread over 20 years, the cost of cancelling the debts of the 52 Jubilee 2000 countries is only one penny a day for each person in the industrialised world. (Source:World Centric)
- Ethiopia, a country with one of the highest mortality rates in the world, the $197m spent on servicing the national debt in 2001 could have fully financed provision of a basic package of health care for mothers and children. (Source:Oxfam)
- The money spent on debt repayments could provide water for around 1.3 billion people. (Source:WaterAid)
- The world's most impoverished countries are forced to pay over $100 million EVERY DAY to the rich world in debt repayments, while poverty kills millions of their people. Meanwhile, creditors use their power over indebted countries to force them to privatise their services, open up their markets or cut essential spending

"I encourage you in your advocacy for total debt cancellation for poor countries because, frankly, it is a scandal that we are forced to choose between basic health and education for our people and repaying historical debt." This was stated by President Mkapa of Tanzania in the Annual International Conference of the Jubilee Debt Campaign in 2005.

Historic Legacy towards Creation of Politically Congenial Environment in favour of MDG VIII

The Millennium Development Declaration underscored the results of the pioneering conferences of the nineties, such as the World Conference on Human Rights and the Fourth World Conference on Women, and confirmed human rights documents such as the Universal Declaration of Human Rights and CEDAW. The MDGs were extracted from the Millennium Declaration as a "road map" by the UN Secretariat, in close cooperation with the UNDP, the International Monetary Fund, the World Bank and the OECD. In due course, 8 goals were defined, together with 18 time-bound targets and 48 indicators, which are to be achieved by 2015, at the latest. Several Task Forces are working within the framework of the "Millennium Project" in order to further develop the targets and indicators and to strengthen the coherence between the goals. A Millennium Campaign is geared to raise awareness and commitment at a broader level. Most of the signatory states are preparing reports on the implementation of the MDGs. The UN Secretariat is promoting the MDGs, considering them to be the panacea for the solution of the most pressing problems of humankind. Many institutions of development cooperation use them as a frame of reference. The original drive, however, seems already to have weakened. There is little doubt that there are positive aspects to be found in the MDGs: For the first time the international community agreed on measurable time-bound goals and targets – at least in some areas – which can be used in monitoring and lobbying activities, and are easily understood by a broader public.

It is, however, problematic that these long-term issues of civil society and the social movement have finally been addressed, but in a way that lacks a true human rights spirit, and does not address the underlying reasons for poverty and "underdevelopment".

"The frustration for many has been the concern that the MDGs have met the letter of civil society's demands for accountability, but not the spirit. That is, they seek to solve critical problems with measurable targets, without adequately addressing the roots of these problems."

Critical Remarks from a Development Perspective

The crucial problem is that the MDGs are based on a concept of development which denies the necessity of structural and political transformations, and tries to solve problems such as hunger, illiteracy, disease and marginalisation by material incentives, investment, consumer goods and technologies, and the overall incorporation of the targeted sectors into processes of modernisation and industrialisation.

The framework strategy, and what is seen as the infallible panacea for the realisation of all MDGs, is the integration of the so-called developing countries into the concept of a neo liberal market economy, which has already proved to contribute to rising poverty and injustice. Recently even World Bank officials admitted that without equal distribution growth, poverty reduction will never be achieved: There is increasing evidence, that growth and the prospects for long-term poverty reduction can be held back by inequality.

Contradictions such as the fact that countries in the South are forced to privatise and to deregulate in areas such as health care, education, energy, transport and communication, and on the other hand are called upon to invest in just the same areas in order to attain the MDGs, are not dealt with. Similarly the devastating effects of international agricultural policy and of the TRIPS agreement pushed by the WTO and other powerful macro-economic players on poor countries and poor people are ignored.

The nation-states are asked to come up with national framework to achieve the MDGs. However, this national-level work will have limited chance of success if the root causes of failed development are not addressed. These lie primarily in the overarching framework of the global economy, and in the systems and rules of trade and finance which are failing to deliver on critical development objectives.

There is an urgent need to change the thrust of macro economic policies in favour of just, fair and sustainable trade from the point of view of the poorer nations. To empower the developing countries the following measures are inevitable.

The WTO must

- Develop further an open trading and financial system that is rule-based, predictable and non-discriminatory, includes a commitment to good governance, development and poverty reduction— nationally and internationally.

- Address the least developed countries' special needs. This includes tariff- and quota-free access for their exports; enhanced debt relief for heavily indebted poor countries; cancellation of official bilateral debt; and more generous official development assistance for countries committed to poverty reduction

- Address the special needs of landlocked and small island developing States

- Deal comprehensively with developing countries' debt problems through national and international measures to make debt sustainable in the long term

- In cooperation with the developing countries, develop decent and productive work for youth

- In cooperation with pharmaceutical companies, provide access to affordable essential drugs in developing countries

- In cooperation with the private sector, make available the benefits of new technologies— especially information and communications technologies.

Gender Blindness in MDG VIII

One of the most striking flaws of the MDGs is, as has been stated already, the fact, that the role and the needs of women in trade and development, in financial transactions and debt relief are not taken into account in Goal VIII. As has been widely evidenced, the negative impact of the neo-liberal orientation of the economy falls disproportionately on women, because of their lower economic and social status. Due to the capitalist economy dominated by male values, more and more women are impoverished and marginalised.

The indicators on **development cooperation**, which are considered to be important for achieving the goal of a "global partnership", do not once refer to women or gender relations, neither is a special target formulated in this context, though a great deal of research and planning has been carried out in this field. During the first three World Conferences on Women, especially in Copenhagen and Nairobi, specific measures were formulated in order to gear development cooperation to the needs and the possibilities of women. The approach gradually developed from "women in development" to "gender and development". Development cooperation must be considered as the first and foremost area where gender mainstreaming should be applied, as has been proposed in the **BPFA** as well as in the **Gender Resolution** (1995) and the **Gender Regulations** (1998 and 2004) issued by the European Union.

It would therefore be essential to include, among the indicators on development cooperation, one that measures the degree to which women benefit from development programmes and projects, in particular in evaluating their access to **basic social services**.

Additionally a new target should be formulated which aims at increasing **official development assistance** by industrialised countries, with a clear emphasis on the involvement of women as important development agents.

The indicators dealing with **market access** and **debt sustainability** completely neglect social aspects and the concerns of poorer and vulnerable groups, especially of women. The dramatic impoverishment of many women as a result of the "**debt crisis"** and **in** particular of Structural Adjustment Programmes has been widely documented. Therefore, any measure geared at debt relief has to consider women's needs. This should be reflected in a separate indicator.

The women's rights organisations all over the globe have demanded from the UN that:

- Introduce a strong and holistic **human rights-perspective** within the MDGs and enhance the effectiveness of human rights instruments.
- Express a strong commitment to the universal ratification and the progressive implementation of **CEDAW.**
- Call for the implementation and further development of the strategies elaborated in the Beijing Platform for Action **(BPFA),** with the participation feminist experts, NGOs, grass-root groups and networks.
- Reorient international **financial, monetary and trade policies** from the perspective of human rights, gender justice and sustainable development.
- Ensure **coherence between** measures in the field of development cooperation and financial, monetary and trade policies.
- Support the integration of a strong and comprehensive **gender-perspective** on the basis of CEDAW and the BPFA into all MDGs and widen the scope and the targets of Goal III, in order to pursue the following sub-aims:
- Safeguard the fundamental **rights, needs and capabilities** of girls and women in the field of nutrition, health – with an emphasis on reproductive *rights* – and education.
- Combat **violence** against girls and women at all levels in the public and private spheres.

- Strengthen the **economic rights** of girls and women within the household and the subsistence economy, in the informal and the formal sector, by recognising, adequately rewarding and supporting their manifold reproductive and productive activities; by securing their access to land, property, capital, credit, training, guidance and counselling, technologies, tools, infrastructure and transport; by ensuring their right to income and equal remuneration, to satisfying working-conditions and to social security.
- Ensure the equal treatment of women and girls in the **inheritance law.**
- Promote the **empowerment** and **political agency** of (adolescent) girls and women at all decision-making levels, from their personal environment to the parliamentary and governmental level.
- Strengthen the **collective agency** of women and girls by giving support to structures of mutual **cooperation** and **networking** at the local, regional and international level and by supporting their **political strategising** in all these spheres.

Decision Making for the Global Governance

We will have to change the direction of macro-economic policies that has rendered the toiling masses faceless and devoid of dignity. We can achieve all the MDGs only when we are able to reduce the North South Gap in the quality of life. Decision-makers across the globe must strive collectively and see to it that resources and fruits of development and economic prosperity are distributed justly among countries, within countries and among all human beings thereby eliminating poverty. This will ensure everyone access to food and nutrition, shelter, health services, safe transportation, right to information, education, justice, culturally rich leisure-time activities. Use of jingoistic sycophancy to hike military budget must be challenged tooth and nail and the demand of diversion of military funds to development efforts to attain all the MDGs must be made by the people's organisations of each and every country. Demilitarisation by the industrialised world can release massive resources for fulfilment of MDGs and will also set example for the developing countries to do the same. To deal with this crucial task force, we will have to evolve high levels of participatory democracy in governance so that we can improve lives and freedoms of peoples in all parts of the globe.

22

Emerging Issues from the Seminar

Leni Chaudhuri

Prof. Rupa Shah, the Vice Chancellor of the SNDT women's University in her presidential address expressed her concern at the pace of the country's economic development. She mentioned that the deadline of 2015 in not very far away but India is nowhere close to achieving the goals. She expressed her dismay at why India is still a "developing country" even after fifty-eight years of Independence. She mentioned that India is a country of planners and thinkers. The country has great plans for its people but implementation of the plans is something the country lacks. She emphasized that for individual as well as national development self-discipline is essential and all the components of the society lack the same. She harped on the economic development of the country, which needs to be treated as priority. She mentioned that the Millennium Development Goals can be achieved only if women are actively involved in it because women have special managerial skills. She mentioned that her university primary concern is to facilitate women's participation and furtherance of gender equity. She said that for improving the status of women in this country, men have special role to play. To which there are evidences in the history, social reformers like Ram Mohan Roy,

Mahatma Phule and Dr. Karve have worked towards women's empowerment. She mentioned the seminar should come up with a resolution should not be empty rhetoric but very precise and workable in nature.

Key Note Address by Madam Sayeeda Hameed

Madam Sayeeda Hameed began her presentation by congratulating the P.G. Department for organizing the symposium. She said that that the symposium is being organized at a time when two important bills are being passed in the Parliament. The Domestic Violence Prevention Bill has finally seen the light of the day and the Hindu Women's Succession Bill has been passed by the parliament. The Employment Guarantee Scheme has also come through. These are landmarks in social justice in the history of the Parliament. MDGs, she said are indicators of the country's human development and are of very little significance if they cannot change people's life. As a planning commission member her concern are gender equity the health of women and children and she wants to see how the MDGs can help.

Critiquing the MDGs she said that they have a targeted approach to development, which fail to take into cognizance regional imbalances. The numerical indicators have a scope for data to be forged in order to show the country in good light, and larger goal is often limited or reduced to theory

According to her reducing gender equity in education one of the targets of MDG but it is meaningless if women continue to be victims of violence, if they are denied right to property and patriarchal values are not questioned.

She appreciated the governments' decision on having its own targets, which are cognizant of the socio economic reality of the country. It is good that the Government is targeting to bring down the infant mortality rate to 45 by the year 2007 and to 28 by the year 2012, but the government is silent about under five mortality. The other positive efforts by the government are the target of attaining universal education by 2007 and universal ICDS program. She said that with the Sarva Shiksha Abhiyan education as really reached the remote areas.

She said that there is a need to widen the target for women's equality. She expressed her concern on why reproductive and sexual health is expunged from the MDGs. One of the lacunae of the MDG is that they fail to address the gender issues sharply. She mentioned that if gender concerns are to be addressed one needs to go beyond the traditional understanding of women's' issues and identify other things which also affect women's life. For eg. the area of conventional energy resources is badly neglected in our country when it is a well known fact that women spend around thirty million hours in gathering fuel. Infrastructure, like water, electricity affects the lives of women. It is amazing that in spite of technological development women in our still lead life in drudgery.

Quoting Kofi Anan she said that without economic self reliance in terms of access to property women cannot move ahead. Referring to the demands of a women's group she said that, the group looks at each MDG in a different light and demands the following rights. According to the group-

- The MDG target of eradicating Poverty can be met by increasing women's access to land.
- Gender equality can be achieved by reducing poverty.
- Maternal and child health targets can be met by improving access to livelihood opportunities.
- The other demands are environmental sustainability, equitable resource allocation, scope for active participation in decision making, rights on common lands etc.

Referring to Goal 8 i.e., Global Partnership for development, she mentioned that the developed countries have the obligation to assist the developing countries in achieving the first seven goals. She mentioned that the developed countries who have acquired their share of growth any way contribute less so why should we absolve them from their responsibility. The MDGS are in conflicting terms with the Washington consensus which only talks about fiscal prudence and market and not about the health of the social sector. It is important that the developed countries are told that the developing countries constitute of the majority of the world's population who are not standing in the queue for charity. Today majority of the world's population consists of young people, investing in them is investing for the future. She reiterated that the only road to peace and security is through people centered development. Again quoting Kofi Anan she said that a country with hungry children cannot talk about achieving freedom.

In her concluding remarks she expressed her faith in the Civil Society. Civil society organizations are closer to the people so they have better knowledge of the ground reality. The civil society should play a very vigilant role and follow up on the target and implementation of the same. The need of the hour is that the government and the civil society should come together and direct a broad based social movement.

One has to see that the MDGs do not become absolutes or ceilings but yardsticks to measure progress and not an end in itself.

She assured the group that she will diligently play the role of a messenger to the planning commissions about the concerns and issues emerging from this symposium.

Validictory Session

The valedictory session had two stalwarts. Mr. M. N. Chaini, President, Maharashtra Economic Development Council, Mumbai and Justice R. A. Jahagirdar, Retired Judge of Mumbai High Court.

The valedictory session started with Dr. Vibhuti Patel, introducing both the guests. The session was chaired by Mr. M. N. Chaini and the valedictory address was given by Justice Jahagirdhar.

Mr. Chaini said that it is special privilege to address an educated and enlightened group. She said that even through MDGs are expressed in numbers and are time-bound, they are actually goals of lifetime, which were there in the past and will also be there in future.

He mentioned that the MDG targets, which are particularly relevant to India, are that of :

- poverty alleviation,
- Universal primary education.
- Gender equity
- Improving maternal health
- Combating HIV/AIDS.
- Improving the economic condition of the country by increasing productivity.

Referring to the situation in India he said the incidence of poverty is extremely high in India. The health status of the vast majority of Indians is in a poor shape. Maternal and infant mortality rate are high, diseases like T.B, Malaria and HIV/AIDS have reached alarmingly high levels. The access to facilities in health care also reflects wide variation. There exist sharp disparities between the rich and poor. Quoting Micheal Carter – he said looking at the disparities in India, one feels there are two worlds where a vast majority are left behind from availing the facility of public services.

To combat this, he suggested or multi-pronged approach should be adopted. First and foremost, the economic growth should be raised to a double-digit figure. Heath and education should be the next priority. Conservation of natural resources and gender equity are the two most important concerns. A holistic approach to growth, which takes cognizance of the above, mentioned factors could only take India forward.

He said the MEDC's concern is development of infrastructure without which the national development is not possible. In his concluding remark he said that meeting the MDGs is a big challenge for which we need progressive policies, effective communication, increases in awareness and proper implementation of plans is essential.

The valedictory address was given by Justice Jahagirdhar.He said that the biggest evil, which is affecting India, is poverty and we need to address that at the earliest. He said even though poverty affects all sections of the societies, women are the worst affected. He said all other problems in the country like poor health, illiteracy etc, are results of acute poverty. The government and the other actors in the society should work towards social and economic development with assistance from the international community. According to him globalization is an inevitable reality. India has to work out its advantages within that. The positive aspects of globalization like – increased trade, new ideas, development of science and technology, greater employment opportunity etc. should be made use of for our advantage.

He said the another major problem, which has been affecting India's social and economic growth, is corruption. We need to free the country from this evil. Referring to the economists he said that the country needs economists who can influence policies and not arm chair economists.

The session was concluded by Dr. Vibhuti Patel's response where she mentioned that all the participants in the symposium are activists in different fields, and don't believe in only in theoretical discourses. She gave the assurance that all the presenters, guests and participants will carry forward this discussion in their own fields, which will also influence their action in the filed.

Index

A

Absolute Poverty, Global
    Protection, 19
Adarsh Gram Yojna (AGY), 296
Adivasis, 233
Agrarian
    Distress, 32, 36
    Economy, 17, 29
Agricultural Development, 32
AIDS, 220, 222, 223, 226, 227, 262, 264-266, 268-270, 272, 278, 313
    Control Organization, 286
    Deaths, 266
    in India, 286
Alcohol Drug Disengagement, 272
Alma-Ata Declaration, 277
Alopathy—Siddha, 220
Ambani-Birla Report, 108
Aman Ikhatiyar in Malaysis, 49
Ambedkar, 100
Andhra Pradesh, 221
Andhra Pradesh, Kerala, Punjab, 35
Anti-Poverty Program, 36
ASEAN Countries, 130
Asset Creation Zone, 79
Awade, Sonale, 149
AYUSH, 173

B

Backward Caste, 35
Balwadis, 89
Bangladesh, 232
    China, Columbia and India-Vietnam, 64
    India and Ethopia, 61
Bangladesh—Maharashtra, 58
BARC, 307, 308
Basic
    Education, 100, 101, 103, 111, 114, 119, 120
    Social Services, 322
Beijing, 185
Beijing Platform for Action, 185, 322
Beijing Women Conference, 1995, 155, 156
Below Poverty Line, 76
Bhutan, 232
Book Banks, 91
Brazil—Thailand, 64
Breast/Urine Cancer, 136
Bride Burning, 135
British Rule, 114

C

Canada—Japan, 250
Caste System, 99

CEDAW (Convention To Eliminate All Forms of Discrimination Against Women), 179, 195, 196, 318, 322
CEHAT (NGO), 135
Central
  Advisory Board of Education (CABE), 111
  Pollution Control Board, 302
Chaini, MN, 328
Child
  Labor Act, 1986, 132
  Labour Ban, 122
  Marriage, 122
  Mortality, 30, 306, 313
  Prostitution, 133
  Sexual Abuse, 133, 134
China, 63, 66, 136
Chitale, MP, 295
Classic Welfare Economics, 30
Coalition Governments, 30
Commercial Sex Workers, 286
Commercialization, 36, 37, 136
Commission on Sustainable Development, 291
Common Minimum Program, 236
Communicable Diseases, 223, 278
Community Development, 46
Community Health Workers, 235
Conference on Human Environment, 290
Constitution of India, 101
Contraceptives, 137
Control of AIDS, 25
Conventional Energy Resources, 327
Crash in Prices, 18
Credit System, 47
Crimes, 161
Crop Pattern, 36

D

Dalit/Tribal Women, 128
Data Collection Methods, 204
Debt Crisis, 316, 322
Decentralization, 235, 258
Decision Making, 32, 48, 127, 138, 158, 189, 323
Degradation of Environment, 128
Demilitarization, 324
Developed Market Economies, 234
Developing Countries, 22, 29, 32, 38, 41, 64, 81, 138, 166, 289, 292, 309, 310, 324
Developmental Planning, 23, 293
Development of Women and Children in Rural Areas (DWCRA), 23, 201
  Indira Awas Yojna (IAY), 23
  Maharashtra Rural Credit Project (MRCP), 23
  Mahila Samridhi Yojna, (MSY), 23
  NABARD Sponsored Programs, 23
Developmental Strategies, 38
Dharmapuri, 76, 77
Dichotomy, 75
DIFID, 217
Directive Principles, 101
Disadvantaged Class, 105
Disadvantaged Social Groups, 99
Discrimination Against Women, 127
District Institute of Education and Training (DIET), 91
District Primary Education Program (DPEP), 21, 89-91, 95, 117
Domestic Violence Prevention Bill, 326
Domestic Violence, 43
Dowry, 135
Dowry Deaths, 135
Drought Prone Area, 145
Drug/Alcohol Abuse, 43
DWCUA (Development of Women & Children in Urban Areas), 45

E

Earth Summit Agreement, 291
East Asian Economies, 86
Economic and Social
Development, 84, 99, 100
Development, 66, 73, 86, 115, 325, 330
Distress of Farm Family, 18
Growth and Development, 176
Growth, 19, 25, 29, 55, 58, 63, 66, 67, 157, 285
Liberalization Policies, 131
Reforms, 23, 218
Transformation, 56
Economy, 25, 73, 111, 128, 308, 321
Capitalist, 321
Industrial, 32
Political, 220, 224, 234
Rural, 219
World, 56
Ecosystem, 292, 294
Education, 20, 21, 24, 43, 83-88, 99-101, 103, 105-109, 113-115, 118, 120, 124, 128, 156, 159, 168, 184, 220
and Empowerment, 178, 186, 187, 189
and Health, 66, 75, 77, 84
and Health Services, 31
Compulsory, 101, 102, 106, 107, 110
Elementary, 87, 109, 168
Universalization of, 20, 115, 119, 120
Elementary-In India, 20
Expenditure, 109, 110
For All (EFA), 115
Free, 106
Free/Compulsory, 115
Govt. Expenditure on, 107
Policy, 124
Post Independence, 107
Policy, 1986, 111
Primary, 30, 83, 85-88, 102, 106, 113, 115, 116, 122,
Basic Objectives, 113
Expansion of-, 123
Universalization of-, 20, 92, 99, 112, 116, 118, 306
Privatization, 134
Sector, 108
Technical, 116
Universal, 20, 99
Educational
Attainment, 159
Policies, 103, 106
Status of Depressed/ Oppressed Classes, 99, 102
System in India, 106
System, 103, 107, 109, 111, 114, 122, 124
Electoral Policies, 30
Electronic—Agro Industries, 128
Emerging Economies, 234
Employment, 75, 77, 78, 100, 116
and Asset Creation, 35
Generation Bill, 36
Generation Schemes, (EGS), 20, 35, 36, 326
Generation, 85
Insecurity, 42
Opportunities, 285
Promotion Sector, 156
Empowerment, 45, 48, 71, 80, 81, 102, 145, 146, 149, 151-153, 178, 180, 184, 186, 187, 190, 191, 192, 203, 308
Definitions, 180
Economic, 23, 207, 307
Indicators, 166
of Women, 21, 166, 306
Policies, 21
Political, 158, 209
Social, 207
Socio-Economic, 23
Entrepreneur Development Program, 210, 213

Environment Sustainability, 308
Environmental
Degradation, 29, 229, 289, 292, 293, 294
Entrepreneurship Program (EEP), 301
Hazards, 43
Sustainability, 289, 290, 291
Epidemics, 136
European Union, 321
Europe—Australia, 234
Export Industries, 128

F

Family
Planning, 138, 219, 227
Welfare, 171
Welfare Program, 253
Farmers, 18, 35
Caste, 35
Entrepreneurial Spirit, 38
Indebtedness, 35
Indian, 39
Suicide of-, 35
Farming Practices, 37
Female
Child Mortality, 159
Economic Activities Rate, (FEAR), 129
Field Agents, 150
Financial Services, 19
First Irrigation Commission, 294, 295
Fishery Mission Activities, 78
Five Year Plans, 115, 116
Foreign Direct Investment (FDIs), 130
Foreign Exchange, 56
Forest Development Project, 81
Formal Savings Program, 47
Free Markets, 67
Free Trade, 56, 57
Fundamental Rights, 119

G

Gandhi, Mahatma, 101, 114
Gangavane, Vasant, 295
Gender
Based Violence, 194
Blindness in MDGs III, 321
Budget Initiatives (GBIs), 166
Equality, 22, 29, 30, 127, 155, 159, 175, 178, 184, 187, 188, 192, 306
Resolution, 321
Girl Child
Labour, 128, 132
Workers, 132
Global
AIDS Prevention Strategy, 287
Education Monitoring Report, 2005, 105
Markets, 217
Partnership, 313, 314, 321
Partnership, Issues Before-, 314, 315
Poverty, 19
Warming, 136, 289
Globalization, 19, 29, 38, 55, 121-133, 140, 166, 217, 330
Economic, 140
Gokhale, 100
Gokul Prakalp Pratisthan, 295
Gram Panchayats, 88, 96
Gram Shikshan Samities, 88
Grameen Bank in Bangladesh, 49, 53
Growth Rates, 65, 67, 72,73, 75, 84
Gujarat, 221, 224
Gujarat Carnage, 140

H

Haryana and Punjab, 76
Health and Education, 18, 30, 158, 176, 247
and Nutrition, 83, 84

Care Services, 258
Education, 248, 279
For All, 228, 277, 279
Sector Reforms Program, 217
Sector Reforms, 134
Services, 128
Workers, 136
Health/Basic Services, 18
Hindu Women's Succession Bill, 326
HIV, 266, 284-286
Infection, 184
Positive, 262, 284
Rate, 136
Transmission Prevention, 230
HIV/AIDS, 24, 25, 176, 177, 187, 217, 230, 231, 233, 264, 265, 267, 270, 271, 277, 278, 281, 283, 284, 286, 329
Children, 261
Combat, 283, 306
Epidemic, 25, 284
Facts, 262
In India, 284
Infection, 280
Prevalence Rate, 136
HIV/AIDS/STD, 133, 136
Hormone Replacement Therapy (HRT), 137
HPV, 133
Human Development, 29
Human Development Index (HDI), 19, 66, 161
Human Resource Development, 20, 66, 83-85
Human Rights, 17

I

IFAD (International Fund for Agriculture Development), 202
Immigrant Women, 131
Immunization, 219
Impact of Migration, 44
Imports and Exports, 39
Income Distribution, 19, 41, 63
Income Generation, 45, 77, 79, 80
India's
Public Health Program, 231
Socio-Economic Status, 25, 284
Indian
Agriculture, 293
Constitution, 86, 87
Economy, 292
Educational Institutions, 114
Population, 257
States, 17
Indo-China, 130
Indo-German Watershed Program (IGWDP), 296
Indonesia, 191, 218
Industrial Countries, 47
Industrial/Traffic Pollution, 43
Industrialized Countries, 56
Infant Mortality Rate, 231, 232
Infrastructural Facilities, 96
Inheritance
Law, 323
Rights, 100
Injecting Drug Users (IDUs), 286
Insurance Services, 47
Integrated
Child Development Schemes, (ICDS), 20, 77, 168, 233, 326
Rural Development Program, 220, 230
International
Community, 330
Conference On Population and Development, 185
Covenant for Economic, Social and Cultural Rights (ICESCR), 228, 29, 231
Economic Agency, 55

Financial Institutions, 38
Labour Organization, (ILO), 131, 157, 191
Markets, 38, 247
Monetary Fund (IMF), 317, 318
Irrigation Policy, 293

J

Jahagirdar, RS, Justice, 328, 329
Jalan, Dr. Bimal, RBI Governor, 51
Jalna, 96
Japan Bank for International Cooperation, 78
Jawahar Rozgar Yojna, 44, 220
Joterao Phule, 101
Jubilee Debt Campaign, 318

K

Karad City, 146
Karve, Dr., 101, 326
Kashmir, 224
Kerala, 30, 31
Kofi Anan, 327
Konkan Region, 296
Kothari Commission, 111

L

Labour
Concentration Camps, 130
Intensive Growth, 38
Markets, 44
Latin American Countries, 63
Least Developed Countries (LDCs), 57
Liberalization, 63, 220
Liberalization Policies, 39
Liquor Industry, 136
Literacy, 30, 75, 100, 102, 111, 190, 218
Female, 91
Indicators, 189
Rates, 102, 103, 159, 168
Scheduled Caste/Tribes, 103
Lok Jumbish (LJP), 21, 118
Low Income Countries, 19, 55

M

Macro Economic Policies, 55, 127, 128, 134, 137-140
MACS (Mutually Aided Cooperative Societies), 49
Maharashtra, 18, 30, 35, 90, 93, 94, 145, 151, 221, 253, 257, 294, 295, 303
Agriculture, 294
Educational Institutions in-, 93
Employment Generation Act, 1977, 36
Farmers, 32
Health Schemes, 253
Rural Credit Project (MRCP), 202
Maharashtra—Tamil Nadu, 129
Mahatma Phule, 326
Mahatma Phule Shikshan Hami Yojna (MPSHY), 88, 96
Mahila Arthik Vikas Mahamandal Ltd. (MAVIM), 202
Mahila Milan Bank, 49, 50
Malaria, 24, 176, 218, 233, 277, 278, 280, 313, 329
Manmohan Singh, 277
Mann Deshi Mahila Sahakari Bank (MDM), 145-149
Market Economy, 124
Market Reforms, 63
Markets, 18
Maternal Health Program, 253
Maternal Mortality Rate (MMR) in India, 232
MAVIM, 210, 213
MCH (Maternal and Child Health), 161, 247

MDM Mahila Hat, 151,152
MDM, 148, 150-152
Medical Education, 226
Medicine Systems, 219, 220
MEP's Impact, 128
Micro Finance Institutions, (MFIs), 51
Micro-Credit, 48, 51, 201
Micro-Crediting Organization, 47
Micro-Finance, 19, 41, 46, 48-50, 52
Micro-Finance Institutions, 153
Mid Day Meals Scheme, 168
Migrant Labour System, 46
Migration, 49
Millennium
- Campaign, 318
- Declaration, 17, 29, 159, 175
- Development, 99
- Goals, 29
- Project, 318
- Summit of UN, 289

Millennium Development Goals (MDGs), 17, 19, 21-23, 25, 29-31, 71, 83, 85, 128, 129, 140, 175-177, 184, 187, 188, 190, 194, 196, 217, 228, 229, 231, 233, 234, 247, 248, 250, 277, 283, 286, 290, 291, 292, 304, 313, 314, 317, 318, 319, 322, 323, 325-329
- Environmental Sustainability, 17, 25
- Eradication of Poverty and Hunger, 17
- Gender Targets, 189
- Global Development, 17
- Goals, 189
- HIV/AIDS, Malaria, TB, 17

Maternal Health, 17
- Promotion of Gender Equality& Employment, 17
- Reduction of Child Mortality, 17
- Strategy, 232
- Targets, 329
- Universal Primary Education, 17
- Goals, 177, 186
- Health Goals, 229

Milllennium Development Goals III, 127
Minimum Needs Program, 227
Ministry of
- Health & Family Welfare, Goals, 172
- Human Resource Development, 124
- Rural Development, 293, 297

Modernization and Industrialization, 319
Monetary and Trade Policies, 322
Mukherjee, Pranab, 111
Multilateral Agencies, 217
Mumbai—Chennai, 136
MYRADA in India, 43

N

Nakusa, 146
Nanded (Marathwara), 204
Nanded—Mahur, 205
Narasimha Rao, 277
Nasik—Ahmedabad, 310
National
- Development Strategies, 68
- Disease Control Program, 227
- Health Policies, 277, 279, 280
- Health Policy (NHP)-2002, 231
- Health Program, 235
- Malaria Control Program, (NMCP), 278
- Movement, 100
- Planning on Education, 91
- Policy for Education (NPE), 1986, 106, 119

Policy on Education, 1987, 117
Rural Health Mission (NRHM), 171-173, 235, 237
Sample Survey, 92, 93
Sample Survey Org., 221, 224
Slum Dwellers Federation (NSDF), 49
TB Program, 278
NBFC (Non-Banking Finance Companies), 49, 51, 52
NCAER, 21
NCW (National Commission for Women), 167, 168
Nehru Rozgar Yojna, 45
Nepal, 232
New Economic Policy, 277
New Reproductive Techniques (NRTs), 137
NGOs, 24, 47, 49, 96, 118, 135, 139, 140, 196, 205, 221, 258, 287, 290, 310, 322
NHRC (National Human Rights Committee), 237
Non-European Union Countries, 316
Non-Governmental Organizations (NGOs), 21
Non-Renewable Resources, 289
North East States, 224
NSDP, 75
Nutrition Program, 20

O

Occupation Segregation Indicators, 192
Oil Producing and Exporting Countries, 56
Old Age Pensioners, 20
Operation Black Board, 21, 89, 117
Orissa, 76
Other Backward Class, 102

P

Panchayat Samiti, 91
Parisar Bhaginis, 306-309
Parisar Bhagini Vikas Sangh (PBVS), 304
Pay Commission (5th), 223, 228
Peace and Security, 17
Planners, 325
Planning, 80, 100, 155
Planning Commission, 115
Planning Micro Level, 90
Planning Process 1950-2005, 21
Platform for Action at Beijing, 1995, 156
PM's Integrated Urban Poverty Alleviation Program, 45
PM's Rozgar Yojna, 89
Policies
and Measures, 29
Macro-Economic, 17, 21
Population Policy, 138
Pornographic Filming, 133
Poverty
Alleviation, 41, 71, 77, 79, 80, 247
Program, 18, 19, 35, 310
Schemes, 20, 77
Education, 43
Eradication, 156, 159
Policies, 32
in India, 41, 44
Causes and Remedial Measures, 41
Reduction, 19, 22, 38, 55, 58, 61, 63, 65-67
Structure in Tamil Nadu, 20
Syndrome, 43
Rural/Urban, 41
Urban, 42, 44, 45
Primary Education
in India, 113, 120
Problems Faced by-, 120
Measures for Development, 115, 116

Scheme, 90
Primary Teachers in Science Education, 116
Project DILASA, 135
Public Distribution System, 128, 139, 307
Public Health, 217
Care, 24, 259
Centres, (PHCs), 221, 236, 279
Facilities, 30
in India, 247
Infrastructure, 247
Movement, 248
Nurses, 236
Program, 227
Services, 277
System, 30

R

Rajasthan, 118
Ralegan Siddu, 294, 296
Ram Mohan Roy, 101, 325
RCH (Reproductive and Child Health), 253
Reforms, 32
Reproduction Rights of Women, 138
Reserve Bank of India, 146-148, 153
Rio de Janeiro (Brazil), 291
Rupa Shah, VC SNDT, 325
Rural
Poverty Alleviation, 44
Poverty in India, 44
Poverty, 32
Under Employment, 131
Women, 145

S

Sado-Masochistic Relationship, 133
Salem and Erode, 75
Samaj Mandir, 210
Sarva Shiksha Abhiyan, (SSA), 21, 90, 91
Sayeeda Hameed, 326
Scheduled Caste/Tribes, 99, 101, 102, 105, 224
Population, 95
Scheduled Caste, 233
Scheme of Urban Micro-Entrepreneurs, 45
Scientific and Technical Institutions, 108
Second Irrigation Commission, 295
Second Water and Irrigation Commission, 295
Sector,
Agriculture, 32, 73, 75
Employment in Organized, 129
Health, 219
Indian Public, 30
Public Health, 219, 222, 223, 228, 234
Social, 30, 168
Self-Determination, 23, 203
Self-Employment, 46
Self-Employment Activities, 43
Self-Help Groups, (SHGs), 19, 23, 48-50, 96, 147, 148, 150, 202-214
Activities, 212
Federation, 146
Members, 210, 212, 213
Movement, 209
Women, 210
Service Training Program, 118
SEWA (Gujarat), 49, 52
Sex
and Sexuality, 284
Ratio, 135
Tourism, 133
Trade, 136
Workers, 136
Sexual Abuse, 132

SFDA, 201
Shiksha Karmi Project, 21, 118
Shramdan, 210
SIDBI, 50, 51
SIM Card Technology, 150
SJSRY (Swarn Jayanti Shahari Rozgar Yojna), 45
Slum/Pavement Dwellers, 43
SMART Card
    and Expenditrue, 150
System, 151
    Technology, 150, 151
Smokeless Chulha, 210
SNDT Women's University, 52
Social
    Change, 100
    Infrastructure, 44
    Opportunities, 17
    Reformers, 101
Security, 219
Services, 18
Structure, 205
Society, 25, 41, 99, 100, 159, 177, 203, 207, 248
    Civil, 140, 225, 258, 328
Socio-Economic
    Issues, 32
Status, 203
    Transformation, 50
Soil Degradation, 37
Solid Waste Management, 307, 310
South Africa, 46
South Asia, 131, 177
South Asian Countries, 130
South East Asia, 131
South East Asian Economies, 218
South Korea—Brazil, 234
SPARC (Society for Promotion of Asia Res. Centres), 49
Sponsored Poverty Alleviation Programs, 45, 46
STDs (Sexually Transmitted Diseases), 133, 136
STI/HIV, 286
Stree Mukti Sanghatan, Women's Liberation Org., (SMS), 302, 304, 306-309, 311, 312
Structural Adjustment Program, 131, 138, 322
Sub-Sahara Africa, 119, 168, 177, 192, 316
Subsidies, 39, 219
Suicides, 18
Sukhomajari, 294
Support System, 18, 36
Suvarna Jayanti Shahari Rojgar Yojna (SJSRY), 305
Swedish International Dev. Authority, 118

T

Tagonre, Rabindranath, 101
Tamil Nadu, 19, 71-73, 75-77, 284
    Afforestation Program, (TAP), 20, 78, 80
    Economy, 72
    NSDP, 72
    Poverty Reduction Strategies in-, 77
    SHDR, 72
Teachers Training Institution, 116
Teaching Learning Material (TLM), 97
Technological Revolution, 145
Technology, 36, 249
New, 21, 100, 145, 148, 149, 153, 219
Tenure Insecurity, 43
TFR (Total Fertility Rate), 253
Thailand, Peru and Malawi, 259
Thrift Credit, 19
Trade Reforms, 314
Trade Unions, 131
Training Programs, 210
Transaction
    Banking, 46

Services, 46
Transnational Corporations (TNCs), 129
Transnational Corporations/Multi-National Corporations, 140
Transparency, 167
Tribal Areas, 116
Tribal Students, 89
TRIPS Agreement, 319
Tuberculosis, 24, 176, 218, 220-223, 227, 233, 277, 278, 280, 313, 329

U

Uganda, 191
UN (United Nations), 178, 185, 188, 192, 290, 291, 318, 322
Agencies, 229
Commission on Environment Development, 291
Development Fund for Women (UNIFEM), 155
Progress, 190
Development Program, 155, 318
Environmental Program, 291
General Assembly, 71, 179, 195, 291
Human Development Report, 1995, 178
Member States, 283
Millennium Declaration, 228, 277
UNESCO, 177, 190, 217
Report, 106
Uniform Labor Standards, 131
Universal Primary Education, 85
Unsafe Sex, 286
Urban
Basic Services for Poor, 45
Poverty in India, 44
Poverty, 18
US, 179
USAID, 217, 227
Uttar Pradesh, 30
IMR, 31

V

Vastishalas, 88, 96
Vibhuti, Patel, 330
Victims of Violence Retirement Scheme, 131
Village
Development Council Training Program,. 210
Education Committee, 90
Kolhapur, 94
Panchayats, 210
Sajol, 95
Violence Against Women, 133, 161, 180, 184
Voluntary Organization, 88, 114
Vyas, Girija, 168

W

Wage
Discrimination, 131
Labourers, 147
Wardha District, 35
Waste Pickers/Picking, 303, 310, 312
Water Harvesting, 79
Watershed
Based Strategy, 293
Development Program (WDP), 296, 297
Organization Trust (WOTR), 296
Women
Decision Makers, 21
Health Workers, 139
Waste Pickers, 304
Workers, 129, 135
Women's
Economic Participation, 156
Economic Rights, 185
Empowerment, 22, 23, 155, 159, 192, 193, 201, 205
Labour Force Participation, 156

Rights Organization, 140, 322
Rights, 180
Workers Rights, 131
World Bank, 55, 61, 67, 89, 91, 178, 184, 210, 217, 220, 225-228, 317, 318, 319
World
Conference on Human Rights, 185
Conference on Women, 318, 321
Declaration on Education for All, 1990, 119
Economic Forum, 156
Economy, 217
Education Forum, Dakar Senegal, 105
Gini Index, 66
Health Organization (WHO), 217, 226
World Report on Violence and Health, 193
Social Forum, 2004, 140
Social Forum, 21
Summit on Social Development, 185
Trade Organization (WTO), 39, 131, 319, 320
Treaty, 225

Z

Zila Parishad, 91
Zila Parishad Primary Schools, 89, 91